A NEW DEAL
FOR
BRONZEVILLE

A NEW DEAL FOR BRONZEVILLE

HOUSING, EMPLOYMENT & CIVIL RIGHTS IN BLACK CHICAGO, 1935–1955

LIONEL KIMBLE JR.

Southern Illinois University Press / Carbondale

Furthermore:
a program of the J.M.Kaplan Fund

This publication is partially funded by a grant from Furthermore, a program of the J. M. Kaplan Fund.

Cover illustration: "Picket line at Mid-City Realty Company, South Chicago, Illinois"; John Vachon, photographer; Library of Congress Prints and Photographs Division.

Library of Congress Cataloging-in-Publication Data

Kimble, Lionel, Jr., 1973–

A New Deal for Bronzeville : housing, employment, and civil rights in Black Chicago, 1935–1955 / Lionel Kimble Jr.

  pages cm

Includes bibliographical references and index.

ISBN 978-0-8093-3426-1 (pbk. : alk. paper)

ISBN 0-8093-3426-7 (pbk. :alk. paper)

ISBN 978-0-8093-3427-8 (ebook)

1. African Americans—Illinois—Chicago—History—20th century. 2. African Americans—Illinois—Chicago—Social conditions—20th century. 3. African Americans—Civil rights—Illinois—Chicago—History—20th century. 4. Civil rights movements—Illinois—Chicago—History—20th century. 5. Chicago (Ill.)—History—20th century. 6. Chicago (Ill.)—Social conditions—20th century. 7. Chicago (Ill.)—Race relations. I. Title.

F548.9.N4K55 2015

323.1196'073077311—dc23   2015002884

For Hazel and Paul

CONTENTS

ACKNOWLEDGMENTS

THIS BOOK grew out of my desire to better understand many of the stories my maternal grandmother would share about her childhood on the black South Side of Chicago. Unlike the tales many of my friends were told, my grandmother's stories were neither of the Great Migration nor of the American South. My grandmother was a product of the city. She was born in Chicago in 1926 and, to my knowledge, had never spent any considerable amount of time in the South nor expressed the slightest interest in doing so. In our home, then, there were no laments about the harshness of agricultural work or Jim Crow. There were no stories of African American disfranchisement or pains of powerlessness.

Her narrative, instead, was that of a city girl who witnessed the diversity and dynamism of African Americans in the city where she was born. From my grandmother I learned of a community that had ties to black singers and entertainers, gospel music innovators, and heavyweight boxing champions; that established the first nursing school for African American women and lay the foundation for African American History Month; and that was the home of U.S. senators and congressmen and the president and First Lady of the United States. While these nationally and internationally prominent figures bring a certain degree of prestige and pride, to judge the community solely by its famous residents is a mistake. In doing such, I eventually discovered, we run the risk of completely ignoring the countless nameless individuals who, while mostly forgotten to history, played an important role in the black communities of the city.

I took all of these ideas with me when I went away for college and my graduate studies at the University of Iowa. The faculty at Iowa, especially Shelton Stromquist, Leslie Schwalm, Colin Gordon, and Robert F. Jefferson, provided the necessary support and encouragement that aided me with this project. I am confident that without their guidance, this project would have never happened. Together they instructed me in how to be a historian, taught me a great deal about the complexities of the New Deal, and instilled in me enthusiasm and insight about African American historiography and African

Acknowledgments

American veterans. But faculty input, as important as it is, can carry one only so far, and this book has also benefited from the hours of discussions and the ready support of my graduate school classmates and friends Paul Young, Patricia Reid, Jennifer R. Harbour, John McKerley, Eric Fure-Slocum, Robert Bionaz, David Lewis-Colman, and Michael Innis-Jimenez.

When I left Iowa and moved home to Chicago, I was fortunate to get adopted into the intellectual community on the South Side. Special thanks are due to Robert Cruthird and Jeanette Williams of the Chicago Branch of the Association for the Study of African American Life and History; all of the people on the Chicago Council on Black Studies; Lyn Hughes of the A. Philip Randolph Pullman Porters Museum; my colleagues in the Departments of History and African American Studies at Chicago State University; my graduate student, Alexis Mayfield; and Michael Flug, Robert Miller, Cynthia Fife-Townsel, and the entire staff of the Chicago Public Library's Vivian G. Harsh Research Collection at the Carter G. Woodson Regional Library. Michael, in particular, with his "your-money-is-no-good-here" policy for microfilm copying, helped ease my financial burden during the preparation of the book. Special thanks are extended to Timuel Black, Robert Starks, and especially my friend and mentor Christopher R. Reed, all of the Black Chicago History Forum. These three have arguably forgotten more about black history in Chicago than I will probably ever know. It is indeed an honor and a privilege to be able to learn from them.

No one writes a book alone, and historians cannot do what we do without the support of research money and the hard work of library archivists. The bulk of the initial research was completed using research funds, which included the Huggins-Quarles Dissertation Award of the Organization of American Historians; the King V. Hostick Award from the Illinois Historic Preservation Agency; the Louis A. Pelzer Dissertation Fellowship from the University of Iowa; and a Competitive Scholarly Research Grant from the University of Illinois at Springfield and Center for Teaching and Research Excellence at Chicago State University. Special thanks go to Ida Jones of the Moorland-Spingarn Research Center at Howard University; the late Walter Hill of the National Archives in College Park, Maryland; and Aaisha Haykal and William Adams of the Chicago State University Archives. Without the dogged investigative work of the individuals named here and those at the National Archives Office in Chicago, the University of Illinois at Chicago, and the Chicago History Museum, I am not certain that this project would have seen the light of day.

My family is my rock and has sustained me with inspiration and encouragement through this entire process. "Grateful" could not begin to explain how I feel. Even though my father, Lionel Sr., and my mother, Sharon

Stingley, have witnessed my journey, they probably secretly wished I had completed my degree in chemical engineering. They, along with my sister, Jennifer, and my aunts, uncles, nieces, nephews, and cousins, have been some of my most ardent cheerleaders. My children, Nita and Charles, have given me much joy and were always a welcome distraction through the completion of this project. It is my sincere hope that this book not only teaches them much about the richness of black life in the neighborhood we call home but also tells them something about who they are. Last, my wife, Courtney, has been my sounding board, my keenest critic, and my most diligent editor. You helped me more than you will ever know and believed in the book even when I did not. I know this project took entirely too long to complete. But I would not want to imagine undertaking this endeavor without your constant support.

A NEW DEAL
FOR
BRONZEVILLE

INTRODUCTION

> There has been a kind of informal and unplanned division of
> labor with the "accepted leaders" negotiating and pleading for the
> Negroes, while the "radicals" turned on the heat.
> —St. Clair Drake and Horace Cayton, *Black Metropolis*

IN 1944 the Carnegie Corporation commissioned Swedish economist
Gunnar Myrdal to prepare a comprehensive study of the short- and long-
term ramifications of World War II on race relations in the United States.
This examination, *An American Dilemma*, unearthed a dangerous contradiction
between the dominant trope of American liberalism, which privileged individual liberty and opportunity and served as the basis of American society, and institutional racism, which both permeated nearly every aspect of
American society and contributed to the perpetuation of the so-called Negro
Problem.[1] Myrdal's observations suggested that America could live up to
the principles of liberty and freedom by developing fundamental strategies
to end this contradiction, especially at a time when the nation was increasingly viewed by the West as the world's moral compass in the face of fascist
threats. Moreover, only by developing ways to address this problem could
the nation realize its full potential and truly live by the "American Creed."

This study may have been considered groundbreaking in some circles
of white Americans, but for African Americans it was anything but. African
Americans were painfully aware that the contradiction Myrdal outlined
existed and that their entire history in the United States included centuries
filled with struggles to enjoy the benefits of the "American Creed" and
with attempts to force America to truly live up to these ideals. As World
War II progressed, it became increasingly evident to a growing cadre of
early civil rights activists that the changes taking place in the country's
economic and social structure during this period would inevitably afford
them unique opportunities to expand their fight for first-class citizenship.

In a time dominated by the rhetoric of freedom and democracy, by the need to fully mobilize the wartime labor, and by the rhetoric of New Deal liberalism articulated by the Roosevelt administration, African Americans during the Roosevelt era found themselves, in the words of Richard Dalfiume, with "an excellent opportunity to prick at the conscience of white America."[2]

Using Dalfiume's argument as a guide, the trajectory of African American activism during the era, then, can be characterized by the belief that the New Deal and World War II periods fundamentally changed public perceptions of the federal government's role in providing for the welfare and security of all American citizens. Historian Thomas Sugrue, for example, explores these issues in his study on postwar Detroit. Sugrue argues that postwar militancy was fueled by the prevalence of competing notions regarding "rights-based liberalism" ideology held by blacks and whites.[3] While some employed the language of liberalism to maintain the mantle of white privilege in employment, African Americans used similar rhetoric to engage in antiracist programs to subvert old racial and industrial hierarchies. African Americans and their supporters, stimulated by an often-literal interpretation of President Roosevelt's Four Freedoms, gained important venues from which to articulate their "impatience for first-class citizenship."[4]

Even though African Americans undoubtedly echoed many of the high ideals regarding changes in American society, in some cases their activism was focused squarely on more pragmatic and immediate concerns, such as how peacetime economic and social reconversion would affect their demand for increased protection of their rights, particularly in securing jobs. As a way to address these issues, African Americans commonly formed strategic coalitions with other African American activists, labor organizers, progressive politicians, and white liberals to challenge racial discrimination during the Depression, New Deal, and World War II eras.[5] What follows in these pages are but a few examples that focus on the shape and effectiveness of these private/public coalitions and underscore the tenuous interplay between labor activists, local government officials and agencies, and African Americans in Chicago.[6]

The creation of strategic alliances was not a new phenomenon in the history of African Americans. Rather, this strategy, according to *New York Herald Tribune* correspondent Earl Brown and associate editor of *Harper's Magazine* George W. Leighton, was an extension of tactics employed at various times in which African Americans "[kept] asking [the] government, 'What are you going to do about it?'"[7] Brown and Leighton's commentary offers an inside look at a developing popular belief that government intervention, especially during the New Deal, could be demanded or expected as African Americans made steadier calls for greater inclusion in the state.

This expectation gained momentum during the years covered in this study, 1935–55. During these years, federal and local governments were drawn, many times rather reluctantly, into a growing number of civil and workers' rights campaigns initiated by forces on the political left. Unable to extricate themselves from these battles, government officials were forced to choose sides. Activists, in turn, were able to take full advantage of increased exposure of their issues and achieved a number of victories for their constituencies. Successes by the Left also challenged the broader American society to rethink its own ideas about the public's welfare, patriotism, civil rights, and, most important, citizenship during the era. The public discourse taking place during the period casts a powerful light on the transformative effect of New Deal– and Roosevelt-era liberalism on early civil rights rhetoric.

African American intellectuals, of course, were at the forefront of this debate. Rayford Logan's 1944 book, *What the Negro Wants*, contained essays dealing with the question of the advancement of civil rights for African Americans that many hoped would develop after the war.[8] In one of the essays, "The Negro Wants Full Participation in the American Democracy," Tuskegee University president Frederick Patterson wrote, "The Negro wants to become a fully participating citizen in every sense of the word." Patterson continued,

> He wants this participation not only or merely for the sake of himself but also because he believes in democracy as a way of life for this nation and because his concept of democracy leads him to feel that this citizenship status is essential to the complete realization of our national destiny.[9]

Patterson's assertions of course were correct, and a growing cadre of activists from across the political spectrum seized upon the changes in the country's economic and social structure to push for tangible outcomes to improve the black condition.

The African American intelligentsia and civic leaders, like those in Logan's book, used public forums to advance early civil rights claims. Theirs, however, was not the only civil rights narrative that was being written during this era. In a city like Chicago, where local residents commonly concede that "everything is political," black working people demonstrated they thought about and talked about politics daily. The vast majority of them undoubtedly echoed the same high ideals concerning citizenship as those held by black leadership. The difference between these groups lay in the protest ideologies.

Recent scholarship on black middle-class activism argues that some old-line organizations like the Chicago Urban League pushed a political agenda that, in many cases, privileged access to equal opportunities for "better classes" of African Americans at the expense of black workers and the poor.[10] The examples of working-class activism outlined in these pages, however, tell a different story about civil rights. The overwhelming majority of black workers were employed in semiskilled and unskilled professions ranging from laundry workers to general labor to stockyard labor. Thus, as this book examines civil rights activism in Chicago, it does so from the perspectives of those who occupied "jobs," as Drake and Cayton discuss in *Black Metropolis*, rather than of that "small group of people holding down 'positions'—professionals, proprietors, managers and officials, clerical and kindred workers."[11]

When civic and political leadership pushed heavily for racial integration with white citizens, the black working class, more often than not, articulated a civil rights program that pushed for *greater* access to their fair share of opportunities. Even though racial integration may have been a by-product of their organizing, it was never their primary objective. Within these larger discussions about race and the state, working-class commentaries about societal changes that were occurring nationally were usually colored by their position within both the black and white economic hierarchies. As African American leadership worked to advance the race by accentuating the similarities between the wants and aspirations of African Americans and white citizens at the national level, working-class activism focused inward and was concerned with addressing more pragmatic and immediate concerns associated with emerging economic and social realities.

Take, for example, an event that occurred during the spring of 1946. At that time, a group of more than five hundred honorably discharged World War II veterans and their families, many of whom were either formerly or presently employed as cabdrivers, drove to Washington, D.C. They were fully prepared to "stay for 'days or years' through Washington red tape and Jim Crow until their fight against Chicago's cab license limitation [was] won."[12] Included in the group was the hundred-member-strong, all-black Illinois Cab Drivers' Association for Discharged Veterans (ICDADV). African American veterans John Patrick and H. G. Hardy led the group. Two-thirds of the group's membership had been cabdrivers before their military service, but upon their return to civilian life, they, like many of their colleagues, were denied driver's licenses, despite provisions mandating the contrary. This denial cost them the right to operate a cab legally in the city of Chicago. Their inability to secure licenses, and thus economic freedom, was undemocratic and ran counter to federal protections that many of these vets knew they had. This rights-based argument became increasingly popular in the years following World War II and was grounded in the belief held by many that when they "were overseas dodging flak, digging foxholes, and sweating it out," all they wanted was to "come home to the land of the free and plenty; a country where all men are created equal."[13] Unfortunately for some, merely relying on federal provisions proved inadequate in the face of white racism and corruption.

As a way to force local officials to recognize their demands, ICDADV members planned to mobilize their "collective strength," call on their status as veterans to bring about fundamental changes in their economic realities, and force the nation to live up to its democratic principles. In the end, they were successful. According to St. Clair Drake and Horace Cayton, linking their self-interests to the patriotic ideals of the era aided in the overall goal of "racial advancement" and integration and was a crucial element in the fight for democracy.[14] Though mindful of the shape of national and international events, the working class often lacked the public platforms or the notoriety of the black leadership class from which to speak out on political issues. Even without a readily available public space, when opportunities to speak out against racism were presented, they seized the opportunity to do so. As this episode illustrates, emboldened by their military service, African American veterans led the charge for inclusion in the New Deal state by returning home with the "determination that they were going to make a difference" and anticipated that they would win, in the words of one, "increased recognition for his service and . . . access to more opportunities."[15] Regardless of whether or not they realized the larger civil rights implications of their words and actions, many of their battles helped establish a foundation for a larger civil rights movement in Chicago and throughout the urban North.

In the larger scope of the New Deal era, a common theme in rhetoric of the leadership and working people was an inherent faith in the Roosevelt administration. Drake and Cayton noted an anecdote involving an African American clergyman who reportedly told his congregation, "Let Jesus lead you and Roosevelt feed you!" This episode has appeared in different forms throughout African American communal lore. My maternal grandmother, for instance, remembered the saying as "May the good Lord lead you and let Roosevelt feed you." Tiny variances aside, its continued proliferation highlights the high level of reverence African Americans had for the messiah-like qualities of FDR (although his reputation as a race liberal is both debatable and problematic). A number of examples explain his popularity. These range from his appointment of a number of "race advisers" throughout his government to the relative racial openness of some New Deal policies.

Black Chicago enjoyed a special connection to the Roosevelt administration. African Americans Earl B. Dickerson, Robert C. Weaver, Truman

K. Gibson Jr., and Milton P. Webster and white resident Harold Ickes, among others, all contributed significantly to the political landscape of the era. Each worked in a capacity that enabled him to advance an agenda of nondiscrimination in agencies such as the Fair Employment Practices Committee, the War Department, and the Works Progress Administration (WPA). African American residents of Chicago did gain access to valuable government resources such as the job creation programs of offices like the WPA and the U.S. Employment Service, which lessened, to some degree, the effects of the Depression.

The president's reputation in Chicago was enhanced both by his actions and by his words. In a 1934 speech at Howard University, Roosevelt outlined his ideas on the shape of the New Deal, "American liberalism," and what role, if any, African Americans would play in defining American economic recovery policies during the Depression. In his speech, the president remarked, "As far as it is humanly possible . . . there should be no forgotten man and no forgotten races."[16] In reality, however, "liberals increasingly chose to present public issues almost entirely in terms of economics and class" and ignored race altogether, and many others "expressed little interest in remaking individuals or in uniting all Americans into a single moral community."[17] Rather, they reserved their passion for economic reform, and their moral compass pointed to such words as "security," "opportunity," and "industrial democracy."[18] Despite Roosevelt's positive reputation, the overall effectiveness of a number of early New Deal policies failed to alleviate the economic, political, and social stresses of black life during the period, and many more neglected to cement the place of African Americans in the economic recovery plan of the country. Furthermore, his race advisers lacked any real authority.

Even with New Dealers' unwillingness to address issues of race and racism head-on, African Americans still saw that the New Deal and the Second World War provided access to the common yet contested citizenship expressed by liberal democratic ideas. By 1935 African Americans were readily embracing the rhetoric of President Roosevelt and were moving to fully incorporate his vision into their existing ideas about the future direction of the race. The blending of these two philosophical positions transformed Rooseveltian liberalism into a new African American liberalism. This idea, in turn, became the catalyst for an emerging protest movement in the city and democratized the political, social, and economic landscape.[19]

This exploration of racialized interpretations of liberalism is a topic to which a number of historians are devoting more attention.[20] Scholars have noted that challenges to racism and interracial conflicts centered on the important day-to-day issues such as neighborhood composition and access to employment opportunities.[21] Historian Thomas Sugrue, for one, has found that as Detroit developed into a wartime manufacturing hub during this same period, African American workers took advantage of their recently acquired political strength and pushed for greater access to civil rights. Their assertiveness to improve their condition was challenged by conflicting interracial visions "rooted in a newfound rights consciousness" of the Roosevelt era. According to Sugrue, when African Americans moved to assert their rights for equal opportunity, they "faced opposition from working and middle-class whites who claim[ed] the mantle of the authentic New Deal state."[22]

During the 1930s and 1940s, while Detroit was named the "arsenal of democracy," Chicago's wartime output was as high, or in some instances higher, than Detroit's.[23] Given the city's history of interracial tensions, this expansion of the wartime economy along with competition over jobs and space created the necessary conditions for activism. At the same time, black participation in the war effort led to powerful claims of equity and full citizenship, and for support African Americans enlisted the aid of various government and progressive organizations to help achieve these goals. These strategic coalitions of African American activists, labor organizers, progressive politicians, and white liberals developed at just the right historical moment, when a brief window through which to bring about societal change opened. They soon found that taking advantage of this opportunity would be no easy task.

In this work, I examine the scope of these interracial conflicts as they occurred in the black South Side community of Bronzeville—the cultural, political, social, and economic center of African American life in Chicago, if not the Midwest. This area has been one of the most studied black communities in the United States. Many of these studies have taken great care to examine black community formation in a nuanced, sophisticated manner and encouraged scholars to devote significant attention to the interaction of the people, the government, and the institutions of black Chicago with a specific focus on race, housing, and employment.[24]

Arnold Hirsch's *Making the Second Ghetto* uncovers a pattern of "hidden violence" that occurred in Chicago between 1940 and 1960 over the issue of housing. He cites more than five hundred white housing riots that occurred in response to neighborhood integration.[25] For Hirsch, white response, both political and communal, helped reinforced Chicago's reputation for being a city of neighborhoods, which made these battles over housing more intense. Although Hirsch's work provides compelling examples of interracial housing strife, he fails to fully investigate the actions taken by African Americans in this fight. In his study the voices of the black working-class community are silent, their actions hidden from view.

Similar studies dealing with the experiences of African American workers in Chicago, most notably *Making a New Deal* by Lizabeth Cohen and *Down on the Killing Floor* by Rick Halpern, examine how the formation of a working-class political ideology challenged prevailing discrimination in the workplace. Both of these, however, fail to adequately explore how black protests influenced, and were influenced by, the social, material, and political environment that operated in Bronzeville. *A New Deal for Bronzeville* addresses this omission by placing African American historical actors at the center of the housing and employment debate.

Although the theoretical and methodological frameworks of the above-noted works have influenced this study, the scope and focus discussed herein mark a significant point of divergence. First, I argue that the activism that appeared on the South Side was not simply motivated by the "class consciousness" rhetoric of the organized labor movement. Instead, African Americans' demands grew out of everyday struggles for racial justice, citizenship rights, and improved economic and material conditions. Second, while previous studies have acknowledged black agency in early civil and workers' rights campaigns, very few have engaged in a discussion about African American life in Chicago from a "bottom up" perspective. I attempt to explore this issue by focusing on the formation of a black working-class culture through which African American working people interpreted federal and local policies and subsequently articulated their understanding that participation in the American war effort was justification for equitable treatment.

Historians Adam Green, Anne Knupfer, and Bill Mullen have contributed to a current historiographical trend exploring African American cultural and coalition formation between the 1930s and 1950s. In each of their works, meticulous attention has been devoted to how African American culture was influenced by interracial cooperation between, generally speaking, the African American middle class and elements from the Left and how these forces addressed racial discrimination in the city.[26] While this book is also concerned with coalitions, its focus is on those whose lives commonly existed somewhere near the bottom of the economic hierarchy. Thus, if one defines culture as Knupfer does—the process through which "people make sense of their lives and create an identity for themselves and future generations"—one must focus on three interrelated issues to understand black working-class cultural formation in this context: population increase, the legacy of African American protest, and the formations of vital political alliances.

The years between the end of World War I and World War II marked the largest internal migration in American history. Chicago's African American population grew from 109,458 to 337,000 between 1920 and 1940. James Grossman argues that those who participated in the migration "looked to urban life and industrial economy for the social and economic foundation for full citizenship, and its perquisites."[27] Even though this expansion resulted in the second-largest African American population living outside of the South, new migrants found themselves packed in segregated communities because of racist urban planning practices and policies in their search for adequate housing.[28] As they searched for jobs, African Americans saw white unemployment plummet and black unemployment increase and in some cases saw employers recruit white workers from hundreds of miles away rather than employ black workers from the local population.

The rapid increase in the population strained the already racially charged working and living conditions on the South Side and held serious consequences for interclass conflicts as well. African Americans' working-class culture was constantly attacked by their middle- and upper-class neighbors. Major points of conflict often included spirited debates about such issues as mannerism, decorum, and religious and sexual practices. Assailed from without and within, working-class activists developed a civil rights culture that, while often parroting strategies of more established middle-class organizations, clearly reflected their own economic and political interests.

In spite of Chicago's reputation of being the most segregated municipality in the United States, black Chicago experienced a long history of interracial coalition building and industrial activism during the Roosevelt era. The Communist Party and other Left-led organizations, in particular those of the labor movement, attempted to make inroads into the African American community during this period and were often proactive in the fight against discrimination. For a number of African Americans, the implementation of Communist Party and Communist Party–*styled* organizing tactics, especially around job discrimination, was not foreign, and the tactics were integral parts of already established organizing traditions. Embracing this style of political activism provided another platform for spearheading a movement against racial discrimination and was often a crucial outlet for advocating for better treatment of their fellow African Americans locally and nationwide. While it was true that nonaffiliated blacks were willing to employ leftist rhetoric (for example, class-based group solidarity) into their existing protest models, it is vital to note that at the core of these strategic alliances, dissatisfaction with segregated living and working conditions in black Chicago and adverse conditions facing African Americans more often than not trumped any strict adherence to a European, class-based political dogma.[29] Protest activism was amplified at a time when a brief window of opportunity emerged where African Americans and their allies saw a realistic chance to challenge entrenched employment and housing discrimination in the city in the wake of World War II.

Black activism also benefited from the ability to form political alliances with local politicians who were concerned with race relations in the city. For example, Mayor Edward J. Kelly cultivated a reputation as a race liberal and ally of African Americans and a number of their causes. It is not completely clear whether these moves were initiated because of his genuine concern for civil rights or due to shrewd politicking. Nonetheless, Kelly's championing of school and housing integration; realization of the long-term political and social implications of instituting fair employment legislation; donations of monies to African American philanthropic endeavors; and appointments of African Americans to important political positions cast his administration in a positive light with black Chicagoans. More important, African Americans gained considerable access to more and higher-level patronage positions under Kelly than under any other mayor until that point.[30]

Chapters 1 and 2 cover the prewar period (1935–41) and examine community activism in Bronzeville, utilizing the Depression as a backdrop. By conservative accounts, the United States during the 1930s was characterized by three major developments—the Depression, the expansion of the New Deal state, and the growing working-class militancy by African Americans and white citizens. The Depression affected all areas of American life, as the economic crisis was far more complex than simply a stock market crash. For African Americans, the pains of the Depression struck early and severely because they already occupied many of the lowest levels of the occupational hierarchy. The lack of economic opportunity for black Chicagoans could not be solely blamed on the Depression. Discrimination in the hiring procedures of many companies and the exclusion of black people by a number of labor unions, in particular those affiliated with the American Federation of Labor, hampered African Americans' ability to secure work. In addition, African Americans still lacked access to adequate housing and continued to pay disproportionately high rents for slum housing. Despite setbacks, African Americans organized protests and worked with Left-led organizations such as the Communist Party and the Congress of Industrial Organizations to counter job discrimination and made strong appeals to New Deal allies at the local and federal levels for access to public housing. The cases discussed in these chapters highlight the effectiveness and limits of ad hoc insurgency for civil rights during the 1930s. In each, African American workers, in particular, made demands for a fundamental change in the social order and for immediate redress of issues that directly and adversely affected their day-to-day lives. By examining these activities, we gain a better understanding of early civil rights and how African Americans in Chicago understood the promise of the New Deal.

Chapters 3 and 4 cover the World War II period (1941–45) and examine how federal nondiscrimination employment guidelines and public housing initiatives shaped race relations in the city. The 1940s presented a new set of challenges and opportunities for African American civil rights activists in Chicago. With the entry of the United States into World War II, the American economy began to fully recover from the effects of the Great Depression. The expansion of the American wartime economy provided relief from the economic crisis within the African American communities of Chicago because it drew increasing numbers of black workers into war factories and federal employment throughout the city. However, much like in the 1930s, African Americans' presence in these jobs was often unwanted, and they faced resistance from white workers and management. Despite the fact that the stated aim of the war was the protection of democracy, black workers faced steady discrimination on the home front.

African Americans also contended with persistent discrimination in Chicago's housing market. Here, recurring issues such as overcrowding, unsanitary conditions, and high rents continued to shape day-to-day experiences in black communities. World War II offered new chances for black citizens and their supporters to improve both the material and social conditions of the day. At the center of these wartime fights was the enforcement of the nondiscrimination clause of the Chicago Housing Authority (CHA), heated debates in local government over the direction and scope of the CHA's war housing program, and questions about the critical housing shortage faced by families of servicemen and servicewomen and its impact on morale. As during the Depression, during the war African Americans in Chicago resisted discrimination and actively pushed for equal access to jobs and better homes. Civil rights activists were aided by growing intervention by the federal government into local issues. In turn, activists learned how to use changing federal policies and rhetoric as proof the federal government could, and should, take an active role in fighting racism and discrimination, even if no government institution at the time publicly made improving race relations a priority during the war.

Chapters 5 and 6 cover the postwar period (1945–55) and examine how African Americans, especially returning World War II veterans, continued the fight against discrimination in housing and employment. World War II marked a watershed moment for the fledgling civil rights movement in Chicago. During the period, African Americans made rather significant inroads into Chicago's war economy and, working alongside the CHA and local government officials, gained access to both public and private housing. At the conclusion of the war, a growing number of working-class activists feared that as the economy entered a peacetime posture, many of the strides black Americans had achieved during the war would be reversed as the federal government no longer took an active role in the private lives of citizens.

African American activists continued to agitate despite such possibilities. These demands were strengthened as thousands of African American soldiers returned to civilian life expecting equal treatment due to their veteran status and discovered that not much had truly changed on the housing and employment front. In fact, black veterans found themselves squarely engulfed in the postwar debates over economic reconversion and neighborhood integration taking place across the nation. The fights would prove very difficult because, unlike in the Depression and World War II eras, African Americans could no longer rely on support from the mayor's office as Edward Kelly, long an advocate for African Americans, was forced out of office. Nonetheless, the battles against racism and discrimination in post–World War II Chicago set the tone for how New Deal liberalism would spread. Chapter 5 examines both housing policy and how veterans along with the CHA successfully challenged neighborhood segregation. Chapter 6 explores the role that returning veterans played in post–World War II industrial reconversion and how black veterans and black war workers fought for racial equality even in an era in which labor militancy was, in many cases, labeled as Communist activity and therefore subversive.

This study of African American labor militancy and civil rights in Chicago adds to the extensive history of workers' activism in Chicago that already includes such key historical events as the Haymarket Riot and the Pullman Strike during the nineteenth century and the organizing efforts of packinghouse workers in the twentieth century. By focusing on the lives and labors of African Americans who resided in Bronzeville, this project will add to and illuminate the important wartime story of black Chicago that is still being overlooked by historians of African American labor. The questions and answers discussed in this project will shed light on the historical roots of the current shape of African American life in Chicago today. This examination will further highlight how World War II held both racial and political implications for African American working people and will focus on how understanding their roles as workers and soldiers helped define their claims as citizens.

1. BLACK BELTS INSULT US
EQUAL HOUSING AND CONTESTED LIBERALISM DURING THE DEPRESSION

If we were primitive in our habits, black belts would be justified. But we deport ourselves in many instances better than some other racial groups against which there is no residential line of demarcation.

—*Chicago Defender*, July 11, 1936

Here on Chicago's South Side we have thousands of Negroes who have fled from the South to escape the burden of debt slavery. More arrive each month, so that it is estimated that at least 50,000 Negroes here—one sixth of the colored population—have no regular place to abode, begging for their meals at back door and on the streets, sleeping in parks, hallways, or on the floors of already overcrowded apartments.

—Ishmael P. Flory, Chicago Council of the National Negro Congress, 1940

THE STUDY of race and housing in Chicago has long been domi-nated by numerous accounts of interracial violence and intimidation. One of the most notable of these incidents, the "Red Summer" riot of 1919, was an example of how racial tensions in Chicago could turn violent. Between 1917 and 1921 there were more than fifty bombings of homes occupied by African Americans, resulting in two deaths, injuries to both white and black Chicagoans, and an estimated $1 million in damage.[1] The roots of these clashes were many and can easily be traced to a myriad of social, political, and economic pressures outlined by the Chicago Commission on Race Relations in the aftermath of World War I. Within this milieu, access to better housing was a prominent source of racial conflict. As the African American population expanded and sought relief from the housing crisis in Chicago's Black Belt, white Chicagoans responded by working to protect their communities by employing legal and illegal tactics, such as arsons and bombings, to deter an African American "invasion." What provoked these groups to act in such a manner? While the physical realities of neighborhood change undoubtedly played a vital role, the political landscape contributed to both black and white citizens' expectations. Much of this can be attributed to the belief that Roosevelt-era rhetoric gave many Americans hope the state authority would guarantee that their interests would be protected. America's history of racial antagonisms affected the interpretation of these federal guarantees, which would change depending on the viewers' race or ethnicity.

In housing in particular, the policies developed by local and federal agencies during the New Deal exacerbated this already contentious situation. W. Dennis Keating and Janet Smith argue that the Roosevelt era marked "the beginning of a continuing struggle between political and ideological positions regarding the federal government's involvement in urban conditions associated with poverty."[2] In light of these competing ideological and political positions, black and white Chicagoans took sides, each group articulating its vision regarding the access to housing and racial mobility. African Americans and their allies believed federal government intervention would positively address their housing situation. White citizens, on the other hand, held fast to the belief that the laws provided the requisite legal foundation to allow them the justification to shape their communities in their own image. These competing visions made conflict inevitable, and it stood to reason that if the federal government could not reach a consensus concerning how to define its own housing policy, it stood to reason that black and white citizens would experience similar difficulties.

Housing activists on the South Side launched various campaigns to secure improved housing during the 1930s as their growing dissatisfaction with substandard conditions provided a focal point around which black activists, who were fighting for better and more equitable housing, could rally. In addition, there was no singular agenda. Working-class African Americans contended with white South Siders and with middle-class African Americans who sought to acquire housing commensurate to their perceived status in the community. What is important about this discussion is that during this period, public housing became one of the central tenets for shaping local political activism within the working class.

Dramatic population increases that took place during the Great Migration fueled much of the confusion. Southern African Americans were drawn to cities like Chicago for a variety of reasons ranging from improved social and economic conditions to their need to escape racial repression in the South. Chicago met such needs. Black migrants to the city enjoyed greater (although not complete) mobility, education opportunities, and employment prospects than they would have in many other locales in the country. As a result, migrants came in ever-greater numbers. Between 1920 and 1930, the African American population grew from 109,458 to 233,903 (a 113.7 percent increase). While much of this increase grew out of the expansion of economic opportunities during World War I, the population continued to grow during the worst years of the Depression—from 1930 until 1940, the population increased to 277,730 (an 18.7 percent increase). But for new arrivals and the existing community alike, Chicago in many cases proved to be more of a flawed Promised Land than anything else. Much of this developed because as the community continued to grow, the available housing stock on the South Side could not keep pace with the demand.

Chicago's black community experienced one of the greatest population densities in the city. For instance, the area bordered by Thirty-Ninth Street, Forty-Seventh, State Street, and Cottage Grove Avenue housed 51,591 people per square mile during the 1930s. This number skyrocketed to 62,943 people per square mile at the outset of World War II. Comparatively, the white working-class community of Bridgeport, located directly west of Bronzeville, had a population density of 20,695 people per square mile during the 1930s and 20,070 during the 1940s. High population densities and hyper-segregation meant that, over time, African Americans lived in more and more racially segregated communities. In 1920, for instance, 44.8 percent of Chicago's African American communities lived in areas that were between 75 percent and 89.9 percent African American. By 1940, 44.6 percent of all of Chicago's black population lived in communities that were between 90 percent and 97.4 percent African American. At the same time, 19 percent of Chicago's black population were living in communities that were greater than 97.5 percent African American.[3]

Much of the congestion was attributed to the fact that, by custom and by law, African Americans were concentrated in communities with people who looked, talked, and acted like themselves. These patterns of settlement served an important role in shaping the migrant experiences. The difference, though, was that in ethnic white communities there was a very real possibility that movement out of these enclaves was possible and that ethnic white individuals would experience a fuller integration into American society.[4] For African Americans, achieving integration would be virtually impossible. Black mobility in the Chicago housing market was severely hampered by the implementation of restrictive covenants. Originally rooted in English common law, these pacts were "contractual agreements among property owners that none of them would permit a 'colored person' to occupy, lease, or buy his property."[5] When first used, these provisions guarded against encroachment of industrial plants, saloons, taverns, and similar businesses. When initiated in places like Chicago, they restricted access to minority groups by targeting African Americans, Jews, Italians, and others. White Americans who wanted to resist community integration often viewed the covenant system as the key to maintaining racial homogeneity in their communities and to protecting property values. African Americans maintained a different view of covenants. For many, restrictive provisions represented a hindrance to their upward mobility, and they saw the existence of such provisions as an insult to their dignity.

Fighting for dignity has been and continues to be a common trope within African American history. In countless cases, African Americans actively resisted such physical obstacles like lynchings, Jim Crow laws, and political and sexual oppression and overcame various legal setbacks such as the *Dred Scott* and *Plessy* decisions. On the housing front, two cases, *Buchanan v. Warley* (1917) and *Corrigan v. Buckley* (1926), speak to this fight. In *Buchanan*, the Supreme Court found that an "attempt to prevent the alienation of the property . . . to a person of color was not a legitimate exercise of the state, and is in direct violation of the fundamental law enacted in the 14th amendment of the constitution preventing state interference with property right except by due process of law."[6] In *Corrigan*, the Court's ruling noted that those sections of the Fifth and Fourteenth Amendments referring to equal protection under the laws applied only to governmental actions, not to private contracts. *Corrigan* provided legal justification to further place fetters on black citizens' freedom of movement. It was not, however, the only option available to opponents of neighborhood integration. Much like in the post-*Plessy* South, where African Americans' liberties were limited by state-supported segregation, in the 1930s white citizens would again enlist the aid of the government to maintain separation of the races. The Federal Housing Administration's (FHA) *Underwriting Manual* would prove an invaluable tool. University of Chicago sociologist Homer Hoyt was a driving voice in the preparation of the underwriting standard used by the FHA. In 1933 Hoyt ranked fifteen racial and ethnic groups to determine their impact on housing values. Not surprisingly, he found that African Americans and Mexicans embodied the biggest detriment to home values. Following his advice, the FHA concluded that in order to maintain property stability, "it is necessary that properties continue to be occupied by the same social and racial classes."[7]

Emboldened by the courts, community groups throughout Chicago worked at stemming the invasion of African Americans into white communities and enlisted the aid of influential groups such as the Chicago Real Estate Board (CREB). Organized in 1908, by the 1920s CREB, along with forty-five other real estate boards from across the nation, organized and formed the National Association of Real Estate Boards (NAREB). The group established a national headquarters in Chicago. Soon after its founding, NAREB created a system of real estate standards that sought to preserve racially homogeneous neighborhoods. In 1924 CREB contracted the services of a Chicago lawyer, Nathan William MacChesney, to draft the text of a code of ethics for realtors. The final draft of the code included specific language prohibiting realtors from introducing members of any race or nationality into neighborhoods when their presence would damage property values.[8] To enforce this code, MacChesney created a real estate licensing act known as the "MacChesney Act." The act empowered state real estate commissions to revoke the licenses of any agents who violated the code of ethics. Following the adoption of these policies, MacChesney and NAREB drafted the first standard covenant against the selling or leasing of housing to African Americans. This form became a model employed throughout the nation.

NAREB and CREB were not the lone forces driving racial restrictions. Instead, these groups relied on assistance from community-based organizations such as the Cook County Property Owners Restriction Association and other homeowners', improvement, and businessmen associations to actually enforce covenants through programs like the "Choose Your Neighbor" campaign.[9] The purpose of this campaign was to educate white homeowners on the effectiveness of restrictive covenants in halting neighborhood integration. Neighborhood associations had a long history in Chicago, and some associations pressured the city into fulfilling annexation campaign promises. In the beginning, these associations seemed more concerned with the physical conditions of the communities than with their racial composition. During the 1920s, several of the associations were interracial, and some had memberships composed completely of African Americans. Most of these groups focused on such issues as "dissatisfaction with local conditions" and "failure of authorities to sweep and sprinkle streets or provide adequate street lighting, corner signs, and similar equipment." They also urged residents to "utilize night school and 'other public and semi-public institutions'" in the neighborhood.[10]

Among these early groups that were truly concerned with actual neighborhood improvement were the Hyde Park Improvement Protective Club and the Washington Park Court Improvement Association. Formed in 1906 to address vice, the activities of these groups included planting shrubbery and advocating for clean streets.[11] As African Americans outgrew the confines of the Black Belt and encroached on white communities, the missions of these organizations moved away from "neighborhood improvement" to antiblack activism. The Kenwood–Hyde Park Property Owners' Association was one of the most notorious groups on the South Side, famous for using bombings as a way to restrict African Americans. These acts of terrorism were so successful that as early as the 1920s, CREB sent congratulatory letters to the association for its proclamation that "in 60 days it had forestalled Negro occupancy of 57 houses south of Thirty-Ninth Street."[12] This practice soon became the "rage"—"to adopt these covenants [and] spread [them] across Chicago, fueled by the Board and local realtors."[13]

Restrictive covenants, despite their popularity, ultimately failed to completely limit housing options for African Americans. Their searches continued, and more often than not, they looked to the neighboring white communities of Washington Park and Hyde Park for relief. Challenging restrictive covenants did not necessarily occur merely to find better housing conditions. While this was an important issue, the pressure African Americans exerted on the covenant system gained symbolic importance. The existence of race covenants was seen as an insult to the dignity of the African American community—especially to the "most economically secure members for whom social and legal equality were deemed highly important."[14]

As was the case in 1917 Louisville and 1926 Washington, D.C., African Americans in Chicago, defended by the legal departments of organizations like the NAACP, launched legal campaigns to end restrictive covenants in the city of Chicago. One early case occurred in 1938. The Oakland–Kenwood Businessmen's Association filed a suit against John and Blanche Fox, African Americans who resided at 3705 South Ellis. The association asked the court to remove the Foxes because allegedly 95 percent of the property owners along the street had signed an agreement to keep African Americans from living in this section. What is unique about this particular case is that although the covenant was recorded in December 1937, residents on the block declared that "the covenant [had] never been adhered to and this was the first attempt that has been made to enforce it." Also, according to the *Chicago Defender*, the 3700–3800 block of South Ellis Avenue was a virtual melting pot of ethnic cultures.[15]

As claimed in a number of reports, many of the white residents were unaware of the existence of the covenant. A white woman who lived on the block stated she had been in the neighborhood a number of years and found out about the covenant only in the previous week. In addition to African Americans, the 3700 and 3800 blocks of South Ellis had a high number of Chinese, Mexican, Japanese, and white citizens. However, it was unclear whether any action was taken against any other ethnic groups at the time. Monroe Binkley, himself a member of the businessmen's group and one of the named plaintiffs in the case, went as far as to acknowledge that Fox and his wife were "swell people." However, that did not deter him from moving from the 3700 block to the 3800 block of South Ellis when the 3700 block took on a "definite Race color."[16] In a similar case, African Americans living at 417 East Sixtieth Street were forced to move from their home in a contested area after white residents decided to enforce an underutilized covenant.[17]

The Fox case was by no means an isolated event, and in scanning the black press during this period, one encounters dozens of similar incidents. That African Americans continued to move into segregated neighborhoods in spite of the legal and physical threats they encountered calls into question the overall effectiveness of restrictive covenants as a legal tool. One of the most important legal challenges to restrictive covenants occurred when Carl Hansberry, father of playwright Lorraine Hansberry, tried to move into the Chicago subdivision of Washington Park in 1937. The case, *Hansberry v. Lee*, would eventually be argued before the U.S. Supreme Court in 1940. The decision handed down by the Court would strike a blow against covenants locally. Unfortunately, it would fail to set any major legal precedent.

Hansberry moved to Chicago in 1915 from Glaston, Mississippi. By 1923 he had established his own accounting firm, which was on the segregated South Side. In 1927 Hansberry received a patronage job working for the Chicago Board of Education, and in 1929 he was appointed deputy U.S. marshal for Chicago, a position he held until 1931. This steady employment during the Depression helped Hansberry amass enough money to develop his own real estate business, and he went into business managing apartments on the South Side. A 1941 article in the *Crisis* reported that he "owned and controlled over $250,000 in residential real estate, housing over 400 families."[18] By 1937 Hansberry was a wealthy real estate investor and active in the Chicago Branch of the NAACP. Between 1933 and 1940 he served as either the secretary or treasurer of the organization. Although his primary duty was maintaining membership, it was his attempts to acquire property in white communities that bordered the South Side black community that helped shape the housing policy of the local branch.

Hansberry's first engagement occurred when he enlisted the Chicago NAACP in a fight against covenants. In October 1936 he and his family moved into an apartment building at 549 East Sixtieth Street. A white woman, Ruth Hoffman, owned the building. Upon learning of the family's occupancy, Hoffman's neighbors sued her, claiming she had violated a restrictive covenant that governed the community. Hoffman initially claimed that Hansberry was not her tenant but rather a cousin, and she argued she would not expel him or his family. Hoffman also refused to comply with the expulsion demand because for her, any restrictive covenant was a violation of public policy of the state of Illinois. While there were no clear ties between Hoffman and Hansberry, her interpretation of state policy was correct. Under Illinois law, no "municipal corporation in the State of Illinois, shall deny any person, on account of race, color, or religion, the full accommodation, advantages, or facilities."[19] The circuit court, initially, allowed the Hanberrys to remain in the apartment. However, when the case was appealed in 1937, the Illinois Appellate Court reversed the lower court's decision and ordered that Hansberry must vacate the property. White opponents believed they scored a major victory. Their victory was brief.

Hansberry again challenged restrictive covenants in 1937. This time he purchased a property at 6140 South Rhodes Avenue. During his first nights in the building, bricks were thrown through several windows of the home. Several weeks later, members of the Woodlawn Property Owners' League, led by Anna Lee with the support of the University of Chicago, sued Hansberry in the circuit court of Cook County. Early rulings went against Hansberry. However, on appeal to the U.S. Supreme Court, the Court ruled that the particular restrictive covenant did not have the required number of signatures and was therefore invalid. This legal victory, although won on a technicality, marked an important moment in the civil rights fight in Chicago and proved to the public that African Americans could use the courts to break down residential segregation. This ruling opened Washington Park to select groups of African Americans looking to escape the confines of the Black Belt.

This case, like the ones discussed earlier, had little bearing on the experiences of members of the black working class, who were quick to differentiate their problems from those of their wealthier neighbors. Some within the community could take no joy from the case. In a letter to the editor printed in the *Chicago Defender*, one reader seemed less than sympathetic to the problems of "one or two of Chicago's leading Race citizens," who all but ignored the poor who "would have to remain here in the filthy atmosphere" even if other options were made available.[20] This sentiment developed out of the irony of restrictive covenants, at least in their earlier forms, in that segments of the black middle class actually supported the fundamental idea behind these agreements, especially when they were aimed at new southern migrants. While they abhorred the racial components, the standards of living and behavior that covenants demanded were important as segments of the black middle class worked to prove themselves worthy of the benefits their social standing afforded them. In some instances, the desire for recognition put them at odds with newly arrived southern black migrants. Nowhere was this more evident than when they cautioned new arrivals to "abandon their 'obnoxious' country habits and adopt the customs of their new homes."[21]

During the early migration period, middle-class black residents, working alongside organizations like the Chicago Urban League, urged African American newcomers to conform to norms and behaviors that came with life in the big city. On the one hand, migrants were confronted by the league's behavioral "do's and don'ts" lists, which included such items as "don't make yourself a public nuisance" and "don't keep unsanitary houses or sleep in a rooms without proper ventilation."[22] On the other hand, migrants saw their institutions—for example, storefront churches—attacked by the middle class and their religious practices labeled as lower class.[23]

What motivated the middle class to take these positions is debatable. One can easily assume that they were simply acting in their own self-interests. Michelle R. Boyd argues that the black middle class in Chicago developed a number of strategies that worked toward bettering the "Negro community as a whole and indirectly obtaining citizenship rights by demonstrating the ability of the Negro petty-bourgeois standards of respectability and success."[24] Touré F. Reed similarly argues that the belief that "whites' tendency to judge the race as a whole by the deficiencies of acculturated Afro-Americans prompted [groups like the Urban League] to pursue remedial as well as punitive programs directed toward so-called maladjusted blacks."[25] This fear of white people using the negative behaviors of migrants as a barometer to judge all African Americans was a real concern. A counterinterpretation focuses on the fact that many within the black middle class believed they had a moral responsibility to uplift the race and worked to reform the behavior of the entire community. Historian Victoria Wolcott, for instance, says that "in urban neighborhoods potent symbols such as clothing, modes of transportation or state of a front yard or stoop signaled the level of respectability to others." A neighborhood that could accomplish this beautification effort, she argues, could "'communicate' the residents' respectability to the rest of the city."[26]

On the South Side, the Urban League conducted public experiments aimed at demonstrating how working-class African Americans had the capability of sustaining clean and beautiful communities. The league's Department of Civic Improvement embarked on a campaign in 1936 to stimulate civic pride and chose Bronzeville's red-light district—the area between Forty-Third and Forty-Seventh Streets and South Parkway and Michigan Avenue—as its testing ground. The community was a center for vice. It housed a number of taverns that harbored criminals and other disreputable characters, claimed sixty illegal gambling and policy stations, and was frequented by prostitutes. Moreover, the area was overcrowded, underemployed, and underserved—thirty thousand people were cramped into a space suited to house only five thousand. Some 74 percent of the community were employed in private industry or domestic service while another 25 percent were receiving some form of government relief. The immediate area had three churches, no schools or playgrounds, and poorly lit streets, and abandoned, dilapidated cars and trucks lined the curbs.[27]

The campaign achieved some successes. By August 31, the Urban League reported that "out of the 620 front yards in the area, [only] 116 had not been beautified."[28] In addition to these beautification efforts, the league organized lectures of neighborhood improvement, sixteen block meetings, and the Washington Park Federation of Improvement Clubs to coordinate future efforts. But much to their disappointment, the Urban League and its supporters were forced to face something that almost all African Americans were aware of—race took precedence over any perceived class similarities. Irrespective of one's ability to maintain viable neighborhoods, to most residents of white communities, in the words of historian Thomas Philpott, "all blacks still looked like 'low grade plantation niggers.'"[29]

For those without the financial resources to engage in drawn-out court battles, court challenges issued by the NAACP were a victory only for those with the resources to physically move out of the Black Belt. In their view, the court rulings did not touch the everyday lives of ordinary African Americans. Realtors and landlords knew that despite the *Hansberry* decision, the majority of Chicago's black residents would still have difficulty moving out of the physical ghetto. Landlords of both races and community activists suggested that Hansberry himself profited from the proliferation of substandard housing, often capitalized on the high internal demand for housing and the low supply of adequate housing, and in some circles gained the moniker of "kitchenette king."[30] In these inner city districts, the use of small apartments called kitchenettes became one of the few options for black people living in Chicago. These units were "large flats [that] were cut into small family units, with existing bath facilities serving a number of families common. Beaver-board partitions were common; closets were converted into kitchens, and living and sleeping space merged."[31]

Chicago's black communities were contained in up to twenty-three square miles of substandard areas. Within the communities, black families lived in homes that were often dark, damp, rat-infested, in need of major repairs, and lacking most of the facilities accepted as necessary for the much-touted American standard of living. The mix of overcrowded and unsanitary conditions contributed to a public health crisis. A 1939 survey showed that within Bronzeville, the tuberculosis mortality rate was "six times the rate for the city and 20 times greater than that of Rogers Park [a white community on the city's North Side]. The infant mortality rate is 40 times greater than the city average and about 2 times that of

Rogers Park."[32] Physically, the buildings were left in major disrepair. In one, African Americans occupied three floors of a four-story property at 4052–56 South Indiana. In this location, the only protection against the elements was the abandoned fourth floor, which served as the roof. In another instance, the Metropolitan Housing Council investigated a location that contained neither functioning toilets nor running water. And in still another, an eighty-six-year-old man and his seventy-eight-year-old wife lived in two rooms on the first floor of a former mansion. Of this space, only one of the rooms was heated, and the home had no running water or toilet facilities. Moreover, any water that the family needed was "carried in from some other house."[33]

High and racially disparate rents compounded the problem as the demand for housing continued to outweigh supply. The Depression severely retarded the building of any new homes during this period. In 1925, for example, more than 5,000 new apartment buildings were constructed annually. By 1926 a construction slowdown gripped Chicago and other metropolitan areas. As a result, in 1928 fewer than 3,000 new apartments were constructed. In 1929 only 1,300 were constructed, and in the following year a mere 330 were built.[34] For landlords, charging high rent was a good business practice because it offered an immediate return on their initial investment. As stereotypes about African Americans and declining property values remained popular, property values in black neighborhoods steadily declined. Realtors and property owners sought ways to effectively manage their investments. As it stood, realtors were left with few options. They could hold on to the land and rent property to African Americans and provide reasonable rents. Or, they could see the investment as a short-term venture, charge exorbitant rents, and turn a substantial profit in return. Many chose the latter.

A report released by the Committee on Negro Housing, "Negro Housing in Northern Cities," found that in "every city in the North, Negro tenants are required to pay not merely excessive rentals for properties occupied, but considerably higher amounts than is paid by other groups for similar properties."[35] This pattern held true for the South Side, where, according to a study conducted by the School of Social Service Administration at the University of Chicago, "the rent paid by Negroes was appreciably higher than that paid by people of any other group."[36] Robert Taylor, the first African American appointed to the Chicago Housing Authority, found that "the median rental in unheated flats was $20 dollars for native whites, $15 to $20 for foreign born white, [and] $25 to $30 for [African Americans]."[37] For heated apartments, Taylor found, the median rent was fifty-five to sixty dollars for white citizens and sixty-five to seventy dollars for African Americans. Disparate rents were not limited to good quality apartments. The Committee on Negro Housing found that even in the vice districts, rents averaged between seventy and eighty dollars per month.[38]

Greed, while an important factor, was not the main impetus behind the proliferation of dilapidated buildings. Public indifference played a part. More significant was the action, or rather inaction, of government regulators to enforce minimum standards in black communities. In their defense, city regulators did not always have adequate funds for inspections. Even though the federal government began to devote more attention to the conditions of cities during the Depression, the Roosevelt administration did not provide direct assistance to cities.[39] In addition, African Americans often lacked allies in the courts willing to compel landlords to make improvements in housing, as many landlords were concerned only with the profit that could be had in renting these apartments and took no interest in making repairs for their tenants or providing basic services like water. Bronzeville resident Felix Washington reported that during the five years he resided in his apartment, he used five-gallon cans and obtained water for drinking, washing, and operating toilets from a local elementary school. In interviews with the city's fire chief, the inspector chief of the Board of Health, and the secretary of the Illinois State Housing Board, the Metropolitan Housing Council discovered that no more than cursory health and fire inspections had been performed at Washington's location and no attempts had been made to remedy the many obvious sanitary deficiencies at the residence.

The Depression decade also saw an increase in the number of evictions for nonpayment of rent. However, it was in this arena that working and poor residents encountered some opportunities to help better their living conditions. The Communist Party and other organizations on the Left were active in fighting high rents and evictions during this period.[40] Anti-eviction actions during the early 1930s provided Communist organizers valuable inroads into the South Side black community. This was especially true among the working class and the poor. For these people who, in the wake of *Hansberry*, realized that the legal tactics of the NAACP did little to address their condition, aligning with the Communist Party seemed a natural course of action.[41] This "new crowd," according to Beth Tompkins Bates, embodied a more militant style of protest, which at times was more confrontational and direct.[42]

Chicagoan Dempsey Travis, for instance, recalled in his autobiography that during the 1930s "everyday someone was evicted on our block for nonpayment of rent. Before the bailiffs had put the last piece of furniture on the street, someone would contact the Communist Red Squads that met in Washington Park."[43] These direct action campaigns garnered the Communists a great deal of trust from African Americans in the community.

These acts of open defiance over rent controls and living conditions eventually culminated in the 1931 Chicago Rent Riot, in which the Communists and African Americans in the community clashed with Chicago police. During this riot, the police killed three African Americans—John O'Neil, Abe Gray, and Thomas Paige—three policemen were injured, and several bystanders were wounded. This violent resistance prompted the courts to suspend evictions within the African American community and forced government officials to implement a "no-rent" policy and to reevaluate the sources of relief available for the unemployed of Chicago.[44]

While the Communists were very active, other activists, with and without leftist sympathies, also expanded their own agendas for better housing conditions during this period. The Consolidated Tenants Association (CTA) was one such organization fighting against high rents and for access to low-rent housing throughout the United States.[45] Another group was based in Harlem. Although led by prominent Harlemites, this organization engaged in a number of coalition activities with organizations from across the political spectrum—the NAACP, the Communist Party, the International Defense League, and several black churches— that initiated successful campaigns against high rents and evictions and concerning other social issues affecting New York City.[46] The association in Chicago engaged in similar activities and was very active in challenging racial issues in housing and highlighted the blending of public and private cooperation.

The CTA was founded in 1937 to attack high rents after residents living in an apartment at 437–439 Oakwood received letters stating that property management would no longer include the cost of heating and cooking gas in the monthly rent. Residents of the building were instructed to contact the gas company and make arrangements to have gas meters installed for their units in their own names.[47] Joseph Jefferson, a resident of the building and a member of the political organization of the powerful African American alderman William L. Dawson (who served as the group's president), interpreted this action as an indirect rent increase and refused to pay the higher rates. Jefferson, supported by Dawson's political clout and pro bono legal advice, organized residents against this action and refused to comply with the measure. The protesters refused to give in to the demands of the building owners, and the CTA's actions eventually forced the realtor to rescind his orders. Eventually the association expanded its efforts to other buildings and organized rent strikes in cases where landlords increased rents.[48]

The CTA was not alone in its organizing efforts. The National Negro Congress (NNC) organized its Tenants' League in 1940.[49] Several of the group's members—NNC field organizer Ishmael P. Flory, Committee on Housing chairman Joseph Johnson, and Chicago NNC chairman Evelyn

McDowell—joined the fight against high rents when McDowell's landlord attempted to raise her rent and evict her from her apartment at 4320–22 Forrestville Avenue. Out of this incident, the NNC launched a community rent strike by up to 2,300 tenants living in properties owned by the Mid-city Realty Company.[50] The NNC campaign called for the organizing of African American tenants against what Flory and Johnson called "abominably high rents fleeced out of the Negro people by predatory landlords and agents."[51]

The relative success of these two groups aside, merely challenging high rents would not solve the overall housing shortage. More housing needed to be developed. For this, African Americans looked to privately financed subsidized housing. In the early stages of the development of low-income housing, private philanthropic efforts added to the number of adequate dwellings. The construction of the Michigan Boulevard Garden Apartments, also known as the Rosenwald, was one such effort. Started in 1929, the financing of this housing project was provided by philanthropist Julius Rosenwald, who controlled Sears, Roebuck and Company. The construction of the Rosenwald was part of a larger trend where white philanthropists funded the development of private housing for higher-income black residents. Other projects included Marshall Field's Marshall Field Garden, opened for white Chicagoans living on the city's North Side, and John D. Rockefeller's Thomas Gardens in New York City. Covering a full square block, the Rosenwald project contained an enclosed, spacious landscaped courtyard that provided green space for its residents. Although segregated, this facility's 420 or so units were looked upon by some as the "first step to wiping out 'black belts and slums.'"[52]

The ambitiousness of the project did have its critics, as some civil rights activists questioned the segregated nature of the project. The black press, for one, charged Rosenwald with "keeping the colored man out of white institutions," while other Rosenwald ventures, such as his funding of an all-black YMCA, led to accusations that he created institutions for "colored only."[53] While the critiques may have been valid, the five-story building, bounded by Forty-Sixth Street on the north, Forty-Seventh on the south, Wabash Avenue on the east, and Michigan Avenue on the west, offered modern facilities and affordable rents.

Unfortunately for residents and their supporters, economic realities of the Depression forced many would-be investors to abandon any follow-up projects, thus ending strictly private ventures in public housing. This failure demonstrated the limits of privately operated public welfare ventures.[54] More often than not, African Americans increasingly turned to federal and local governments to ease their housing burdens. Nowhere was this truer than with the 1935 proposal to construct a public housing project on the

South Side. The development, which would later be named after Ida B. Wells, symbolized a degree of hope for black residents that an increase in and better housing was coming to their community. At the same time, this proposed development solidified many of the fears held by neighboring white communities of an expansion of the Black Belt.

During the 1930s the federal government instituted of a number of housing initiatives, ranging from direct loans for private and public building programs to the formation of a federal office responsible for slum clearance and the construction of public housing projects. One of these measures occurred in 1934 with the passage of the National Housing Act. This act helped the Federal Housing Administration to oversee the construction of both private and public housing units. In 1937 the housing act was amended. Under this new act, instead of just providing funds for construction, according to Mary Watters, federal policy now "added housing to its program of social reform" and "set out to subsidize slum clearance and low rent housing for the 'one-third of the nation, ill-housed, ill-clad and ill-nourished.'"[55] The 1937 act also provided for the creation of local housing authorities to construct and administer building projects. By using the language of New Deal liberalism to address the housing crisis, the federal government was not simply declaring its assumed responsibility to ensure the public welfare of its citizens. What the federal government did, in essence, was to affirm that access to adequate housing was a guaranteed right for all citizens. The National Housing Act, like most New Deal programs, defined a social welfare component that purposefully made no allusions to race, choosing rather to continue the language of opportunity. The rhetorical color blindness of the program notwithstanding, African American public housing advocates viewed new public housing initiatives as having a direct impact on their people and interpreted housing policy squarely from the perspective of their race. This was easy for them to do since those who resided in substandard housing were keenly aware that phrases such as "slum clearance," "low-rent housing," and "ill-housed" more than accurately reflected their housing realities.

Scholars who have studied the creation of large-scale public housing projects have noted that the program did contain some significant flaws. The most glaring was the federal government's "decision not to disrupt pre-existing racial patterns of neighborhoods"[56] and thus stay above the civil rights fray with its "neighborhood composition" rules.[57] Under these rules, public housing would not be permitted to change the racial composition of a neighborhood. While this interpretation may have had some merit, when interpreted through the lens of African American liberalism, we see that residents embraced public housing, flaws and all, because they depended on these apartments to alleviate overcrowding and the federal government was now making provisions to give it to them. This opportunity offered, according to Rhonda Y. Williams, "a way out, a chance, and a plausible strategy for obtaining adequate, affordable, and sanitary housing in respectable neighborhoods."[58]

In Chicago, the construction and administration of public housing fell under the purview of the Chicago Housing Authority. Created in June 1937 by Mayor Edward J. Kelly, the CHA was given "considerable powers in buying, leasing, or condemning sites, erecting and operating housing projects and issuing obligations on mortgages secured by them."[59] Holding various levels of prestige and prominence, the commissioners of the original body included T. J. Carney, vice president of Sears, Roebuck and Company; Victor A. Olander, secretary-treasurer of the Illinois State Federation of Labor; Coleman Woodbury, director of the National Association of Housing Officials; John R. Fugard, architect and president of the Metropolitan Housing Council; and W. J. Lynch, a building contractor connected to, among others, the Field Museum. But the person who had the greatest influence in shaping the policy of the CHA was executive secretary Elizabeth Wood. A graduate of the University of Michigan, Wood held several citywide and state positions, from head of staff of the Metropolitan Housing Council to a post on the Executive Housing Board. During her tenure with the CHA (1937–54), Wood challenged the "neighborhood composition" policy and guided the CHA into eventually adopting a nondiscrimination position in all public housing matters.[60]

By the time the CHA began operation, four housing developments either were in the planning stages or were underway through the Public Works Administration (PWA). The Jane Addams, Julia C. Lathrop, and Trumbull Park Homes were listed as "white projects."[61] The fourth development, the Ida B. Wells Homes, was to be constructed for African American residents on the South Side. Although construction of the original site was approved in 1935, work on the project would not begin until 1939. Like most of the issues outlined in this chapter, the delays at the Wells project had much to do with legal challenges, planning controversies, and debates about rights, citizenship, and liberalism. Put simply, if African Americans were going to use public housing as a way to articulate their definition of the liberal state, then whites Chicagoans could be counted on to do the same.

"The Project," as residents often referred to it, held a significant psychological impact for African Americans. For many of them, the Ida B. Wells Homes development was seen as a stepping-stone for those "respectable lowers who wanted to make the mobility step to the lower middle class."[62] The project's name also was relevant to community residents. Originally named the South Parkway Garden, community groups rallied to have the building named for a resident who once lived a few hundred feet from the construction site, "a crusader whose pen and voice had been silenced by death" in 1931.[63] The homes were to be constructed on a parcel of land bordered by Cottage Grove Avenue, Thirty-Fifth Street, Thirty-Seventh Street, Pershing Road, Langley Avenue, and South Parkway, but progress on the buildings remained slow. Some within the black community believed that "the long delay in construction of the project has caused a great deal of distrust of public officials by the voters of the South Side."[64] Joseph Jefferson was especially critical of both the governor and the mayor because of their apparent unwillingness to exert political pressure to expedite construction.

Federal and local housing authorities proved convenient and logical targets of community frustration. While ultimately responsible for home construction, the PWA was limited in its acquisition of land by the justice system. Construction on the Wells project was hindered by a court ruling, not in Chicago, but in the federal courts of Louisville, Kentucky. In it, the court ruled the slum clearance and low-rent housing construction were not included in the government's power of eminent domain.[65] The Kentucky ruling had serious consequences for advocates of public housing in Chicago. To make room for the new project the federal government had purchased necessary land, and in the process hundreds of African American families were forced to move from their homes with few relocation options. Race-restrictive covenants hampered efforts at finding housing in other parts of the city. For residents on relief, relocation was an especially difficult situation. There was no place to go, and neither the local nor the federal government made any provisions for their welfare. For those forced to move, uncertainty about the future heightened the levels of fear that existed in the community. CHA officials, left with few options, "turned to the slower process of direct purchase from property owners."[66] When construction funds finally became available, the Illinois General Assembly had to grant Chicago, through an endorsement, the power to expropriate private property for public use through eminent domain. The first draft by the state did not, however, include an open housing provision. As a result the first draft was rejected by the city council. A second draft, with the open housing provision, was approved by the city council and forwarded to the General Assembly in Springfield for passage.[67]

The site selected for the Wells project presented a familiar problem for the white residents living in Hyde Park. Cottage Grove Avenue was the de facto western border between the Black Belt and white Hyde Park–Kenwood. White residents were threatened by the development's close proximity to their neighborhood. To forestall a potential black invasion, the same groups working to restrict black mobility into the Hyde Park area focused their efforts on resisting the construction of the Ida B. Wells Homes. Much of the opposition was led by the Woodlawn Property Owners' League, the organization that had formulated the original restrictive covenants. Initially, its strategy was to get the city to reconsider the site's location. Opponents presented a number of alternate sites to local and federal officials. These locations were farther west, away from Lake Michigan, on property closer to the Union Stockyard, a community of first- and second-generation European immigrants.

Project planners refused to consider this plan, and finding no audience for their suggestion, a delegation of white real estate representatives traveled to Washington, D.C., to take their protest directly to Harold Ickes, secretary of the Interior and head of the PWA. In retrospect, even if they had been successful in their attempts to meet with Ickes, it is unlikely that delegation members would have found a receptive ear in the secretary. Ickes, a strong supporter of African American rights, once served as the president of the Chicago NAACP. In his work for the Roosevelt administration, Ickes was the first cabinet member to establish a race relations office, upon which all others were judged.[68] Moreover, under Ickes, African Americans occupied at least one-third of all the housing units built by the PWA and occupied 41,000 of the 122,000 dwelling units built during 1937 and 1942.[69] Instead, the protesters met with Colonel Horatio Hackett, Ickes's assistant, who informed the real estate representatives that "he did not believe that the protest would be acted upon by [Ickes]" and that "the government had determined to proceed with the project."[70]

It looked as if this was a victory for housing advocates. But, undeterred by their trip to Washington, protesters returned to Chicago and launched a massive letter writing campaign to pressure officials to reconsider. White protesters united with other groups already fighting to restrict African American mobility to the black community. These included the Oakland Business Men's Association, the Hyde Park Property Owners Association, the Drexel State Bank, and the Oakland–Kenwood Property Owners Association. Together these groups, alongside CREB, engaged in legal action to halt the Wells project and approved a number of measures to hinder "any and all low-cost housing projects anywhere near the lakefront."[71] In the face of the efforts of the white community, African Americans stood behind efforts to construct these new homes. One resident characterized these actions by housing opponents as "just another example of how racial trouble is started . . . [and] I'm growing rather damn tired of being told by a bunch a grafting shysters where I could spend my money and how to spend it."[72]

As public housing advocates prepared themselves for conflicts with protesters, new battles would be waged with the federal government. In the years following the initial housing proposal, advocates found that the road to improved housing would not be a smooth one. Housing advocates set out to accomplish several goals during the initial stages of the project. These included obtaining adequate compensation for all land purchased by the federal government, ensuring that African Americans could secure skilled and unskilled jobs on the project, and increasing the number of decent homes for deserving people.[73] This multilayered agenda, although potentially beneficial, helped set the stage for a larger debate that would continue until the end of the Second World War.

Additional controversies arose when African Americans called on the CHA to appoint more black workers to construction jobs on the project. In 1933 Ickes issued an order forbidding "discrimination on the basis of color or religion in employment for public works."[74] Enacting such policy was difficult in some arenas. Since local contractors often employed all-white construction crews, incidents of racial discrimination were high. The Chicago Federation of Labor, in some cases, acted to curb discrimination associated with the development. This was complicated. Despite the federation's view that organized labor was the only institution that stood for equality for African American workers as far as their economic matters were concerned, according to union president John Fitzpatrick, "employers can and do restrict their employees to all Negros or all whites," concluding, "We [the federation] have no say in such cases, we just proceed to organize the workers, regardless of creed, color or nationality."[75]

The CHA sought to curtail this problem and established policy language that explicitly listed guidelines for African American representation on work crews. In outlining its position, CHA officials defined discrimination as the "failure to pay a minimum percentage of the skilled and unskilled payroll to Negro workers"; these percentages were determined by the 1930 occupational census of each U.S. city.[76] In light of the other setbacks associated with the Ida B. Wells Homes project, it came as no surprise that many residents still remained cautious of promises of equality. CHA actions did succeed in placing a small number of African American workers in some skilled and unskilled positions. But in the long term, they were inadequate to prevent African American demands for increased inclusion into public works projects.

An example of this protest is seen in response to the CHA's handling of the appointment of African American architects to design the Wells Homes. In 1938 an all-white architectural firm contracted to oversee the construction of the development was replaced. One of the partners in the new firm, Fugard and Thielber, was CHA chairman John Fugard. Forced to resign his position on the CHA in 1938 because he, in a violation of municipal policy, failed to maintain an address in the city, Fugard and his associate were assigned positions on the architectural staff. His successor on the CHA was J. W. McCarthy. Before his chairmanship, McCarthy had been one of the chief designers with McCarthy, Epping, and Smith—the firm originally tasked with overseeing the design and construction of the multimillion-dollar housing project. By Chicago standards of political corruption and scandal, this particular controversy regarding the composition of the CHA board may have seemed relatively insignificant. For African Americans, though, this event was quite serious. By changing firms, Mayor Kelly reneged on a political promise to employ more African American workers on the project as architects and engineers should any vacancies occur. By implementing such a program, Chicago would follow a trend that was developing in other locations—such as Langston Terrace in Washington, D.C., the Harlem River Project in New York City, and the Brewster Homes in Detroit—where projects were designed by or staffed by African American professionals and laborers.[77]

A number of organizations, including the NAACP, the NNC, and the Chicago Council of Negro Organizations, expressed their "disgust" with McCarthy. The most vocal critiques, however, came from the National Technical Association, the *Chicago Defender*, and the CTA. Founded in Chicago in 1926, the National Technical Association's mission was to advocate for the end of race prejudice in the sciences. Upon learning of the CHA controversy, the association commented that "the citizens of the South Side have always doubted the sincerity of the authority in carrying out the plans to build the project at Thirty-ninth and South Parkway."[78] The *Chicago Defender* chastised the city, noted that "we expect to see black men in key positions," and openly wondered "what evil spirit is hovering over us in Chicago" that allowed racial discrimination to continue.[79] A spokesman for the CTA expressed that he did not "think that the Authority is anxious for us out here to know too much about what they are doing about this project."[80] Moreover, he predicted that despite the popularity of Mayor Kelly, this action would leave some within the community believing that the CHA was a "closed corporation . . . and [they] are not going to let anybody in on it especially a member of the Race who might become too inquisitive."[81]

The public outcry failed to secure technical jobs for black workers. However, seizing upon an opportunity to pressure the mayor to shore up his political base, the *Defender* called upon Kelly to appoint a member of the race to the CHA. Kelly responded by naming Robert L. Taylor to the CHA in 1939. Taylor's appointment was not entirely politically motivated.

Throughout his administration, Kelly tapped a number of African Americans for important posts, including the school board, the Board of Commissioners of the Chicago World's Fair, the Committee on the Chicago Exposition, the Chicago Jubilee Committee, and assistant corporation counsel.[82] Appointing Taylor was important because it assured continued black support for the upcoming election, since many saw this as another example of the mayor's willingness to face black issues fairly. Furthermore, Taylor offered African Americans hope, now that they had an ally within the housing authority to protect their interests.

The belief that Taylor would be a strong advocate for African American housing concerns was a valid one. During the city council confirmation hearing for Taylor, Third Ward alderman Robert R. Jackson stated that Taylor "stands high in the Negro community."[83] Taylor, a respected figure among African Americans, was a student of modern housing policy and one of only eighteen African Americans in the United States who held a seat on a housing board. He had been educated at the University of Illinois and Northwestern University and had made extensive studies of European housing. Like many New Dealers, his professional philosophy was that housing for low-income families could not be provided by private philanthropy and that the federal and local government must take an active role in housing issues. This belief held by Taylor would remain true during and following World War II. Taylor's appointment helped the CHA recapture much of the support it had lost during the previous three years and played a significant role in shaping local housing policy regarding race. In addition, the development provided much-needed jobs for a number of South Side residents. Black workers, both skilled and unskilled, benefited from the construction of the Ida B. Wells Homes. Taylor, who would eventually rise to chairman of the CHA, and Elizabeth Wood, executive secretary of the agency, would advance the CHA's policy of nondiscrimination throughout their tenure. However, this policy would itself come under attack in the coming years.

2. POOR BUT NOT POVERTY STRICKEN
EQUAL EMPLOYMENT CAMPAIGNS IN 1930s CHICAGO

Why do they make us live in one corner of the city? Why don't they let us fly planes and run ships?
—Bigger Thomas from Richard Wright's novel *Native Son*

The industrial situation of the Negro presents difficulties not encountered by white workers. The Negro has often been refused admittance to the skilled trades on account of his lack of skill, and then when he became skilled, refused likewise because of color.
—A. L. Foster, Chicago Urban League

CHICAGO'S AFRICAN American community found itself especially hard hit by the social and political upheavals of the Great Depression. During the 1930s, approximately 18 percent of Chicagoans receiving some form of poor relief were African American, despite the racial group being only about 8 percent of the city's population.[1] In addition, three of the highest relief districts—the Archer district, Washington Park, and Oakland—each had black majorities. For their part, local government agencies found themselves increasingly ill equipped to deal with an unemployment crisis of such scale. In 1932 alone, Chicago's unemployment rolls listed nearly 200,000 people—40 percent of the city's workforce—and of that figure, 130,000 were on some sort of public assistance. The total cost of these benefits totaled nearly $2.6 million. To put this in further context, only 13,000 families had been on the relief rolls two years earlier, and those families had collected only $167,000 in public assistance.[2] These numbers notwithstanding, African Americans in Chicago did not suffer in silence. Instead they engaged in a variety of strategies, with varying degrees of success, to find assistance wherever possible. Their willingness to work with the Communists, labor unions, African American community organizations, and the state and federal government demonstrates how working-class African Americans were savvy in how they sought solutions to oppression and racism.

In Depression-era black Chicago, "over one half of the Negroes employable were out of work; for they were the first to lose their jobs and the last to secure new employment, even in work created in governmental bodies."[3] The ability of a great majority of the African American community to successfully weather the economic crisis was hindered both by a lack of a centralized unemployment assistance mechanism at the state or federal level and by the general inability of public officials, at any level, to provide solid, workable solutions to the relief and public assistance questions. For those not involved in the public assistance system, racist hiring and employment practices of white-led unions engaged in publicly and privately funded projects severely limited opportunities for African Americans to work their way out of the economic crisis.

Federal and local relief agencies were often inundated by more requests for assistance than they could fulfill, and other community-based relief efforts sponsored by churches or civic organizations were often unable to adequately address the economic realities of the Depression. African Americans and their allies seized upon these times to initiate a number of community-based protest programs to gain a measure of economic security while speaking out against economic discrimination. This was especially true in regard to public works projects. The realities of the Depression era provided an atmosphere conducive for various expressions of political activism. As a result, many African Americans embarked on campaigns to improve their economic status.

As was the case in the equal housing campaigns of this period, African Americans' demands for employment equality were inspired by the perceived social openness of the Roosevelt administration's liberal rhetoric. Nowhere was this more evident than in the formal and informal letter writing campaigns of African Americans. During the 1930s, African Americans continuously wrote New Deal administrators either seeking assistance in navigating the federal relief programs or directing New Deal officials' attention to cases of racial discrimination in federal programs. Quite often, writers would make reference to the president's own allusions to a universal citizenship where all citizens, regardless of race, could find some relief. In a 1935 letter to President Roosevelt from B. J. Jennings, president of the American Consolidated Trade Council, Jennings tells the president:

> We heard your speech Sunday night Mr. President over the
> radio; we know the President is sincere and intends to be fair to
> all the people, but those who are responsible for carrying out the
> President's great work programme, certainly have failed you Mr.
> President and have failed the black man all over this land.[4]

Letters like Jennings's spoke to the ideological battles raging in American
society where the idea of "equality of opportunity" competed with the
American notion of the "liberty to run one's business as one pleases."[5] Severe
unemployment on the South Side, coupled with the growing dissatisfaction that African Americans were good enough to spend money in white
establishments in Bronzeville but could not work in those establishments,
elevated the level of resentment toward white merchants.

Between 1929 and 1938 the American labor market changed dramatically with the appearance of more than twelve million unemployed workers.
A 1931 study commissioned by the Urban League examined the effects
of the Depression on African Americans. Of the 106 American cities examined, "with a few notable exceptions . . . the proportion of Negroes
unemployed was between 30 to 60 percent greater than for whites."[6] With
essentially no state or federal welfare agencies in place to provide relief for
the unemployed, African Americans had to rely almost solely on support
from religious and civic organizations within the community.

A number of groups arose during this period seeking to address these
disparities. Among them was the Communist Party. As noted in the previous chapter, the Communist Party was active in fighting against the large
number of evictions on the South Side. It did the same in advocating for
adequate relief. One of the ways the party accomplished this was by organizing the unemployed, primarily through the Unemployed Councils.
The councils were first formed in New York City in 1921. After a failed
attempt to establish other councils nationally in 1924, the Communist
Party again set out on a program to develop Unemployed Councils in
other cities across the United States. The platform of the Unemployed
Council movement consisted of a call for federal employment insurance and
federal appropriations for federal relief; a formal structure describing the
relationship between local, county, state, and national groups; and a written constitution.[7] In addition, the party was very influential in organizing
drives to bring African American workers into the ranks of organized labor.

The Communist Party and the Unemployed Councils provided services and opportunities to African Americans in the city that other civil
rights organizations, such as the Chicago Urban League or the Chicago
Branch of the NAACP, could not or would not exploit. So Sam Parks, an

African American labor activist who was influential in organizing workers in Chicago's stockyards, aligned himself with the Communist Party because he, and others like him, believed that the party was useful in "bringing about advancement in economic and working conditions for workers— black and white; [bringing about] community living for blacks and whites; [and] bringing about the end of discrimination."[8] In contrast, the Chicago Urban League established a Workers' Bureau during the Depression to stimulate black activism but failed to make considerable inroads as the "Negro upper-classes could not whole-heartedly commit themselves to the [militant] course dictated by the masses."[9] The Chicago NAACP, on the other hand, challenged the Communists in Chicago to determine which group would take the leadership role in fighting for rights for the working class. However, in some instances, the NAACP was unwilling to participate in open protest activities that, in the words of historian Christopher Reed, were "primarily social and economic in nature."[10]

The influence of the Communists (and by extension organized labor), while important, was only one avenue available for African Americans to secure employment. By the late 1920s, African Americans within Bronzeville formed a number of their own groups to push for change in the neighborhood. Some of these community-based entities engaged large chain and department stores operating on the South Side and challenged these venues to change their racial hiring practices. These fights held serious economic consequences for both the white retailers and the black residents on the South Side. Residents of the community became more outspoken over the fact that while their dollars made white merchants wealthy, store managers often refused to reinvest profits into the community or hire local African Americans to work in their stores.

These African American–led protest groups often rallied under a banner proclaiming "If our money is good enough to take, our boys and girls are good enough to be given a chance to make a living."[11] Black churches and other civic and fraternal organizations formed their own protest groups, and across the South Side, according to a *Chicago Defender* article, ministers were advising their congregations to stop making rich those merchants who refused them a living.[12] In 1930, the *Chicago Whip* became a vocal leader in the coordination of community protests by supporting the efforts of James Hale Porter, who coined the phrase "Don't Spend Your Money Where You Can't Work."[13] In its pages, *Whip* editors Joseph Bibb and A. C. MacNeal encouraged African Americans to follow Porter's advice and participate in formal boycotts. Among their first targets were three Woolworth stores on Forty-Third Street, Forty-Seventh Street, and Garfield Boulevard. The Woolworth stores proved logical targets because they were, according to

Oliver Cromwell Cox, the only major stores in the immediate area that did not employ black clerks.[14]

The action against Woolworth proved no easy endeavor, and at the onset there was considerable controversy among organizers regarding strategy. Initially, activists settled on the use of boycotts as a protest strategy. However, this proved rather ineffective. Because the stores offered a variety of inexpensive items to families often with limited incomes, black shoppers continued to patronize the stores. As a result, the economic boycotts failed to satisfactorily pressure the chain to alter its hiring practices. It was not until protest leaders began to employ picketers to march in front of these locations that significant movement was made. By the end of the thirteen-week Chicago campaign, "at least 2 dozen young black females won jobs as counter clerks at the four Woolworth's stores located in Black Metropolis."[15] By the end of 1931, as Cox found, not only did African Americans work at the store, but African American women made up approximately 25 percent of all Woolworth clerks in the area.[16]

Although ultimately successful, controversy within the South Side community tarnished the victory. While some white residents supported the pickets and the black masses almost unequivocally supported the action, critics argued that since Woolworth agreed to hire only twenty African American women as clerks, the protest failed to bring about significant economic changes for African Americans in Chicago. Not only was the scope of the protest too limited for some, but conservative critics in the community believed employing picketing as a protest tactic was too drastic. The possibility that Woolworth would respond to a confrontational strategy by discharging what few African Americans it employed in its stores nationwide was, to some, too risky. Also, some middle-class blacks feared that the campaigns were overly Communist in character. On the other hand, critics from the Communist Party condemned the campaigns for not being radical enough, and one protester argued, "It is indeed possible on occasion to kick up enough of a row big enough to force a Woolworth store in Chicago to make a promise. But, what has this to do with thousands of Negro workers in the coal, iron, steel, oil, automobile, and packing industry?"[17]

Despite these differences in interpretations, the protests succeeded in demonstrating the power of African American collective action and foreshadowed future civil rights activism. Chicago's protests inspired African Americans in other urban areas such as New York, where "Harlem newspapers were filled with appeals by ministers, politicians and businessmen to follow Chicago's example and launch a broad based protest campaign that could unite African Americans across class lines in other cities like Baltimore, Detroit and Cleveland."[18] While more-established civil rights groups such as the national office of the NAACP and the Urban League failed to publicly support more radical collective action campaigns by black Chicagoans, the Chicago offices of these two stalwarts quietly realized that combined civil disobedience and legal challenges would indeed be essential in securing equal protection of African Americans' rights during the 1930s. For the local civil rights agencies, this philosophical change would be important for developing a broad base from which to advocate for civil rights.

No amount of community organizing, though, could overcome the economic depression, and effective welfare protocols needed to be implemented. Organizations like the Chicago Urban League were active here. In September 1930 the Urban League brought together local leaders in an effort to raise funds to help unemployed residents on the South Side. While the meeting was well attended, it was less than a financial success.[19] Despite the best planning, the fact remained that churches and other all-black institutions were dependent upon poverty-stricken masses for support, and the majority of the African American community were unable to provide any funds to alleviate their condition.

The general inability to provide adequate relief was not a problem unique to private charities. Illinois governor Louis Emmerson formed a statewide Commission on Unemployment whose duty was to raise funds to assist local charities. In the commission's first two operating years, it raised more than $15 million. However, even this was far below the minimum amount of funds it needed to raise. By 1932 the Illinois State Legislature created the Illinois Emergency Relief Commission and succeeded in appropriating $19 million for statewide relief. In Chicago the Joint Emergency Relief Fund of Cook County took the lead in distributing funds to private relief agencies throughout the city. The available funds helped alleviate some suffering in Chicago. To supplement these funds, the city received monies from pre–New Deal programs such as the Reconstruction Finance Corporation, and the money was used to aid the most severe poverty cases in the city. But even with this influx of money, the city's welfare rolls increased by 168,000 cases.[20]

African Americans attempted to use New Deal initiatives to help fight unemployment. One of the most important instruments they used was the Works Progress Administration (after 1939 called the Work Projects Administration), or the WPA. Established in May 1935, the WPA was the largest New Deal agency, employing millions of people and affecting most every locality. Until its close in 1943, the various programs of the WPA added up to the largest employment base in the country—indeed, the largest cluster of government employment opportunities in most states. For those with access to WPA projects, in northern areas in particular, the WPA offered the best chance for economic relief because it prohibited discrimination in public works and mandated that all those "qualified by training and expertise to be assigned to work projects shall not be discriminated against on any grounds whatsoever."[21] African American supporters of the WPA applauded the significance of the agency. Contemporary economist Robert Weaver noted that the WPA was a "godsend," while the *Crisis* commented on the "great gains for the race in areas which heretofore have set their faces steadfastly against decent relief for Negroes."[22] The creation of the WPA and its nondiscrimination language came at a good time as roughly half of all African American families in the community relied on some form of public assistance; without this aid, the ability to meet any minimum standard of living remained difficult.

Even though some African Americans enjoyed relatively easy access to the programs, incidents of discrimination in the program existed. Here, too, African Americans were vocal about their dissatisfaction with racism in the WPA. Often they took complaints directly to President Roosevelt. In their appeals, African American workers requested that the administration intervene because it was the moral course of action and pointed to the fact that many had begun to carry the banner of the Democratic Party in local and national elections. Indeed, the 1930s saw a number of African American voters change party affiliation from the Republican to the Democratic Party. Many thus believed that since their votes had helped Roosevelt capture the White House, the Roosevelt administration owed them the benefit of federal protection of civil rights. In some cases, African Americans made appeals for federal protection during the New Deal by articulating their loyalty to and support for the Democratic Party and, by extension, New Deal liberalism.

Wallace Pettigrew, in a letter written in 1937, appealed to WPA administrator Henry Hopkins:

> Will you please help me get my job back . . . they are laying off all colored and hireing [sic] white in our District. Yet we have the same experience they have. . . . I'm an American citizen registered voter one hundred percent Democratic voter. Give all my support as a citison [sic]: hope you will give me some assistance as soon as possible.[23]

Similarly, Robert Lewis, an individual removed from his WPA position, sought assistance from the Roosevelt administration in securing employment. Like Pettigrew, Lewis pointed to his political affiliation as justification for receiving help:

> I am a Negro man, a Democrat, a committee of one for Mr.
> Roosevelt administration's reelection. Now Mr. McIntyre, I
> don't want to be classified as a beggar but I do think a first class
> Democrat should not be butchered in preference to a Republican.
> I have worked ha[r]d, and my record will show to make our party
> a success and to get our President re-elected.[24]

Lewis concluded his letter by stressing that there were others being retained on his WPA project "who have cursed our party going and coming and who are not registered Democrat voters."[25]

In industrialized regions in the North, New Deal programs actually encouraged the displacement of African American workers in favor of white workers or prompted widespread violations of wage and hours agreements. By the mid-1930s, stimulated by growing participation of African Americans in the Congress of Industrial Organizations (CIO) and by the ever-increasing support of African Americans for the Democratic Party and President Roosevelt, African Americans gained increased access to New Deal programs. But by the late 1930s, this situation changed.

In theory, the increased participation in CIO activities should have protected the interests of African Americans encountering opposition securing work. But in reality, since a large number of unions in the city (particularly those in the building trades) maintained racially discriminatory practices, African Americans seeking to work in some skilled trade positions continued to find it difficult to access higher wage jobs. This discrimination was especially prevalent within the organizations affiliated with the American Federation of Labor (AFL). Started in 1886, the AFL was dominated by skilled craft workers—which in many cases completely excluded African American workers or organized them on a segregated basis. This provision had long-lasting effects during the New Deal because one of the requirements of employment called for each worker to hold membership in an AFL union. Black workers found limited opportunities in these organizations and were thus deprived of their constitutional rights within these bodies.

According to sociologists St. Clair Drake and Horace Cayton, the WPA assured African Americans that they would be "able to maintain their accustomed standard of living despite the fact they were on WPA." Some, the authors concluded, were "even able to improve on [their living standards]."[26] However, aside from jobs, the most important benefit offered by the agency was the opportunity for black workers to apply many of the job skills they already possessed. Because the WPA played such an important role in easing the effects of the Depression in Chicago, instances of discrimination

Poor but Not Poverty Stricken

encountered by African Americans in gaining access to WPA jobs and training were not taken silently. Bronzeville resident Sarah Harris wrote a letter to President Roosevelt in July 1937 detailing her experiences with discrimination in local WPA projects:

> I was working on a WPA clerical project here in Chicago and a foreman by the name of Chester Lesawski had me put off under false pretenses. . . . They were forcing the majority of colored women with good educational qualifications to either take maid work or get off W.P.A.[27]

In another letter to the president, Vera Simmons questioned the hiring practices of the WPA:

> If the W.P.A. Projects were set up for the benefit of the needy, why is it that these who have other means of support are able to maintain their W.P.A. positions [and] if the Works Progress Administration Projects are not for any particular racial group of people, why should my supervisor, Mr. Charles H. Good, send a requisition to the Personnel Department of the Adult Education Program of the Works Progress specifying WHITE?[28]

Frank Ferrill also questioned the reasons behind African Americans' inability to secure equitable treatment within the WPA. He wrote,

> Seemingly, there is a tendency to exclude Negroes from positions of trust and responsibilities, especially on various projects. While I realize that a few Negroes are filling certain places of authority and trust; they are not [being] given the proper placement in proportion to the number being employed.[29]

Jessie Taylor commented that on

> April 18, 1937, I was reclassified from a Junior Clerk to a Home Economic Instructor. Miss Bates, the Project Technician, informed me that she would not increase my salary, but upon the recommendation of Mrs. Crosby [project supervisor] she classified a white woman from Interviewer, Class 1, to a Home Economic Instructor, with an increase in salary of $20.00 per month. This woman has had no special training in any branch of Home Economics.[30]

It is unclear what effects these protests had in ending discrimination in the WPA. What is important about these instances and others like them was that protests against discrimination were common in the everyday life of the Black Metropolis. Moreover, these examples show how black citizens maintained expectations that the federal government carry the burden of protecting equity and equal protection of their rights. African Americans viewed New Deal programs, like the WPA, as a mechanism to facilitate the restructuring of the U.S. economy, but many also viewed such programs as an avenue to restructure American society despite racial division.

Unemployment was not the only issue that challenged African Americans in Bronzeville; another serious problem was underemployment. A small number of African Americans managed to secure jobs in higher salary positions as brick- and stonemasons, carpenters, painters, and plumbers. A larger number of black workers made significant inroads into more lucrative semiskilled positions in the food industry, slaughter and meat packinghouses, and the iron, steel, and chemical industries. But even as some African American workers secured various skilled positions, an overwhelming percentage of employed African Americans were still working in jobs that were often classified as unskilled and low wage.

Drake and Cayton discovered that during the early Depression 25 percent of African American men and 56 percent of African American women were employed in domestic service and over 50 percent of black men were employed as manual laborers in industrial fields like coal, meatpacking, and steel. The percentage of African American women in these same fields was about 15 percent.[31] But when massive unemployment struck the United States during the 1930s, African Americans were often the first to be laid off. This is not to say that African Americans were altogether excluded from white-collar jobs. A small segment of Chicago's African American population was employed in clerical or professional occupations. To illustrate, there were 448 African American letter carriers and 458 African American teachers in Chicago. However, these individuals worked almost exclusively within the Black Belt itself. Despite their small number, skilled African American workers in Chicago had made significant strides into the skilled trades by the onset of the Depression.

Aside from the activities of the WPA, the federal government implemented additional programs to address African Americans' employment woes in other areas of Chicago's economy. The Labor Department initiated job programs to "conserve for Negro workers those jobs which had been theirs [and] to reopen those avenues of employment to Negroes which were there in prosperous times."[32] At first glance, the actions to protect jobs for unemployed African Americans held some benefits. However, when one considers that African American workers were anything but secure in such low-paying occupations, especially when unemployed white workers often displaced African Americans for such occupations in times of crisis, it is not difficult to see how such conservation would prove less than beneficial in a long-term economic downturn. Nonetheless, in Chicago, this duty fell chiefly upon the U.S. Employment Service (USES) office and the WPA's Central Labor Office.

The USES office, at Forty-Seventh and South Parkway, was established in 1918 as a result of lobbying efforts of African American state legislators and, during the Depression, was responsible for placing the overwhelming majority of unemployed African American applicants throughout Chicago. To a lesser degree, the Central Labor Office, at 1021 South State Street, primarily served Chicago's downtown Loop district and was chiefly concerned with providing common labor to local businesses. USES was able to assist applicants in locating and securing employment on public works projects as well as in private industry. Like other New Deal agencies, in theory, the USES offices should have served all applicants without regard to race. In practice, however, USES had no clear-cut policy in regard to black citizens.

James B. Hamlin, manager within the Illinois State Employment Service, witnessed this discriminatory policy firsthand. According to Hamlin, although the Chicago USES offices had a policy of nondiscrimination, "as a matter of fact, few offices other than the South Parkway office serve[d] Negroes."[33] Hamlin also found that other employment offices routinely referred African Americans to the South Parkway office. As a result, some regional offices largely followed local racial patterns. Not only did USES accept discrimination by taking employment calls from potential employers looking for "whites only," but the office also discriminated against African Americans by classifying black workers in traditional occupations regardless of their individual qualifications, training, or advanced degrees.

L. S. Gregory, in a letter to President Roosevelt, reported taking a WPA exam and attaining a score sufficient enough to be classified as a timekeeper or skilled foreman. However, when he reported to his job site, he was assigned a laborer position.[34] George Webster, a licensed physician and former medical examiner for the state of Illinois, received a work card from the WPA to "go work in a park as a laborer" even though "needy white physicians are placed here in research work, sanitary projects, CCC camps and the like."[35] Similarly, Clarence Lymore, an electrical engineer, reported that the foreman on his WPA assignment refused to give him any work because of his race. The fact was made more than obvious following a conversation between Lymore and the foreman in which Lymore inquired where he would be working. The foreman told him to "work with the 'niggers.'"[36]

Limiting African American applicants to the South Parkway office limited that office's effectiveness in serving the public, and there was a concern that staff would be unable to handle the growing number of applicants. Top-level officials within USES such as Lawrence A. Oxley echoed this sentiment and determined that "such unwise concentration of Negro applicants greatly handicaps the South Parkway office."[37] Furthermore, some within the service believed that this discrimination would facilitate the growth of "various radical groups which are now active in fighting for the recognition of Negroes."[38] Nonetheless, this office continued to place as many applicants as it could.

Between July 1935 and June 1936, 54.8 percent of the total workers placed by the South Parkway office received only temporary positions. Of that figure, the number of African American women placed through the office outpaced that of African American men, 2,343 to 1,901. In contrast, between July 1, 1934, and June 30, 1935, the South Parkway office had placed 2,374 men and 1,996 women.[39] Despite the high placement numbers for African American women, the jobs they secured were primarily in domestic service fields. Furthermore, many of these jobs were temporary and rarely WPA positions. This inability to secure permanent work led some officials of USES to conclude that African Americans were receiving temporary jobs in numbers that were "far too high" and that "a great deal of work was needed in pushing for new openings of a more permanent nature, especially in industry."[40]

Civil rights groups in the city investigated allegations of discrimination within the WPA. In 1938, William McMillan, a white supervisor on a WPA project, claimed that project supervisor Jefferson Davis Hardy ordered him to transfer seventy-five men to the Merrick Playground located at Ninety-Sixth and Halsted Streets. Hardy's written orders stipulated that all seventy-five hires should be "white men," and he cautioned McMillan to "be sure and not send any Niggers to the Merrick Playground."[41]

The Cook County Young Democrats called for diligence within the Roosevelt administration in securing nondiscrimination in the WPA and emphasized the political consequences if this discrimination continued unchecked. Clarence Carraway warned WPA administrator Harry Hopkins that Republican Frank Knox and former congressman Oscar DePriest could benefit among black Democratic voters because "your offices [are] very unfair to our people."[42] Carraway also pointed out that "if a war should occur between America and some other country, the Polish, Italians, and other non-American groups your organization is favoring will be first to run to the Old Country."[43]

African American unemployment and underemployment was worsened by African Americans' often-adversarial relationship with organized labor during this period. In Chicago, with a few notable exceptions (such as the United Packinghouse Workers), nonunionized black workers and unionized white workers were in stiff competition with each other for jobs. The Chicago Commission on Race Relations' 1922 study, *The Negro in Chicago: A Study of Race Relations and a Race Riot*, had paid particular attention to the Great Migration and its impact on labor relations.[44] The study concluded that several factors worked to shape race relations in Chicago industry and gave some idea on the obstacles facing African American workers. These included (1) the attitudes of the management when black labor was introduced; (2) circumstances under which black workers were hired, whether because of a recognized labor shortage or as strikebreakers or to reduce labor cost; (3) the attitudes and characteristics of the particular African American employed; and (4) the attitudes of the white worker toward the black worker as a result of previous contacts with African Americans.

Understanding these attitudes is important to any discussion of race and the labor movement during the interwar years because as the economy slowed following World War I, Chicago soon became more of a flawed promised land concerning labor and racial violence. Because of these sentiments, labor tension between African American and white workers in some labor organizations inevitably grew. Nonetheless, African Americans stayed in Chicago because "Chicago at that time was a hotbed [of economic opportunity]. This was a place where you could make money and there were jobs there."[45] This soon changed following the stock market crash in 1929.

Employers' attitudes also played an important role in the growing black unemployment in Chicago, although black workers made strides in securing jobs in a number of industries in the city and in many cases worked side by side with white workers. Employers sometimes justified discrimination by claiming an unwillingness to lose or offend white customers who would resent being served by African Americans, despite the care taken in regard to the appearance, training, culture, and poise of the employee. Employers maintained that white customers would protest using goods, food in particular, that had been handled by African Americans. Bronzeville resident Timuel Black, who worked at the Union Stockyards as a teenager in the 1930s, recalled the disdain in the eyes of white tourists in the plants as they witnessed African Americans handling hams that were being prepared in the yards. According to Black, management often took extra care to assure that consumers never witnessed African Americans handling food in the plant.[46] This argument was by no means the only one used. While some employers harbored very racist attitudes toward African Americans and refused to hire them based on these reasons, for others, these excuses were used so as not to give the appearance that they were racist.

Another reason given by white employers for discriminating against African Americans fell under the guise of preserving workplace harmony. Some employers explained that white labor would refuse to work if they were forced to labor alongside black workers. A personnel manager of an iron and steel manufacturer in Chicago stated that he did not employ African Americans in his particular plant because "he felt that the introduction of colored workers would cause dissatisfaction among other employees."[47] Portraying the white workforce as racist could help employers argue that discrimination was a way of avoiding workplace tension. Using such language, companies hoped to avoid public attack from protest groups or the black press.

Because of the great number of African Americans on relief, some white citizens believed that black workers were unemployable or simply had no desire to work. To the contrary, many unemployed African Americans did whatever they could to secure any type of work. As the streetcar companies began laying new track through Bronzeville using gangs of white laborers, African American men, many of whom were unsuccessful in securing jobs with the streetcar companies, surrounded the white workers, took up their tools, and demanded the jobs for themselves. The notion of the "unemployable African American" prospered despite much evidence to the contrary in private industry.

African Americans who did manage to secure jobs within the city often struggled to keep them. Black workers found that they were often the last hired and the first fired in many situations. This phenomenon was all too prevalent during the Depression. According to representatives of the Chicago Urban League, during Depression years employers showed a tendency to employ white workers even in positions traditionally occupied by African Americans. This practice more than guaranteed that during times of economic troubles, companies would first dismiss black workers before white workers. To find an illustration of this last point, one need only look to Chicago's stockyards during the 1930s. It was often customary for white supervisors to mark the timecards of African American packinghouse workers with black stars. Then, in times of economic crisis, when it came time to lay off a portion of the workforce, supervisors simply collected those timecards marked with black stars and terminated those individuals.[48] The dismissal of African Americans before white employees was magnified by their concentration in heavy industry and manufacturing. When these industries laid off workers on Chicago's South Side, black workers suffered larger proportions of unemployment than those in other communities.

In addition to targeting black workers during economic hard times, some companies targeted black workers even in the face of perceived public pressure. In 1935 the Chicago-based Coca-Cola Company terminated its entire African American workforce and replaced those employees with white laborers. Despite the fact that many of the African Americans who were fired held membership in the carbonated beverage bottlers' union, union officials made no calls for revocation of the company's National Recovery Administration (NRA) Blue Eagle, nor was there any official complaint made to the local NRA offices in Chicago. Many of these workers came to believe that the sole reason they were terminated was because the company was relocating from its South Side location to a facility in a predominantly Italian community on the city's West Side and "didn't care to have Race men working in the plant."[49] Since no action was taken on their behalf, some African American unionists responded in several ways. A smaller, symbolic campaign took place as J. Levirt Kelly, president of Local 444 Waiters, Bartenders, and Waitresses' Union, instructed his members to refuse to handle Coca-Cola products.[50] More commonly, workers came to believe that neither New Deal policies nor the unions represented their best interest and that the NRA and other initiatives designed to protect the rights of organized labor failed to apply to African Americans. As a result of these events, African American unionists often found themselves at odds with management and with fellow union members.

The conflict with Coca-Cola illustrates one of most challenging obstacles facing African American workers—organized labor. Some have argued that various unions, especially those in the building trades, had in place mechanisms to exclude African Americans' access to jobs. These unions included those for carpenters, steamfitters and plumbers, machinists, electricians, and motion picture operators. Historian Arvarh E. Strickland found in his study of the Chicago Urban League that "unions in the construction trades tried to secure as much of the available work as possible for their members and to maintain wage scales on relief projects at a level comparable to those on private jobs."[51] Taken together, this almost ensured that African Americans had limited access to high-paying skilled jobs in this sector.

The often-strained relationship between African Americans and organized labor contributed to steady levels of unemployment, especially in heavy industry and on public works projects, as unions, particularly in the building trades, controlled access to many WPA projects. During the Depression, organized labor instituted ways to ensure that only unionized workers obtained employment on those projects. Because so few African Americans belonged to unions during this period, many were locked out of these jobs. To make matters worse, relief administrators who were unfriendly to the plight of the black working class "used racial policies of unions as a convenient excuse for their own discriminatory inclinations."[52]

In 1939 a group of African American plumbers filed a $10,000 lawsuit against the Chicago Journeymen Plumbers' Benevolent and Protective Society (AFL) in an effort to reverse the union's discriminatory practices. The plaintiffs listed in this suit alleged they were denied jobs because they did not belong to the plumbers' union. This suit grew out of a long and bitter history between African American plumbers and the union. Since the early 1920s and well into the 1940s, black plumbers were offered membership on the condition that they work only for black contractors and only in black communities. When African American plumbers refused to accept discrimination at the worksite, they were often denied jobs on housing projects and war jobs.[53] African American workers claimed that they were prevented from practicing their trade by the white union. It was further alleged that builders who hired African American plumbers were threatened with a strike of all union labor unless the African American workers were taken off the job.

Another case concerning the exclusion of black workers by unionized white workers centered on the use of milk drivers' helpers and African American milkmen by local milk distributors. Early in the campaign, local dairies seemed willing to employ African American milkmen if the union accepted black workers into its ranks. The local unions refused to comply with this request, and in addition to not accepting nonwhites into the union, labor leaders mandated that all drivers' helpers, many of whom were African American, be denied employment. The Negro Labor Relations League was one South Side group that fought this practice and asked all South Side businesses using milk to "order only from dairies employing [African American] drivers."[54] The strategy was to "affect the business of the dairies [so] that they themselves will force the unions to change its [sic] attitudes towards Race drivers."[55] This action gained support throughout Chicago's black community. African American community groups responded to this action by calling for milkless days to force the employment of African Americans as milk delivery drivers. Activism for this measure spread through appeals to the consumers made by churches, the press, member organizations of the Chicago Council of Negro Organizations, and sound trucks in the neighborhoods to cancel all orders for milk from white drivers and other stores using Jim Crow drivers. Two weeks later, the protest received support from other African American organizations, including the Chicago Post Office Clerks' Union through the National Alliance of Postal Employees and the Chicago Urban League.[56]

Not all unions were hostile to black membership; in particular, many unions affiliated with the CIO opened their ranks to African American workers. As historian Philip S. Foner writes, "The CIO policy from the first was to open its doors to all black workers on an equal basis. There were no constitutional bars, no segregation of blacks into separate locals, no Jim Crow ritual."[57] There were occasions when the practices of local CIO unions contradicted the public nondiscrimination stance of the organization's leadership. However, the CIO sought to maintain its position and to include African American workers. Foner notes, "Black organizers were employed in all initial CIO campaigns . . . to demonstrate that the policy of nondiscrimination was more than empty words and would be carried through."[58]

In Chicago the CIO was very active in the Chicago stockyards.[59] African American involvement in the stockyard union had a rather mixed history. According to scholars such as James Grossman, during the early twentieth century, African Americans' participation in packinghouse unions was weak for several reasons: union racism, antiunion leadership within the black community, unfamiliarity with trade unionism, and intimidation by employers. More important, as Grossman points out, "black workers from the South ultimately rejected union appeals because they analyzed the situation in racial rather than class terms."[60]

However, by the mid-1930s, relations between some labor unions and African Americans began to improve. This was especially true in the Chicago meatpacking district. Not only did black workers begin to embrace the class-consciousness rhetoric of the packinghouse union, but some, like I. H. Bratton, went as far as to connect the unions' class-based message with existing civil rights arguments that were occurring in communities like Bronzeville. Upon receiving a lifetime membership in the United Packinghouse Workers in 1939, Bratton commented, "For 50 years I've fought for an industrial form of union. For 50 years I've fought for full equality for the Negro worker. Today, I've found those things in the C.I.O."[61] Bratton's sentiments were by no means atypical, and black workers constantly employed rhetoric that linked their struggle for workers' rights with their existing struggle for civil rights.

By 1935 there were five thousand African Americans in the Amalgamated Meat Cutters and Butcher Workmen who lived in Chicago. African Americans made such significant inroads that in one Amalgamated local—although they made up only 35 percent of union membership—the president, vice president, recording secretary, and financial secretary were all African American. Ultimately, however, African Americans began to reject the Amalgamated union. They did so primarily because, in the words of one member, "they [AMC] would separate us—put the whites in one local and the coloreds in another."[62] By the time the CIO began organizing drives during the mid-1930s, African Americans were becoming fully involved with the unionization efforts in the yards. As a result, African American unionists entered the ranks of the organization and became "more militant and more effective trade unionists partly because of what they brought on to the shop-floor and into the union hall."[63]

Another African American union of the period was the International Brotherhood of Red Caps. Originally incorporated in Chicago under the AFL, both the Brotherhood of Sleeping Car Porters and the American Railway Clerks claimed jurisdiction over the new union. The Red Caps eventually split with the AFL and functioned as an independent union where African American and white unionists shared organizational leadership. By the early 1940s, white unionists withdrew from the union and created a separate local. This was motivated by, in the words of one white unionist, the refusal of

> a lot of employers . . . to negotiate with a Negro at all. When we first formed this organization, we had our officers—first a black one, then a white one, then black, then white, and so on. This was all wrong. If you want real equality, you wouldn't take special care to see that Negroes were elected, you would simply elect the men who were best qualified for an office.[64]

Undeterred by the exodus of white members, the Red Caps continued to organize. By 1939, as a member of the CIO, the Red Caps changed its name to the United Transportation Service Employees of America. As a CIO-affiliated union, this group helped fight discrimination within the CIO itself. The experiences of individual African Americans in the packinghouses, the BSCP, and the Red Caps often proved to be the exception rather than the rule. These organizations worked within often-racist organizational structures to combat these acts of discrimination.

These cases illustrate that despite growing levels of working-class activism in Chicago's South Side black community during the 1930s, the many efforts failed to bring about significant changes in the position of African Americans in Chicago's labor market. In order to secure work, African Americans sometimes employed a variety of pressure tactics like "Don't Buy Where You Can't Work" campaigns, using picketing, strikes, and boycotts to push for better employment opportunities. Some of the demands made by pressure groups included complete equality in wages, hours, and working conditions for black and white employees; nondiscrimination within industry and unions; and equitable unemployment and social insurance. Many of these efforts failed to bring about complete change in any particular industry but offered some short-term changes. However, to completely characterize labor activity as a failure would not address the significance of their actions. By World War II, this activism would gain momentum due, in part, to the changing federal and local policy over the issues of housing and employment.

3. HOUSING THE SOLDIERS OF THE HOME FRONT

Justice for minority groups is the ultimate test of our domestic
process and this commission must proceed fearlessly to lead in this
grave problem for Illinois and America.
                                    —Reverend Bernard Sell, Illinois Commission
                                                    on Interracial Relations, 1944

IN THE early months of 1944, two events occurred that shed light
on the dangerous conditions in which many working-class and poor African
Americans lived. The first happened in January when a fire at a kitchenette
apartment at 4022 South Parkway killed several residents and left more than
one hundred residents of the building homeless. Two of the victims were
Edna Dabney, forty-two years old, and her seven-day-old baby. Several
other residents of the building, many of them mothers with young children,
suffered injuries, some critical.[1] The second event happened in February: a
three-story apartment building collapsed and buried three of the building's
residents under the debris. The January fire was but one in a long line of
fires that occurred during the 1940s. After this particular incident, there was
little public outrage or demand for an investigation into how such a tragedy
occurred. Similarly, media coverage of the collapsing building was extremely
unsympathetic to the human victims. Marion Baxter, a journalist with the
Chicago Bee, commented that much of the Chicago media found the February
incident unworthy of significant coverage and that one report "concerned
itself with the pathos of a mongrel dog whose six puppies were victims."[2]

Barton believed that such events, along with the many fires that occurred
in the South Side African American community, underscored "Chicago's
eyesore, slum housing and the hazardous and substandard living conditions
of the South Side."[3] Indeed, it is not enough to know that most of the
people in the community were poor. Simply acknowledging that African
Americans suffered from a lack of jobs does not fully reveal the perilous

conditions they faced in the housing market. Instead, we must come to a better understanding of the institutional and social obstacles that trapped African Americans in dilapidated housing. The fires and proliferation of dangerous, substandard housing in the city's African American communities are important for our current understanding of this issue as, in the words of Barton, they "focus attention of the dire shortages of homes for members of the race, who were thwarted and hampered by 'restrictions' and 'off the limit' barriers."[4]

As discussed in chapter 1, the Supreme Court ruling against restrictive covenants in the *Hansberry* case provided an important victory in the fight to secure better housing for some living within the cramped African American communities. But the *Hansberry* decision notwithstanding, a great deal more needed to be accomplished to bring about effective change in the terrible housing conditions on the city's South Side. As during the Depression era, the coalition of African Americans and their allies continued to argue that access to clean, affordable, and safe housing was one of the central tenets of citizenship established by the Roosevelt administration. Nothing exemplified this more than in the construction of the Ida B. Wells Homes. Black and white New Dealers alike applauded this effort, and for many within the African American community, the Wells development served as a platform from which to make claims for citizenship, providing tangible evidence that Roosevelt's economic recovery plan included initiatives for the plight of all citizens, regardless of race or gender. This belief would continue, and expand, as America moved closer to entering World War II.

With the mobilization of its wartime workforce, cities like Chicago stood to experience a dramatic rise in the number of migrants coming to the city in search for employment. The *Chicago Tribune* projected that in 1942 alone, Chicago could become home for more than sixty thousand migrating war workers. While this migration would undoubtedly help wartime employers meet production demands, on the South Side, the potential of thousands of people moving into an already overcrowded community held serious consequences for the community and for the morale of black citizens participating in the country's war effort. The Metropolitan Housing Council issued a statement in its 1942 annual report detailing the problem of housing in the black community: "Approximately 25,000 Negroes have moved here since 1940, and constitute in themselves a tremendous problem, one which had potentialities of disaster even before the war, since it has been estimated that in 1938 the Negro community in Chicago contained 50,000 more people than it had facilities for."[5] Similarly, the Mayor's Committee on Race Relations found that "most Negroes in Chicago are doubled-up, pay extremely high rents for substandard property, [and] suffer the ills of slum living."[6] In response to these statements, local governments were forced to develop strategies to balance the influx of black migrants while avoiding racial antagonisms and interracial violence.

The enforcement of the national wartime housing policy fell under the jurisdiction of the National Housing Agency (NHA), created in early 1942. NHA director John Blandford managed the day-to-day operations of the Federal Housing Administration, the Federal Home Loan Bank Administration, and the Federal Public Housing Administration. As the need for housing in manufacturing centers increased, the NHA used the resources of these agencies to provide initially private, and later public, housing units to meet the growing needs of migrant workers looking for work. During the course of the war, the NHA operated with a total budget of $2 billion for the construction of 945,000 temporary homes.

Early on, the NHA pushed for enforcement of such programs as the Home Utilization and War Guest Program. Under this program, the federal government worked with private homeowners to either lease available rooms or convert rooms not currently being used as living space for rentals to house war workers. The government would oversee the rentals for a maximum of seven years. After this period, the property, with all of its improvements, would revert back to the landowners. The agency envisioned that over half of the housing created under this program would be private and available at the market rate. By doing this, communities that lacked adequate housing before the implementation of this program would gain improved housing, and this new stock would be made available for residents once the war was concluded. If sufficient private homes did not exist in a particular community, the policy also established alternatives: where private housing could not meet the need for lower-income war workers, government war housing would be programmed. In these latter cases, where the NHA suggested that government war housing be constructed, housing developers had to estimate how many homes they thought could be used after the war. If developers could not determine a significant need for war housing, the NHA suggested that temporary war apartments be provided for war workers. The NHA also urged communities to increase existing housing conversion programs and called for local governments to exercise ingenuity in avoiding the use of critical materials.[7]

In spite of these contingencies and the urgency under which the need for new housing was developing, by the time America entered the war, the conditions in the private housing market were woefully inadequate. This was especially true for African Americans, who received only 0.3 percent of private priority housing. By 1943 this percentage rose to 2 percent, but in 1944 it was still less than 4 percent.[8] This situation did not improve even as it became clear to all observers that African Americans were coming in great numbers after 1942. Their inability to secure home loans from either private lenders or the FHA guaranteed that they could not get better housing. In addition, according to historian Paul R. Lusignan, the federal government reevaluated its existing housing plans and ordered that proposed housing sites be "converted for use solely by war workers and their families, and local housing authorities in strategic defense areas quickly converted unfinished projects from public housing to defense housing."[9] This decision decreased the available housing stock for current Chicago residents because now public housing was reserved for new residents.

African Americans faced many of the same challenges in the public housing market as they did in the private market. However, it appeared that for the long term, public housing offered relatively better access to improved living conditions. The federal government saw that providing housing in industrial regions would be vital in its effort to mobilize the American workforce. In August 1942 the NHA, working alongside the War Manpower Commission, established its policy regarding public housing and the war effort. This policy had five primary objectives:

1. All housing construction would "be limited to that which is essential for the war task."
2. War housing would be constructed in localities of intensive war production activity.
3. New housing would fit into community development and local planning.
4. The design of war housing would "conform as best as possible to local climate and traditions."
5. "Within the limits of available funds and materials, war housing shall be provided with reasonably adequate facilities for recreation, health services, care of children, preparation and serving of food where necessary."[10]

Although this policy seemed promising, it was far from perfect.[11] First, private real estate interests insisted that public housing should not be provided as an alternative to private construction. Second, NHA housing policy was open only to migrant workers who had moved to industrial areas to work in war plants. To alleviate these concerns, the NHA sometimes sought to minimize the number of in-migrants to a given area by directing war industry into localities that could provide the necessary labor and housing. The policy urged "making full utilization of local labor; by farming out sub-contracts to places where labor and housing are available; and by arranging for resident war workers to move, within their localities, from dwellings which are distant from their work to satisfactory existing dwellings near their work."[12] In many cases housing officials encouraged large numbers of in-migrant war workers with families to "come without their families."[13]

The in-migrant rule proved very controversial and problematic. The NHA relied on data gathered from groups within the city's African American communities to determine how many in-migrants could be housed in a particular community. Critics objected to this practice and instead argued that as a federal agency, the NHA had access to better and often underutilized resources by which to more accurately determine housing needs. The NHA also refused to address the issue of residential segregation in its plans and because of this could not accurately predict the amount of housing needed for potential war workers. This led many to condemn NHA efforts and accuse the office of supporting segregation despite an official policy to the contrary. Horace Cayton and Harry J. Walker, two members of the United Committee on Emergency Housing, argued that the NHA housing policy was a failure because of its "deference to the principle of residential segregation."[14] The *Chicago Defender* commented that Blandford "lacked the backbone of a jellyfish" after he refused to take the initiative to integrate Chicago's neighborhoods; in the meantime, 10,500 eligible African American families waited while the NHA constructed a mere ninety-three homes for black Chicagoans by 1944.[15] The most glaring limitation, however, was that the agency naively assumed that most in-migrants would return to their homes immediately following the war. The NHA did not intend to leave any city in a materially better condition in regard to housing than had existed in a region prior to the war. As such, the pressures placed on existing housing, already in disrepair, worsened.

Other critics, like the United Committee on Emergency Housing, argued that the in-migration rule should be abolished and claimed the rule created unusual tension within the city, creating the "potentiality for explosive action."[16] The committee and others suggested that new, more permanent housing be created to provide better options to address the housing shortage in the entire city. The federal government acknowledged the importance of wartime housing but remained cautious and was constantly concerned with material shortage and how this would affect the war effort. This was especially clear in a 1942 memo to local FHA offices that directed them to scrutinize all war housing requests to best determine if there was an "imperative need in the interest proposed of the war effort for housing and the location proposed, and that the location proposed and that the related utility extensions are located and designed as to restrict the use of critical materials to bare wartime essentials."[17]

Providing housing only for in-migrants was controversial, and civil rights and pressure groups continuously challenged those in city government to remain focused on providing appropriate programs to alleviate substandard housing for existing residents. In a missive to NHA administrator John Blandford, one letter writer argued that while new migrants needed housing, they did not "need it more than thousands of other old residents who are contributing everything they have to bring victory to our country at the earliest possible date."[18] With the war raging, activists and others working to address housing issues in the city not only continued to articulate their demands for better living conditions but draped their concerns in the rhetoric of patriotism and military service.

This rhetoric grew popular among those fighting discrimination during this period, especially when they considered how adverse living conditions at home affected the morale and productivity of those in the military. The status of military families remaining in Chicago presented a number of questions for wartime housing policy makers. One observer wrote Blandford and argued that construction of war homes should not have been used only for those coming to work in wartime industry but also for "the families of men in the armed forces [who] are suffering because there is no place for them to live"; as permanent residents, "they are not eligible for the new homes being financed by the Government for which these men are fighting and dying."[19] Public outcries like this one, along with hundreds of letters from African American servicemen and servicewomen, forced the Chicago Housing Authority, the NHA, and housing officials in the city to eventually relax residency restrictions to better accommodate Chicagoans with relatives serving in the military.

In 1943 CHA executive secretary Elizabeth Wood announced that the CHA, in an attempt to help the war effort, would accept service families as tenants in public housing despite in-migration rules and would give preference to families of servicemen who relied on the allowance and allotment system for support. In addition to easing residency requirements, the CHA announced that service families in housing projects would have "their rental charges reduced in proportion to their lower income as the number of fathers entering military service increased."[20] In spite of the patriotic rhetoric associated with the change in housing policy, though, a number of controversies persisted.

War housing coordination was handled through the War Housing Center (WHC) in Chicago. Opened in 1942, the office was designed to address the housing issues facing migrant workers coming to work in Chicago's war plants, primarily through the center's "Share-the-Home" program and the city's dwelling conversion initiatives. Under this program, residents were encouraged to register all available vacant residential space with the WHC. If a home was accepted into the program, homeowners had two options: (1) they could perform renovations to their property to adequately prepare it for incoming war workers, done by securing an FHA or other similar type of home loan, or (2) they could lease their property to the government, which would convert it into additional accommodations for workers and their families, assume responsibility for the mortgage and taxes, and then return the property to the homeowners at the end of the war. While this program held some definite advantages for property owners and allowed them subsidized home improvements, given the lasting impact of residential segregation and the general disrepair of so many of the homes owned by those confined to the South Side, African American homeowners were largely excluded from this program.

By 1943 the NHA opened offices in Chicago and absorbed the duties of the WHC until it closed in 1945. Between 1943 and October 1945, the staff of the housing center interviewed 159,000 families who had moved to Chicago in search of wartime housing. Of these interviewees, two-thirds were white families and one-third were African American families. From this number, 25,000 white and 14,000 African American families qualified for placement into war housing. The WHC placed 20,000 (80 percent) of white families but only 3,000 (21 percent) of African American families.[21] This disparity could be attributed to several factors, including racial discrimination that confined African Americans to all-black enclaves; severe housing problems in the areas African Americans already occupied; unfit dwellings in the community; and the lack of available apartments to convert to adequate housing without displacing a large number of residents.

Even with these impediments, by keeping with NHA policy, the Chicago WHC still sought to renovate several buildings for African American occupancy. One such venue was the Pythian Temple at Thirty-Seventh and South State Street. This building, which was constructed in 1927, was converted into 105 apartments for war workers. Another building, at 5925–27 South State Street, provided 24 apartments in a previously fire-damaged building. During the war, the Chicago WHC and the NHA converted and operated 246 apartments in thirteen buildings for African American war workers at a total cost for these war homes of approximately $330 million. Despite this construction, by March 1945 the housing center's South Side office estimated that five thousand eligible families and another twenty-two hundred emergency housing families still awaited housing.[22]

Between 1942 and 1944 the NHA programmed 2,073 privately constructed new housing units for black residents. By 1944 only 444 of these units had been completed, 464 units had been started, and 136 units were in the very early construction stage. The city also discovered that, during this same two-year period, the NHA issued 221 permits for private conversions. Of these, 193 had been completed, 20 were under construction, and 8 were in the early planning stages.[23] These observations clearly show that private home construction would not be the answer to African Americans' housing woes. Private construction, such as the Rosenwald Apartments in the 1930s, was inadequate for providing homes for black workers.

Public housing, on the other hand, offered slightly more flexibility. In the 1930s, Chicago had already embarked on a program to construct low-rent public housing. With the war, the CHA was able to fully integrate its own low-rent housing initiatives into the NHA's war housing program on a nondiscriminatory basis, as per CHA policy. Between 1942 and 1945, the CHA constructed 1,410 public housing dwellings for African American occupancy and was constructing another 1,012 at the end of this period.[24] These new public and private initiatives were indicative of great need throughout Chicago. City housing officials conducted a survey and discovered that 242,000 of the 985,000 dwellings in the city were "below minimum standards."[25] In fact, a Chicago public health nurse lamented that during the course of her work she

> patiently filed reports on unusable homes, windowless rooms—unscreened houses—masses of garbage, unsafe and unsanitary places for so these many years—and to what avail. Houses that I reported in 1912 are still being occupied and still untouched except by the accumulation of successive years of filth and decay.[26]

Public safety, fire, and high rents were also issues that shaped the daily experiences in African American communities,[27] and the city was making efforts to regulate housing conditions even before the war. In 1936 the Metropolitan Housing Council of Chicago attempted to establish a uniform code to enforce minimum standards and a separate housing bureau that was eventually voted down by the Chicago City Council. In 1942 the Metropolitan Housing Council again introduced an ordinance for consideration by the city council. This new ordinance established a Housing Board of Inspection and developed a central records department to make access to housing records more convenient. In several cases, increased building inspections stimulated improvements in substandard housing. But one of the unfortunate consequences was that in the course of such improvements, residents were sometimes ordered to vacate their homes, which only added to the housing crisis. Nonetheless, upon completion of these improvement efforts, some observers found that "Negro housing [has] not only been brought up to a higher standard than they enjoyed before, but they have been painted, tuck pointed, or landscaped so that the neighborhood actually look[ed] better."[28] The inspectors made periodic surveys and visits of all dwelling units, except for those classified as single-family dwellings. If violations were found, inspectors could "order the repair or demolition of structures in violation of the Code, and may proceed to enforce this by vacating the building or by contracting itself with a wrecker to have it torn down."[29] But despite the best attempts of public and private housing efforts in African American communities, housing conditions remained inadequate as overcrowding and racial discrimination continued to force black enclaves to absorb thousands of residents past capacity.

While the physical condition of a building posed a severe risk to residents of the South Side, an exploding rodent population presented an imminent danger even to those African Americans living in the best residences. Chicago set out to rein in the rodent population by establishing a rat control program in 1940, which, during its early stages, killed an estimated 1.5 million rats. By 1942, however, the war in Europe jeopardized the city's program because the most effective rodent poison was produced in the Mediterranean. African Americans and the poor were especially susceptible to the ills of an uncontrolled rat population, and of primary concern was the impact on black children and the infirm. The Welfare Administration of Chicago reported one family where "the baby has had his nose entirely bit off by rats [and] his entire body was lacerated." The child's mother had been "awakened at 3 A.M. to find the child almost smothered by the rodents."[30] Lena Shaw, a fifty-seven-year-old paraplegic, was bitten about the face and neck by several large rats for more than three hours as she was confined to her bed. The attack did not end until she was rescued by her son-in-law.[31]

Fires proved another constant problem, and many, such as the incident that opened this chapter, remained in the consciousness of the black community even when the media ignored the plight of the victims. Between October 1944 and February 1945 alone, there were fifteen major fires on the South Side. In each, between eighteen and thirty families were left homeless.[32] In examining the effect that these fires had on housing in the African American community, the Metropolitan Housing Council uncovered a disturbing development: some black families were so desperate for housing that they "moved their smoke-weighted and water soaked possessions back into rooms with charred walls, without roofs, and without plumbing."[33] In addition, African Americans continued to cram themselves into buildings that were not designed for such numbers. A Chicago building inspector described one such South Side structure as a "virtual firetrap."[34] The building, which originally consisted of a number of six-room apartments, had been divided into smaller kitchenette units. Building inspectors believed evacuation difficulties "would be encountered in trying to get the large number of people in this building removed from it in case of fire."[35]

Pressure groups within the community took action to make sure that this problem would not be ignored. On August 7, 1944, three African American children—Mary Elizabeth Beauchamp, age eight; Delores Beauchamp, six; and Robert Beauchamp, four—were killed in a South Side kitchenette fire at 335 East Garfield Boulevard. The children suffocated after they became trapped in a bathroom while in the care of their babysitter Mary Smith. According to witnesses at the scene, rescue efforts were hampered because the fire, which investigators believed started in the basement, quickly enveloped the only stairway in the building. Barred windows prevented some building residents from easily escaping the blaze. In the aftermath of the fire, African American civic, fraternal, and community leaders met to demand that Mayor Kelly's administration investigate the causes of this fire as well as of three others that had occurred earlier in the year in which children were killed.[36]

The city responded to community pressure by conducting "sweeping" investigations into the fire. Building Commissioner Paul Gerhardt announced that the city would seek to prosecute the owners of the building for building code violations. City coroner A. L. Brodie supported Gerhardt's position and issued a statement that "too many children have burned to death in the last few years and I intend to find who is responsible for tenement conditions."[37] A grand jury was convened to determine who, if anyone, should be held responsible for the deaths of the Beauchamp children. Building owners Harold Rosenstein and Seymour Edwards were arrested and eventually charged with manslaughter due to their negligent upkeep and illegal conversion of the apartment building and were brought before a grand jury.[38] Rosenstein argued that he purchased the building in 1938 and, assuming the building was "in good shape," never made alterations to the property.[39] However, the jurors pointed out that Rosenstein, who was an attorney, "should be cognizant of building and health ordinances."[40] The jurors also pointed out that the building violated various city ordinances by "being overcrowded, containing gas stoves in closets, not having sufficient toilets, not having fire escapes, and not having fire extinguishers."[41]

The disregard for the welfare of African American residents as demonstrated by Rosenstein and Edwards was not uncommon. In 1941 the city's Health Department documented 1,139 court cases (257 in 1941 and 882 in 1942) that sought to increase adherence to existing housing standards. Of these, 136 were successful in 1941 and 758 in 1942. The events surrounding the fire that killed the Beauchamp children and the subsequent grand jury not only speak to the dangers of fire in the Black Belt but show the dangers of apathy on the part of local government and building owners and of exploitation by Bronzeville's landlords. In many cases, law enforcement found it difficult to locate and fine landlords who failed to meet housing standards, let alone prosecute them. In 1942 the city attempted to apprehend a landlord to answer thirty charges of housing violations. Unable to get the man to appear in court, an issue that eventually caused his attorney to quit, police went so far as to post detectives outside his residence around the clock.[42]

High rents and low vacancy rates also placed severe limits on the availability of alternative housing options for African Americans and white residents and gave landlords distinct advantages in the real estate market. Growing concerns about building material shortages along with an almost complete shutdown of home construction during the war provided landlords an opportunity to take advantage of working people in dire need of housing. During the wartime emergency, even though a greater segment of the population looked to enjoy increased economic opportunities, prices for day-to-day goods increased dramatically. Early in the war the demand for canned fruits, meats, and vegetables by the armed services; rising wholesale prices; and the fear that foods such as sugar and flour would be hoarded drove prices of commonly used items to extreme levels. The *Chicago Tribune* reported that by January 1942, the cost of such items as food and clothing had increased by nearly 116 percent over January 1941. Wartime price controls managed to restrain high prices to an extent, but even with policies in place, prices continued to rise. Between mid-January 1943 and mid-February 1943, the cost of food in the city increased 1.7 percent. Of this, the cost of fruits and vegetable increased 5.6 percent, cereals and baking products 1.6 percent, and dairy products 2.6 percent.[43] Prices for household furnishings during this time rose 41.4 percent.[44] Rising costs in consumer goods and food prices mirrored the patterns of higher rents that were occurring all over the city. In Chicago, rents in the private housing market rose 16.2 percent between 1939 and 1942 and 14 percent for the period between September 1942 and December 1944. Wartime price controls were the only effective means of stabilizing rent increases, much to the chagrin of rental property owners who constantly challenged federal efforts.

Rents for public war homes, on the other hand, were more stable and charged on a graduated scale. A family of five with an annual income of between $1,200 and $1,500 could secure a two-bedroom apartment for $26 per month. Families consisting of six or seven people could rent a three-bedroom home for $27 per month.[45] The affordability, physical condition, and amenities provided in these housing units made them extremely desirable. Many of these units included private kitchens, a bathroom, and green space—a luxury not often available in the Black Belt. Although this made them attractive, only 1,500 units were constructed while another 10,000 were needed.[46]

In the private sector, according to the *Chicago Land Use Survey*, African Americans were paying as much rent as or higher rents than white residents living in exclusive North Side communities such as Lincoln Park and the Gold Coast but, in the years leading up to 1941, "paid a larger proportion of [their] income for rents than whites in the same general income class."[47] During the same time frame, in two predominantly African American communities on the South Side, for example, the median annual income was $1,270.25 and $1,312.96 respectively, and black residents paid between $26.29 (24.9 percent of annual income) and $35.27 a month (32.2 percent of annual income) for rent. In two communities with almost negligible numbers of nonwhite residents, annual median incomes were $1,440.52 and $1,322.05. However, in these communities, residents paid $24.00 (20 percent of annual income) and $16.85 (15.3 percent of annual income for rent).[48] The disparity is even more glaring when one considers that the majority of housing on the South Side was substandard.

Stabilization of rents hoped to address this problem. In the private sector, this was the work of the Office of Price Administration (OPA), which, during the war, registered more than 830,000 homes and apartments. Between 1941 and 1945, the office secured equitable rents for 2,364 tenants and protected another 4,160 from forced eviction.[49] The OPA not only eased the possibility of unjustly high rents for African Americans but also provided a mechanism through which tenants could challenge some of the authority wielded by landlords. Andrew J. Williams discovered this after he tried to evict two tenants, Frank Roundtree and Catherine Veasley, from a room they rented at 3345 South State Street. During the eviction process, Williams not only was arrested by the Chicago Police Department for assault, illegally entering the apartment, and removing a stove and refrigerator but also was investigated by the OPA, which questioned whether the steps he took to evict the tenants violated established rent control laws.[50]

Victories aside, the OPA proved an unreliable long-term solution in easing rent burdens for Bronzeville's residents, especially since, during the war emergency, it secured 7,774 rent adjustments for landlords and allowed landlords to evict 4,801 tenants in order to renovate apartment dwellings or to rid themselves of "undesirable tenants" who forfeited OPA protection. Before rent control, African Americans seeking to escape the confines of their neighborhoods could sometimes gain access into white neighborhoods by paying whatever exorbitantly higher rents white landlords would charge. When the OPA froze rents across the city, African Americans lost the ability to buy and bribe their way into better housing that was located in adjacent white communities.

Property owners not only resisted the idea of federal rent controls but also refused to even admit the existence of a rent problem. The South Side Renting Men's Association conducted a 1942 study in which it claimed South Side rents, in one community, increased by only 6.4 percent. However, according to a study by Third Ward alderman Benjamin Grant's office, the Renting Men's study was inherently flawed and failed to give an accurate picture of rents paid by African Americans because so few were included in the survey. Grant's study, instead, tracked the number of complaints about high rents that black residents reported to his office. What was clear about the data Grant collected was that rents for African Americans increased by 11.5 percent—more than nearly double the announced "over-all" increase reported by the Renting Men's group.[51]

But, while the OPA had its drawbacks, two local initiatives helped shape the city's response to the rent crisis. The first was the creation of the city council's Fair Rent Committee (FRC). Proposed by Alderman Grant, the FRC was an eleven-person committee whose membership was drawn from the ranks of organized labor, property owners, and the public. Ninth Ward alderman Arthur Lindell, who was influential in the passage of a local rent control ordinance, chaired the committee and called the fight against high rents as nothing less than his patriotic duty. He also warned, "Mayor Kelly will be asked to revoke all licenses of real estate agents who refuse to cooperate with the committee in keeping rent increases at a fair level."[52] Chicago's FRC and other rent control programs were created at a time when other city municipalities across the country were devising ways to control rising rents. Cleveland's mayor, for example, convened that city's Fair Rent Committee, whose membership included the president of the Futures Outlook League, the district manager of the black-owned Supreme Life Insurance Company, and the president general of the Universal Negro Improvement Association. Cleveland also established a "Fair Rent Day" and encouraged victims of high rents to file complaints with the committee.[53]

Grant also introduced a resolution that sought to direct the OPA administrator, the regional OPA director, and Lindell's committee to declare a significant portion of Bronzeville as "defense rental area" where rent ceilings should be imposed. Editors of the *Chicago Defender* articulated the importance of this resolution because, as they put it, it was "incomprehensible to us that the poorest section of the community should have to pay more rent than other [neighborhoods] have scheduled." Moreover, they claimed, "not only do Negroes pay more rent, they get less services and less comfort for the amount they pay."[54]

The South Side experienced the highest occupancy rates in the city. According to economist Robert Weaver, in the Bronzeville districts of Douglas, Grand Boulevard, and Washington Park, by 1944 "only 0.3 percent of the dwellings were unoccupied. Less than 0.05 percent was for sale and only 0.1 percent was for rent."[55] Even in the face of such horrid conditions, African Americans still worked diligently to both secure and hold on to whatever housing they could acquire. After the federal government purchased the aforementioned Pythian Temple in 1942, two hundred potential residents contacted building management to inquire as to when rental leases would be available before any renovations to the structure were even started.[56] In another instance, a private construction firm that was developing a multi-unit apartment in Bronzeville received twelve thousand applications for the sixty-five available apartments. What makes this even more remarkable was that the deposit for these units was a significant eighty-five dollars.[57]

One high-profile incident occurred at the Mecca Apartments in 1944. Constructed in 1893, this apartment building sat on land owned by the Illinois Institute of Technology (IIT). At the time of the controversy, fifteen hundred people, mostly African Americans, occupied the building. Due to its shoddy condition, all of the residents were to be evicted and the building was scheduled for demolition. In its place, the institute planned to construct a training center where individuals could learn skills for work in American war plants. The school enlisted the services of a local real estate office to secure housing for the residents of the building; however, because of the already limited amount of housing due to restrictive covenants and steady migration, the agent met with limited success.

Residents of this building constantly resisted their evictions. In 1943 an African American state legislator from Chicago, Christopher C. Wimbish, aided their efforts by introducing legislation, which became known as the Wimbish Act, to the Illinois General Assembly that would prevent the razing of any dwelling building in Chicago during the war without the permission of the mayor. If a building owner wanted to tear down a dwelling, he or she would have to petition the mayor, who would be required to "certify that other living quarters were available."[58] This was a very important stipulation for those fighting for better housing for African Americans because Mayor Kelly, in the eyes of some on the Chicago City Council and in the leadership of the CHA, championed housing rights for African Americans.

The Chicago Real Estate Board criticized the bill, claimed it failed to meet constitutional scrutiny, and argued that passage would create financial hardship on landowners, "prevent needed repairs[,] and even prohibit tearing down decrepit homes to make way for new ones."[59] The act nonetheless passed in the Illinois House of Representatives by a 112 to 2 margin. After successfully moving through the state senate, the bill was forwarded to the Illinois attorney general, whose office reviewed the legislation and forwarded it to Governor Dwight Green so he might sign the bill into law. The governor, however, dealt a blow to the efforts of Wimbish and the residents of the building by vetoing the measure and claiming it "violate[d] the constitutional ban on special or local legislation."[60] This move was unusual given the fact that the attorney general's office failed to comment on the constitutionality of the bill. It was also intriguing because Green's own housing committee commented on the substandard conditions in Chicago.

Vetoing the bill meant the legal battles between IIT and the residents of the Mecca Apartments would continue. Cook County Housing Court judge Samuel Heller, in a subsequent lawsuit, refused to permit the evictions and ordered the IIT to take steps to keep the building safe. The court's ruling was partly based on the fact that a number of tenants in the building worked in vital war industries and, according to Heller, "more than 50 boys from this building have entered the service."[61] In making this ruling, Judge Heller took into account the effects the evictions of the families of servicemen would have on the morale of those troops and the overall war effort.[62]

The residents of the Mecca Apartments and representatives of IIT continued their fight for the building even after Heller's ruling. In April 1945 nineteen residents, all of whom were war workers, informed city officials that they tried to pay rent to IIT but were having difficulty finding anyone at the university to accept the payment. To complicate matters, the residents had no formal leases, and thus no legal right, to live in the building and feared that, as squatters, they could be evicted by IIT. The city appealed to IIT and encouraged the school not to evict the residents until adequate housing was available, and at the behest of the city IIT ended the eviction process and informed the tenants that they could occupy the building "at their own risk."[63] The residents also successfully challenged evictions in 1950. But the Mecca Apartments were eventually razed in 1952, despite the efforts of the residents who lived there. The institute not only demolished the building but also destroyed several others as it expanded its campus during this period. But the efforts by African Americans to secure housing in this case were important because they used participation in the war effort as a rationale for equitable treatment.

The idea that housing should be provided for individuals either directly or indirectly engaged in the war effort gained popularity among housing and civil rights activists. For them, better housing not only held important and obvious national security implications but also provided an important platform from which to argue that clean housing was a "right" that should be guaranteed and protected by the state. These demands gained added potency in regard to the demand for public housing. Activists could argue endlessly about the connections between the war and African Americans' citizenship rights, but subsidized housing offered something more tangible. Unlike other government assurances made about African Americans' rights in previous years, providing clean homes demonstrated how the federal government was genuinely (albeit reluctantly) committed to providing for the social welfare of its black citizens—especially those in service to the state.

In the years leading up to the Second World War, the CHA operated four public housing projects. Of these, only one was constructed in a predominantly African American community and was open to African American residents. By the time the United States entered the conflict, the CHA had already developed plans to build additional units: the Francis Cabrini Homes, Lawndale Gardens, the Bridgeport Homes, and the Robert Brooks Homes. Of these later projects, only the West Side projects, Cabrini and Brooks, were scheduled to open on an integrated basis.[64]

Throughout the period, the CHA worked to integrate its existing wartime housing program with new initiatives. For example, in 1942 the CHA started a program called "5 War Homes a Day" that called for the completion of eighteen hundred homes for war workers and their families by 1943.[65] As with the national program for war housing, the CHA program saw that the housing shortages had a direct bearing on war production and that providing housing was extremely important. The program had its roots in 1941 efforts where the city initiated programs for war workers making less than $2,100 per year. The CHA housing program included resources for slum clearance and the rehousing of families living in slum housing to public housing. After the attack on Pearl Harbor, the CHA changed its policy and its use of established housing projects. Instead of slum clearance and rehousing, it began to provide homes for in-migrant war workers.

The CHA did not completely abandon its original rehousing program; rather, it incorporated these wartime measures into the program it had undertaken during the New Deal. Federal policy stipulated that no new public housing could be developed during the war emergency unless it was directed to migrant war workers. However, since the CHA had already begun construction on several housing developments before the United States entered World War II, it was able to continue its housing program and construct more permanent homes that could easily be integrated into existing low-income programs after the war.

The construction of Altgeld Gardens on the far South Side garnered a considerable amount of public support and public protest when the CHA proposed construction in1943. The Altgeld public housing development was originally intended as a temporary housing community; however, in planning it, the CHA convinced the NHA to finance a permanent development.[66] The project, at 130th and Ellis Avenue, was in an area close to heavy industry and had enough space for up to seven thousand residents—many of whom were employed in war work. Altgeld was situated on 157 acres and provided a clean and safe environment for families and their children. Residents of the community also enjoyed access to a commercial center that contained, among other amenities, a supermarket, bakery, barbershop, laundry and dry cleaner, and nine-hundred-seat movie theater. With its construction, it became the city's largest federally funded and operated war housing development.

White residents, both within the community and in other areas of the city, publicly denounced the construction of the housing development, claiming it "would depreciate their property values."[67] Likewise, white business groups like the South Side Business Men's Association, the South End Chamber of Commerce, and the South Side Real Estate Board issued a series of protest statements over its construction. It was intended that their appeals would influence the Federal Public Housing Administration and the NHA to abandon plans to build the fifteen-hundred-unit development close to the predominantly white Calumet area.

Richard L. Hoekstra, president of the South End Chamber of Commerce, argued that the introduction of African American war workers to the region not only would "raise taxes in a territory now requiring none" but also would "deteriorate property values and demoralize civic growth."[68] He further claimed that such an introduction would arouse racial animosity and would lead to rioting, violence, and general civil commotion. Racially coded language and the invoking of terms like "rioting," "violence," and "civil unrest" were often used to mobilize massive white resistance against perceived "invasions" into white territory by African Americans and public housing for them. Such language often achieved its goal and, more often than not, community-wide demonstrations of some whites' visceral hatred toward African Americans followed (an issue more fully explored in chapter 6). This was not the only strategy available to public housing opponents. Instead of using overtly racist language and arguments to protest the perceived invasion of African Americans into all-white communities, white residents often appealed to their neighbors and public officials to resist this integration by citing economic considerations and concerns about property values. In spite of these purported concerns, it is undeniable that racial exclusivity drove much of this rhetoric.

African Americans responded to these protests by circulating petitions in the city's predominantly black South and West Side communities, urging the mayor, the CHA, and Illinois senators and congressmen to "work for the immediate construction of the homes."[69] The *Calumet Index*, which some called anti-Negro and anti–public housing, countered this petition drive by running a full-page advertisement claiming that "not even Negroes want this project." The newspaper called upon white project opponents to reject the "graft and politics" associated with this endeavor, to attend a public mass meeting opposing construction, and to participate in their own letter writing campaign to local officials.[70] The CHA chose not to act on the protest against Altgeld and moved forward with its plans. Black civic organizations and a number of CIO-led unions expressed their commitment and support in the fight for these war homes soon after the demands of the South End Real Estate and the South End Chamber of Commerce boards' demands became public. By November, the Chicago Teachers' Union Local 1 (American Federation of Teachers) endorsed the project. The union argued that Altgeld would

offer incalculable advantages to workers of the area, and [it] would act as a lure to draw many from congested areas and thus benefit not only those who find employment in the Calumet area, but also those who would be relieved of the congestion by their removal to the new development.[71]

In their push to find homes, war workers were not surprised to witness the resistance put up by white residents. In these arenas, African Americans and white citizens often demonstrated that each possessed very complex and competing notions regarding the interpretation of liberalism. Many white residents interpreted liberalism in housing as the innate right to choose their neighbors and protect their communities from detrimental incursions. African Americans countered with their beliefs that the war aims and rhetoric of inclusion carried forth by a host of New Deal liberals cemented their claim for first-class citizenship and increased federal protections of their rights. While most African Americans expected to encounter racism and developed a number of strategies to combat it, how would they respond when the persons discriminating against them were other African Americans? This occurred when the CHA began construction of 250 war homes in the exclusive black South Side enclave of West Chesterfield and upper-middle-class African Americans living in the area protested.

West Chesterfield was a community situated outside of the rigid boundaries of the South Side Black Belt.[72] Touted by residents as "the finest Negro residential development in the United States," the racial and class composition of this community made it "the only one of its kind in the United States and a demonstration to the world that Negroes can, on their initiative and without public or charity financing, overcome the economic handicaps of their race and develop a home community comparable with any white neighborhood."[73] This area was bordered by Ninety-First, Ninety-Fifth, State Street, and South Parkway, and between 1939 and 1944 the *Chicago Defender* reported that seventy-one new homes were constructed in the neighborhood. Each of these units ranged in cost from $6,000 to $44,000.

The CHA proposed the construction of the $1.5 million development for war workers in 1944. When construction began, community residents, many belonging to the Citizens Committee of West Chesterfield, filed a lawsuit to stop the project and submitted a petition signed by more than two hundred residents who objected to the project. Opponents employed a number of rationales to support their demands. Initially, they argued these units would detract from the overall aesthetic of the surrounding neighborhood, even though the new buildings would look like other houses in the community. When this failed, property owners proposed an alternate South Side location where housing projects "[could] be erected without detriment to existing property values."[74] Protesters even took their appeals to end construction to the president of the United States.

These strategies appeared to be nothing out of the ordinary and were, in fact, commonly employed against African Americans by white citizens in their efforts to maintain neighborhood homogeneity. But as this particular episode progressed, what was clear was that the obvious class tensions developing between community homeowners and public housing occupants were taking on a rather unusual tone. Homeowners, invoking rhetoric similar to what white individuals employed to protest black residents, said public housing residents would be "slum dwellers" and "riff-raff" and would not be "up to the standards of their community."[75] Project residents and their allies charged black homeowners, many of them doctors, lawyers, and real estate owners, of being "Negro hating Negroes" whose "fine homes [were] made possible by the profits they make from the poor slum-dwelling clients."[76] Individuals from both sides of the debate eventually took their conflict to the local press, where representatives wrote letters published in both the *Chicago Tribune* and the *Chicago Defender.* In one particularly heated exchange, project resident Lillian E. Bates accused West Chesterfield residents of "Uncle Tomism" and pointed out that "as long as there is 1/100th or less Negro blood in their fine veins—to the white man who they want so badly to be—they are Negroes."[77] Homeowner Leo H. Ellis Jr. responded by saying that while he would not "come right out and say that Miss Bates is stupid in her beliefs," which in fact he does, he did call her greatly misinformed.[78]

Personal attacks aside, the West Chesterfield controversy caught the attention of a number of groups from inside and outside the community.

A coalition of West Chesterfield residents, alongside residents from the adjacent community of Lilydale, formed the Community Council of West Chesterfield and Lilydale to support the housing development. Support also came from the Chicago chapter of the National Negro Congress; labor leaders from the Douglass–Washington Center; representatives from the United Autoworkers; Willard Townsend of the United Transport Service Union Employees; and members of the Mayor's Committee on Race Relations. The National Negro Congress was one of the most outspoken of all the critics, denouncing the neighborhood protests and challenging the community to drop them and stand with others who were "willing to exert concerted actions against anti-Negro opposition threatening the public housing program, which it was agreed, has meant the difference between disease-ridden, rat-infested, sub-standard hazardous slums and decent, livable homes."[79] This last issue was extremely ironic given that several months later, the homeowners found themselves with strange, and perhaps unintended, allies—Floyd Haas, editor of the *Calumet Index*, and a group claiming to be the Ku Klux Klan. While the Federal Bureau of Investigation cast serious doubt as to the involvement of the Klan, Haas stated he supported the homeowners because he supported restrictive covenants: "they keep out undesirable people . . . just as these other people [West Chesterfield homeowners] do."[80] The CHA, as it had already done, stood by its decision to support nondiscrimination in housing. It responded to the controversy by pointing out that not only was it not building a slum project, but the homes were for war workers and were to be sold after the war to private parties or to individual homeowners.

In the end, neither the opponents of Altgeld nor of West Chesterfield were able to forestall efforts to build low-rent homes in their communities. The move to build for war workers and members of service families would have a significant impact on African American demands for better housing during the war as well as in the years following the war. Protests by both white and black citizens, like the ones that took place in the Calumet and West Chesterfield areas, highlight the difficulties some African Americans faced in their search for better homes. Each group framed access to housing and homeownership as a way to define their interpretations of democracy and citizenship.[81] However, working-class African Americans had their own interpretation regarding the meaning of "adequate." Better housing provided real proof that their allies within local, state, and federal government could be called upon to support them and their public protests.

Even in cases where the assistance rendered by government agencies was at best minimal, African Americans realized that they were still able to draw upon the mere existence of such programs as a way to support their own agenda and remained proactive in this struggle. The fact that the war provided extra leverage to their demands was also important. African Americans understood that invoking the language of patriotism and military sacrifice provided an important weapon that could open a number of doors in the quest for adequate housing. However, as the war drew to an end, one could only speculate about how the landscape would change. With the end of hostilities, thousands of veterans, black and white, would return home to Chicago. Their mere presence, and the resulting stress their numbers would place on an already contentious situation, stood to heighten interracial tension. Many were left to wonder if the inevitable postwar debates and physical confrontations between African Americans and white residents over access to both public and private housing would recreate the violence that had occurred in the years following World War I.

One thing was certain. At the municipal level, the policy of local control in housing would remain very important. The war created an environment where the meaning of democracy, liberalism, and housing was constantly being negotiated. Black citizens' demands and efforts to break down the physical constraints of residential segregation would continue to grow into an issue that would occupy the energies of politicians, civil rights groups, and community activists. This was especially true if, and only if, key allies in the mayor's office and the CHA remained in power.

Planning group meeting of the Chicago March on Washington Committee in the home of Ethel Payne, 1941. Members pictured (*left to right*) are Rita Baham, Ethel Payne, Clementine McConico Skinner, and three unknown members of the group. Clementine Skinner Papers, box 10, folder Photos 006, Vivian G. Harsh Research Collection, Woodson Regional Library, Chicago Public Library.

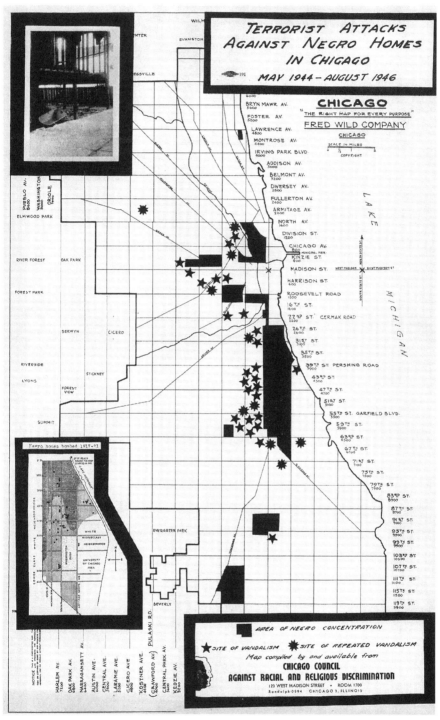

Map showing locations of attacks on black homes, 1944–46. George
Cleveland Hall Branch Archives, box 11, folder 137, Vivian G. Harsh Research
Collection, Woodson Regional Library, Chicago Public Library.

Your Prayers Are Needed

"Trumbull Park" cartoon originally published in the *Chicago Defender*, July 31, 1954. Chester Commodore Papers, box 19, folder 839, Vivian G. Harsh Research Collection, Woodson Regional Library, Chicago Public Library, courtesy of Lorin Nails-Smoote.

Chicago mayor Edward J. Kelly arriving at the White House for a conference with President Roosevelt on the Illinois political situation, January 18, 1938. Courtesy of the Library of Congress, LC-DIG-hec-23921.

African American woman painting the fence around her "pavement garden," April 1941. Courtesy of the Library of Congress, LC-DIG-fsa-01569.

Fair Employment Practices Committee member Milton P. Webster. Webster was also an influential figure in the Chicago division of the Brotherhood of Sleeping Car Porters and served as the organization's vice president. Courtesy of the Library of Congress, LC-USZ62–97539.

African American women war workers recondition-
ing used spark plugs in a large airplane plant, Melrose Park, Illinois. Courtesy of the Library of Congress,
LC-DIG-fsa-8e11110.

War worker Zed W. Robinson tightening the bolts of a cylinder barrel
of an airplane engine, Melrose Park, Illinois. Courtesy of the Library of
Congress, LC-USE6-D-005588.

Ferdinand Smith (*left*, national secretary of the National Maritime Union), Alderman Earl B. Dickerson of Chicago (*center*, Fair Employment Practices Committee member), and Donald M. Nelson (*right*, War Production Board member). Along with his work on the FEPC, Dickerson was an attorney who represented the Hansberry family in the *Hansberry v. Lee* lawsuit. Courtesy of the Library of Congress, LC-DIG-fsa-8e10738.

Ida B. Wells housing development. The development was constructed between 1939 and 1941 as a Public Works Administration project to house black families in Bronzeville. Courtesy of the Library of Congress, LC-USW3–000616-D.

4. THE GREATEST NEGRO VICTORY SINCE THE CIVIL WAR
FAIR EMPLOYMENT POLICY DURING WORLD WAR II

Negroes,
Denounced and Deprived of Democracy,
Insulted and Inveighed in Industry,
Shunned and Shamed in Society,
Murdered and Mangled,
On the very land for which they must fight!
They shall have some of it!
—Rhonda Walker, "I Believe
in Democracy So Much"

IN THE minds of those looking for access to better housing, World War II provided a prime opportunity to make significant strides as the resources available during this period provided the necessary financial and political support. Focusing on where war workers lived during the war, though important, tells an incomplete story. Like residential segregation, job discrimination threatened the wartime home front, and black workers, as they did during this entire period, took proactive measures to lessen the impact of economic racism and carve out a place for themselves in the changing wartime economy. African Americans' attempts to break down economic barriers during wartime had a long history. Dating back as early as the colonial era, African American men and women made increasing demands for equal justice through demonstrations of patriotism.[1] World War II presented new opportunities for increased labor activism, and African Americans drew upon the idea of the basic protection of civil rights outlined in the Constitution and reiterated in the Four Freedoms by the federal government as a way of defining their citizenship. They held this conviction and expressed it in their numerous complaints to the federal government and through their everyday acts of resistance.

In 1941 Earl B. Dickerson, Chicago alderman and future member of President Roosevelt's Fair Employment Practices Committee, gave voice to this sentiment. Appearing on the CBS radio program *Wings over Jordan* to discuss the seventy-eighth anniversary of Abraham Lincoln's signing of the Emancipation Proclamation, Dickerson touched on such issues as the war in Europe, American democracy, and the position of African Americans in the coming effort. Dickerson noted that, although "Lincoln's Proclamation of 1863 freed us physically[,] Roosevelt's proclamation [which would ban discrimination in wartime contracts and industry] is the beginning of our economic freedom." He continued,

> We [African Americans] are in this war to the finish—hoping, believing, and fighting for a democracy that will mean an end to all forms of racial prejudice and Hitlerism. And, we know that allied victory must inevitably mean new advances in the battle against the poll tax, lynching, and all discrimination.[2]

For Dickerson, as well as for other civil rights advocates, Roosevelt's executive order, which created the FEPC, would indeed be a second emancipation and would provide African Americans a platform from which their economic rights would take center stage and their refusal to reinforce the status quo could be articulated.

Dickerson's belief that the outcome of the war was tied to the status of African Americans was emblematic of the "Double V" campaign that occurred in both the African American press and in the larger African American community during the 1930s and 1940s. This campaign called for African Americans to seek victory against fascism abroad and an equally certain victory against racism at home. In addition, Dickerson's comments demonstrate how African Americans linked the aims of the war (fighting to protect Democracy) with their interpretations of Roosevelt-era policies and initiatives.[3] For instance, in 1941 Dickerson and the National Negro Stop-Hitler Committee sponsored a rally at DuSable High School on the city's South Side. Each of the speakers, including individuals such as Judge William Hastie, then civilian aide to the secretary of war; Canada Lee, of the play *Native Son;* and Herbert March, of the Cook County CIO Council, commented on the fact that African Americans had two jobs during the course of the war. According to Hastie, these were "winning full citizenship for the Negro at home and fighting off the dangers of Hitlerism from abroad."[4]

Historian Richard Dalfiume comments, "The war crisis provided American Negroes with a unique opportunity to point out, for all to see, the difference between the American creed and practice."[5] For him, "the democratic ideology and rhetoric with which the war was fought stimulated a sense of hope and certainty in black Americans that the old race structure was destroyed forever."[6] But, as African Americans challenged the old social order, white Americans resisted the increased participation of African Americans in the military and the workplace, and persistent racial discrimination served as "a rationale for denying this group its full rights of citizenship."[7] As the American economy mobilized for war, African Americans' participation in wartime industries still was not "commensurate with their proportion of the labor force."[8]

The Roosevelt administration, civic activists, and labor leaders nonetheless continued their work to educate the American people about the importance of mobilizing the nation's entire workforce. Racism and workplace discrimination had a real chance of derailing this goal, and in the years immediately preceding the war black workers were still the last hired and the first fired in the turn toward full employment. To address this, in the summer of 1940 President Roosevelt resurrected the World War I–era National Defense Advisory Commission (NDAC). This commission was charged with overseeing industrial mobilization to prepare the country for war. Sidney Hillman, cofounder of the CIO, was chosen to head the NDAC Labor Division, and economist Robert C. Weaver was appointed administrative assistant in charge of implementing NDAC nondiscrimination policies.[9] Weaver's duty was to develop effective ways to integrate black workers into the mobilization effort. In September 1940 NDAC issued its first policy statement, which mandated that workers should not be discriminated against because of age, sex, race, or color.[10]

Weaver's involvement in the commission was important in the fight against racial discrimination. Under his leadership, the Labor Division developed a nondiscrimination policy for defense vocational training by the U.S. Office of Education, and he secured fair employment pledges from the AFL and CIO. Furthermore, Weaver was undoubtedly influential in helping map out policy for wartime training that appeared in a U.S. Employment Service bulletin published in 1942. This new policy recommended that the efficiency within wartime industry could be improved by "the employment of those employed or by transfer of workers from jobs in non-defense industry . . . [and] by upgrading programs for the development of semi-skilled into skilled labor."[11] The policy further sought "to assist defense industries in meeting their manpower needs by training within each industry each worker to make the fullest use of his best skill up to the maximum of his individual ability, thereby enabling production to keep pace with defense needs."[12]

Regardless of the established guideline, getting employers to adhere to any nondiscrimination policy proved difficult. Nonetheless, the creation of such policy was important because it implied that the utilization of all available labor would be necessary in winning the war. This move by NDAC could be seen as the federal government's first attempt at a de facto nondiscrimination policy. However, NDAC lacked the authority to force nondiscrimination in the industrial training and hiring of African Americans. Without effective investigative and enforcement power, any policy suggested by the commission would fail to bring substantive change in discriminatory practices. Contemporary social scientist Leon Ransom noted that despite national policy it was not uncommon to find employers still asking for "white mechanics" or "white machine operators."[13] One way African Americans fought this practice was through organizing.

The most famous group was the March on Washington Movement. Founded in January 1941, the organization was concerned with instituting fair employment in defense jobs and desegregating the armed services.[14] What made this organization different from others concerned with the status of the African American working class—in particular, the Communist Party—was that during a 1941 meeting in Chicago, delegates voted to open membership only to African Americans.[15] This move "precluded Communists packing the conventions with white Communists" and all but guaranteed that African Americans' demands would not be co-opted by other pressure organizations.[16]

The threat of a march on the nation's capital pressured the Roosevelt administration into signing Executive Order 8802 on July 25, 1941. This order called for a nondiscrimination clause in all defense contracts, mandated that industrial training programs be free from discrimination, and established a five-member panel, the Fair Employment Practices Committee. The committee was placed under the Office of the War Manpower Commission (WMC). The primary duty of the FEPC was to investigate discrimination and recommend appropriate actions if any discrimination was found.[17] The committee had some roots in Chicago; two of its members, and the only African Americans, were from the city: alderman and attorney Earl B. Dickerson, who in 1940 represented the father of Chicago playwright Lorraine Hansberry and successfully argued before the Supreme Court for an end to restrictive real estate covenants, and Milton P. Webster, international vice president of the Brotherhood of Sleeping Car Porters.[18]

In 1941 and 1942 the FEPC launched a series of public hearings to investigate allegations of discrimination in Los Angeles, Chicago, New York, and Birmingham. The first meeting, held in Los Angeles, was convened on October 20–21, 1941, and concluded without any substantial statements against discrimination being issued. By the time the second group of hearings convened in Chicago in January and April 1942, the committee had changed tactics. During these meetings, the committee took a hard line with companies that violated the executive order. FEPC investigations forced several businesses that employed no or very few black workers to change hiring practices. The Studebaker Company and Western Electric, which represented more than fifteen thousand employees, were two such companies. But after appearing in front of the committee, each reported "they found Negro workers, skilled and unskilled, to be intelligent, efficient, and reliable."[19]

Not all of the investigations ended in such a positive manner, and while some progress was made, further work was needed. Companies like Buick's airplane motors plant, for instance, maintained a policy of hiring African Americans only as janitors, despite their qualifications for other positions. The committee even confronted the state director of the Division of Training for the WPA in Illinois, F. H. Sherlaw, to determine why few black workers were in the federal training program. As a federal agency, it was expected that the employment service would have been more than familiar with Executive Order 8802. But, after his testimony, Sherlaw was chastised by the FEPC for knowingly "disobeying the letter and spirit of the President's order."[20] The Chicago meeting emboldened the FEPC. As its investigations continued, the committee started to issue cease-and-desist orders to companies with government contracts who still submitted discriminatory employment orders to federal and state employment agencies. It also began to request written notice from all employment agencies of their willingness to accept minority workers and required monthly reports that would demonstrate their hiring practices regardless of race, creed, color, or national origin.

With its strong links to the FEPC and a long history of labor militancy, it came as no surprise that Chicago became one of the strongest bases for the March on Washington Movement. After A. Philip Randolph postponed the march after the signing of the executive order, the national group, alongside many of the local chapters across the nation, continued organizing in case immediate mobilization was needed. Various organizations within the Chicago March on Washington Movement, though, were not content with the postponement and voted instead to withdraw from the national coalition. The Chicago group traveled to Washington in April 1945 to participate in the Conference of National Organizations Devoted to the Welfare and Advancement of the Negro without support from the national MOWM. While the support of national organizations would have been welcomed in some circles, many African American activists in Chicago knew that if they were able to at least secure local support, many their goals could be met.[21]

African Americans knew they had to put enough pressure on American society to force greater change. They were again aided by several policies enacted at the local level. Mayor Edward Kelly's administration was put in the unenviable position of determining effective strategies to manage labor relations in Chicago and, at the same time, balancing racial tension in the city to avoid racial strife. Kelly's skill in handling labor became apparent during the 1941 strike at International Harvester. According to Kelly biographer Roger Biles, "[Kelly's] crowning achievement, announced January 6, 1941, was the adoption of a resolution by twelve hundred representatives of the AFL and CIO unions pledging no strike and no jurisdictional disputes that would deter war production."[22] However, throughout the war period, Kelly's negotiating skills would be continuously challenged as he tried to prevent racial tensions over access to better jobs and housing from reaching a critical stage.

The first test for Kelly and the city came during the summer of 1943 as race riots in Buffalo, Harlem, Los Angeles, and Detroit erupted. The root of these riots lay with the tensions over jobs and living conditions in the wake of increased migration out of the rural South by African Americans. To avoid similar riots in Chicago, Kelly took steps to deter any problems. To support Kelly, the U.S. Army transferred twelve thousand tear gas and smoke grenades and ten thousand twelve-gauge shotgun shells to the nearby Fort Sheridan army base. Chicago police officers assigned to the South Side encouraged white residents and African Americans to "avoid known areas of conflict" and implemented a plan intended to limit interracial contact and conflict in public space.[23]

However, the threat of military action and racial separation was merely a short-term solution for a long-term problem in Chicago's race relations. To better address the causes of racial discrimination and strife, Kelly created the Mayor's Committee on Race Relations in 1943. This office, one of the first organizations of its kind in the nation, was designed to mitigate the levels of racial tensions like those in Detroit. The staff worked with community, labor, civil, and religious organizations throughout the city to monitor race relations and propose strategies on how to best avoid racial conflict and intolerance. This move was seen by some as a testament to Kelly's proactive posture in regard to issues of race relations. Moreover, the *Chicago Defender* claimed that the creation of offices like this supported the wartime rhetoric of the day. For the *Defender*, those who practiced discrimination during the war were "agents of the enemy," and the creation of the committee was "imperative if we would save our country."[24] Kelly appointed five African Americans and five white Chicagoans to the committee, and Robert Weaver was named executive director of the office in 1944.[25] Throughout this period, the committee addressed race relations in employment, housing, and public schooling, among other issues. The success of this office led to the formation of a permanent office, the Mayor's Commission on Human Relations, which was established in 1945.

Chicago was the first city in the country to create nondiscrimination language that mandated that all contractors for the city not discriminate in their employment policies.[26] This language would be vital in laying the foundation for the city's fair employment practices ordinance that would be written in 1945. Like the policies of the national FEPC, the Chicago policy lacked any effective enforcement measure to ensure equal treatment in city contracts. This issue was one the city officials would continue to confront well into the postwar period. But, much like the FEPC, the city's stance on nondiscrimination had a symbolic meaning. It was further proof that participation in the war effort was key in cementing equal rights and that the local and federal government would back these claims.

The moves to lessen race tensions were significantly aided by the opening of FEPC operations in Chicago. Public support among African Americans for the FEPC grew quickly. Momentum for fair employment in the city started in November 1941 as labor activists formed the Fair Employment Practices Council of Metropolitan Chicago.[27] Its purpose was to pressure state and local government to enact measures in line with the federal FEPC. As a result of this pressure, the Illinois legislature passed a general state fair employment law that banned racial or ethnic discrimination. The law imposed penalties of between $150 and $500 on companies that discriminated. However, the measure provided no investigatory staff or adjustment agency. Because the state passed such a weak measure, the federal committee was charged with policing discrimination in Illinois.

The FEPC established a field office in Chicago in December 1941. Its first director, G. James Fleming, was a native of Philadelphia and had served as editor of the conservative *Philadelphia Tribune*. Fleming was also a member of Gunner Myrdal's research group that was responsible for the book *An American Dilemma*. With the restructuring of the FEPC in 1943, Fleming was replaced by Elmer Henderson, a Chicago native who had served as a research assistant for the Illinois Commission on Urban Colored Population in 1939. Henderson appeared a better choice to lead the Chicago office because his knowledge of the city added to his "intimate understanding of the employment and social problems of the Chicago area."[28] Working alongside Henderson were his assistants in the Chicago office, African American attorney Henry Gibson and labor relations specialist Joy Schultz, who documented and investigated complaints for Illinois, Indiana, and Wisconsin.

The Chicago office faced an uphill battle. In 1940, 52 percent of black men and 24 percent of black women were employed in private industry, while nearly 26 percent and 12 percent, respectively, were seeking work.

When compared to that of foreign- and native-born whites, the percentage of African American employment was particularly low.[29] St. Clair Drake and Horace Cayton found that during this same period, the percentages of native-born white men and women in the labor market were 71 percent and 34 percent, respectively, with 12 percent and 4 percent seeking work. For foreign-born white men and women, the numbers in private sector employment were 73 percent and 19 percent in the labor market and 10 percent and 2 percent seeking employment.[30]

Even with the support of the FEPC and the city, African American workers still faced a number of challenges in the workplace. But as they always have, black workers developed a number of strategies to combat racism. White workers who wanted to limit the opportunities of African Americans were equally resilient and imposed obstacles that ranged from subtle acts of exclusion to overt acts of violence. One of the most common strategies, though, was the use of the wildcat strike. Wildcat strikes were strike actions taken by workers without the authorization of their union officials. Largely sporadic and spontaneous, they were deployed to address particular and immediate grievances by both black and white workers. In regard to issues of race and the expanding wartime economy, however, white workers often chose to use the strikes to protest perceived violations at work and or in segregated social spaces on and around the shop floor by African Americans.

In August 1942 white workers launched a wildcat strike at the Ammunition Container Company in the south suburban town of Harvey, shutting down operations when a black employee, Levi Ellison, started working on a machine in the factory. Management and union officials ended the walkout quickly by offering those who objected to working with Ellison the option of either returning to work or leaving permanently. According to the *Chicago Defender,* none exercised the latter option. The largest area wildcat strike occurred in December 1944. White workers employed at the Pullman Standard Car Manufacturing Company went on strike after the company appointed an African American pipefitter, Bonnie Morgan, to serve as a group leader of interracial workers. Early on, only 175 pipefitters walked off the job.[31] A week later, approximately 1,100 workers from every department were involved in the stoppage. If left unchecked, the Pullman strike would have negatively impacted the war effort since the company built many of the naval landing crafts used in overseas invasions. Officials from the navy, the U.S Conciliation Service, the regional FEPC, the Chicago Civil Liberties Committee, and Local 2928 of the United Steelworkers unsuccessfully attempted to get the men to return to work. The company refused to negotiate and took a position that was squarely against the strike.

According to company officials, the upgrading of black workers to group leaders was "nothing new at the plant" and Morgan was "one of the most capable workers in the shop and was upgraded solely because of his ability."[32]

In the view of the company, the strike was motivated by nothing more than a small cadre of "anti-Negro agitators" whose actions threatened to "deal a blow to democracy."[33] White workers, on the other hand, tried to deflect these charges. They claimed that their actions were not motivated by racism but by the belief that a white employee, John Aenhorn, who had less seniority but was "years ahead of [Morgan] in ability,"[34] was somehow more qualified for the position. As the strikers downplayed the racial rhetoric, the Chicago Civil Liberties Committee interceded. The group appealed to the Mayor's Committee on Race Relations and the company to work on a compromise that would permit the strikers to abandon their demands to upgrade Aenhorn to group leader and end the strike. In exchange, the company would take all the men back to work without retribution. The company refused and continued to stand by its upgrading policy despite the strike.

Not all cases of wildcat strikes were as blatant as the previous examples; some were more subtle and nuanced. Nonetheless, they still conveyed the unwillingness of white workers to work alongside African Americans. In the Pullman case, jobs and work responsibilities were central issues that aroused white protest. For some white workers, even the mere presence of black employees in work spaces that were perceived as being "for whites only" was intolerable. Two African American women, Elizabeth Smith and Edna Toombs, filed a complaint with the FEPC that detailed one such incident.[35] Both were employed at the Ahlberg Ball-Bearing Company, which had a government contract producing parts for the military. During a fifteen-minute break period in November 1943, Smith and Toombs entered one of the female break rooms in order to sit and relax with other employees, all white. Following the break, the two women were called to the personnel department office and told that some of the white women had complained because Smith and Toombs had been "sitting on the bed" in the room. In another incident that same year, one hundred white women walked out of the Republic Steel facility on the far South Side to protest against three African American female employees using the same washroom.[36] And a company representative at the George A. Detterbeck Company, when informed that failing to hire African American women was a violation of an executive order, said that applications for African American women would be taken but that they would not be hired. Lester Detterbeck, vice president of the company, commented that his company refused to hire any African American women because he "[did] not propose to risk losing a single one of his present [white] employees" and that he was convinced that "the employment of Negro workers would entail that risk."[37] He asserted that "he [knew] beyond a shadow of a doubt that a number of women workers would leave rather than work with Negroes."[38]

Complaints made by individuals made up the bulk of the investigations handled by the local FEPC office. In some cases, though, local activists enlisted the assistance of Henderson and his staff to address a variety of issues, many new and some preexisting, facing Chicago's black community. One case involved hiring discrimination in the public transportation system in Chicago.[39] The fight between the city's three major transportation companies and members of such civil right groups as the Chicago NAACP, the Chicago Civil Liberties Committee, the Chicago Urban League, and the National Negro Congress had been raging for more than a decade before the FEPC interceded in 1943. Despite the city's nondiscrimination ordinance and the fact that the companies faced a severe labor shortage, the Chicago Surface Line, the Chicago Motor Coach Company, and the Chicago Rapid Transit system still refused to hire African Americans as motormen, conductors, or ticket agents.

Hope for a resolution appeared to precede FEPC intervention. In August 1943, Fredrick Nolan, general manager of the Chicago Surface Line, was scheduled to meet with representatives of several labor, religious, and civic organizations to discuss the opening of positions for African Americans. Ishmael Flory, vice president of the Chicago Council of the National Negro Congress, hailed this meeting and charged that the discriminatory policy of the company was weakening the nation's war effort. Flory called for the Surface Line to act in the "interest of the war and national unity" and drop all restrictions against African Americans.[40] Unfortunately for Flory and his colleagues, Nolan subsequently reneged on the meeting, choosing to meet only with the more conservative Chicago Civil Liberties Committee.

This cancellation prompted the FEPC to intervene. At a September 23 meeting, Nolan told FEPC officials that his company had no written order mandating nondiscrimination in its hiring practices and admitted the Surface Line had never employed an African American as a motorman. This position, he claimed, came in response to fear of potential hostility toward African American drivers by white passengers and a potential walkout by white employees over black promotions.[41] After a strong appeal from the FEPC, the company reversed its decision. By October the company began receiving applications from African Americans for motormen positions. On October 31, 1943, the *Chicago Bee* reported that the first African American streetcar conductor, Plato Bibbs, began his regular assignment for the line.

By July 1944 the Chicago Surface Line employed an additional 128 African Americans as platform men. Throughout this process, not a single incidence of violence was reported.

The Motor Coach Company and Rapid Transit System moved to hire or promote African Americans in the wake of the actions by the Surface Line. The *Chicago Bee* reported that B. J. Pepperman, vice president of the Chicago Motor Coach Company, requested a list of driver candidates from the Chicago Urban League's Placement Division.[42] In July 1944 the company hired thirty African American drivers, and seventy-seven others were employed in various shops and garages within the company. By December 1943 the Rapid Transit System integrated its workforce by upgrading seven African American porters and car cleaners to trainmen and began to accept applications from African American women for ticket agent positions.[43] These developments highlight how pressure tactics by African Americans and the FEPC could influence how businesses addressed discriminatory practices. However, what made these events extraordinary was that, as Weaver points out, "it represented a departure from the usual emphasis upon minority group placement on production jobs."[44] These cases placed nondiscrimination policy squarely in the public sector and on positions that, while not directly linked to war manufacturing, were nonetheless vital in transporting war workers to their jobs. In addition, they showed how federal policy could be used effectively to reinforce local policy.

By the start of World War II, despite the efforts of the Kelly administration, the WMC still designated Chicago a "Group 1" city, or one that experienced a severe labor shortage. Chicago would remain a "Group 1" city until the end of the European campaign. This classification carried considerable consequences. If the labor issue was not remedied satisfactorily, the WMC could order employers with eight or more employees to limit workweeks to forty-eight hours, funnel all new hiring through the U.S. Employment Service, and prevent the signing or renewal of any federal contract if alternative facilities were available elsewhere.[45] According to a labor supply analysis conducted by the FEPC in 1943, Chicago faced a shortage of 21,400 workers. Even with such a labor shortage, black residents and new migrants who ventured to Chicago in search of work during the Second Great Migration continued to wait for available jobs.[46] By January 1945 African American employment in Chicago had risen from 80,317 (1940) to 222,600. According to historian Mary Watters, "Negroes constituted 55 percent of the number added to wartime employment rolls in this 'arsenal of democracy,'" and the Negro employment ratio exceeded the population ratio by one-fifth.[47] But African American employees still remained underutilized in Chicago industry despite these numbers.

Perhaps the most important areas in which the FEPC operated were war plants and training facilities as African Americans faced discrimination in their attempts to assist the war effort. Many African Americans were quick to articulate the contradiction of fighting a war for democracy while facing persistent racism in the workplace. This strategy of equating patriotism and nondiscrimination was very common both during and after the war. For example, in 1942 an African American man, Henry Tapley, was enrolled in classes for a vocational training program at Chicago Vocational School. This school was located in a predominantly white community on the city's southeast side. Tapley, who had previously been trained to work in a machine shop, wanted to use this additional training opportunity to gain competency on machines and to familiarize himself with new technologies. According to a signed affidavit prepared for the FEPC, when he enrolled, Tapley was placed under the instruction of the assistant head instructor, Mr. McNabb. According to Tapley, McNabb had a reputation of being resistant and hostile to the presence of African American trainees in this program. McNabb neglected African Americans in by limiting their access to training machines and sometimes assigned black trainees to janitorial duties—despite the fact that the school had a full-time custodial staff.[48]

In August 1942 Tapley approached McNabb to request permission to use a lathe machine located in the machine shop. According to Tapley, McNabb told him, "You damn Niggers are too dumb to make tools. You can't run a lathe. Furthermore, I am the boss here and if you don't want to stay where I put you I'll kick you out of here."[49] Tapley related this incident in a letter to the assistant executive secretary of the WMC, George Johnson, who in turn forwarded Tapley's complaint to the FEPC. Tapley said in his letter that he was prompted to report McNabb's behavior because he "felt that was my duty as a loyal citizen to notify authorities as to what was being done to hinder the war effort."[50] Furthermore, Tapley stated that other black trainees at Chicago Vocational were "treated in every way to discourage them and to make them quit."[51] Tapley noted that many of his African American colleagues were afraid to protest against McNabb and that others in his class believed they "are not accomplishing nearly what they might for the national defense . . . and McNabb lets his prejudice go to the extent of hampering production and is a detriment to the very cause he represents."[52]

Another case where this contradiction was apparent involved Isaac L. Martin. Martin, who was employed at the Dodge operations in Chicago, worked in the manufacturing of aircraft parts for the military. Like Tapley, Martin already possessed the skills and training required for manufacturing work. Prior to his employment at Dodge, he had completed 75 hours of blueprint reading and 249 hours of machine shop training at Dunbar

Vocational School. Unlike Tapley, Martin had been trained at a school that lay in the heart of Bronzeville. According to Martin, although he was more qualified than many white workers who lacked machine shop training, he was passed over for upgrading to machinist. When he inquired why he was passed over, he was told that there were no openings on the line, even as white individuals were being hired for line work. Martin believed he was passed over because he was black. The cases of Tapley and Martin demonstrate some of the obstacles African Americans faced in seeking technical training or in fully utilizing the skills they already had. Although little is known regarding how these cases were remedied, the fact that the FEPC provided an outlet for African Americans to speak out against racism while staking claims of citizenship was important.

Racial discrimination against African Americans was not limited to training programs, and discrimination against federal employees and those seeking federal employment was prominent. The following two cases illustrate some of the obstacles facing African American federal employees. The first occurred in the Chicago Post Office and was reported to the FEPC by the National Alliance of Postal Employees (NAPE) in 1942. NAPE forwarded a report, "Brief of Unfair Practices," to the FEPC. In the brief, the postal alliance outlined how black postal employees were "denied equal opportunity for promotion, preferred assignment, and work privileges" and outlined seven cases, each describing incidents ranging from failure to assign African Americans to particular duties to failure to promote African Americans to supervisory positions.[53] Of the seven cases, four were resolved with no FEPC intervention. In the remaining three, each was remedied immediately following notification of the problems to the FEPC.

In the first case, NAPE charged the post office with a number of abuses and injustices toward the African American custodial staff. The workers claimed they were assigned the "least preferred jobs such as cleaning cuspidors, [were] being subjected to abusive talk and intimidation [and] low ratings, and [were] being denied recommendation for increased compensation." In the second case, in a department that serviced mail for mail order companies, workers claimed that the Montgomery Ward Department Store and Sears, Roebuck and Company demanded that African American postal workers not work in close proximity to their employees. In the last case, African American mail handlers complained about limited opportunities for promotions based on race.[54]

In all these cases, NAPE alerted the postmaster's office of discrimination and received no resolution. After a complaint was filed with the FEPC, each was resolved before the committee began any investigation. In the first case, the discrimination within the custodial department was solved by replacing the white head janitor with an African American. After this occurred, it was noted, racial tensions were eased within the department. In the second case, the postmaster did appoint African Americans to the COD department at the Chicago Mail Order Company after corresponding with the FEPC.[55] In the last, not only did an experienced African American receive a promotion, but he was promoted to the superintendent of the South Market Finance Station.

The most interesting applications of FEPC protection came from African American women. As Chicago attempted to address its labor shortage, a concerted effort was made by city officials, the WMC, and employers to attract more and more women, black and white, into the wartime workforce. But because the FEPC had no provisions for the prevention of discrimination based on gender, when faced with discrimination, African American women were, in theory, left with only one recourse—to claim discrimination based on race alone. In some cases, though, black women moved past mere race-based arguments and employed the rhetoric of patriotism, sacrifice, and the induction of African American men into the armed services as justification for better treatment.[56]

Ernestine D. Tyler used this strategy after she unsuccessfully attempted to secure employment with the U.S. Quartermaster in Chicago. Looking for help, she submitted a letter detailing alleged discrimination to Third Ward alderman Benjamin Grant in the summer of 1942.[57] Her letter noted that she interviewed for three civil service positions between March and June 1942. Her first interview, March 25, was at the Sixth Corps Area Headquarters at the post office; her second, April 23, was at the Quartermaster Depot on Pershing Road; and her third, in May, was at the Office of Division Engineer, Great Lakes Division. In each interview, Tyler was told that no positions were available, but if her services were needed, she would be contacted. This process of interviewing and waiting became frustrating and discouraging to Tyler. Throughout these episodes Tyler noted, "It would seem that with so many vacancies needing to be filled, surely by this time I should have been appointed to one of them."[58] Her discouragement was worsened because of the "patronizing method by which the interviews were conducted." Because of this, she questioned the equity of the hiring process. For Tyler, the fact that she had three brothers serving in the armed forces prompted her to question the democratic principle of the hiring process. Tyler asked that if African American men were called upon to defend democracy, "why shouldn't this same Democracy give me a democratic chance of something for which I have long ago qualified?"[59]

In July 1942, fifty African American women arrived at the Armour company seeking work and were refused opportunities to complete applications for employment. Some of the women claimed they were denied because of racial prejudice, and when they left the location, twenty-five of the women present that day filed complaints against the company stating that they were refused consideration based on their race. This event prompted the *Chicago Defender*, the National Urban League, and the FEPC to conduct an investigation into the stockyards on the southwest side of Chicago. The *Defender* reported that African American women who filled out applications for employment were refused the opportunity to submit those applications even while white women completed them. In response to these complaints, the editors of the *Chicago Defender*, the Chicago Urban League, and the FEPC all met with officers in the meatpacking industry to try to compel the industry to comply with federal law.[60]

Sophie Brown was among the twenty-five women who went to the Armour plant and filed a complaint.[61] According to Brown's report, she was standing outside of the employment office waiting to go in to inquire about work. While she waited, white women were being allowed in the office while black women were told to wait outside. Brown quickly spoke up and told the Armour employee she did not "think it was right for the white girls to go in and the colored girls to wait out." When approached by a white male employee who tried to force the black women to leave, Brown told the man she was "speaking up for our rights" and blocked the entrance of the office so that no other white person could be brought in. When asked by one of the white men there, "Do you think you have as many rights as these other white girls?" Brown replied, "Yes I do. Every time they draft a white man they draft a colored man, so wouldn't you think I have as much right to get a job as the white girl[?]"[62] As a response, the man pushed Brown to the ground, called the police, and had her arrested. Upon Brown's arrest, five other black women who were standing in line demanded that they be arrested along with Brown to show solidarity. This arrest is significant because it epitomized A. Philip Randolph's call that "a citizen is morally bound to disobey an unjust law." Randolph believed that "all Negroes [had] to join the movement for non-violent civil disobedience," and he challenged, "If Negroes [are to] secure their goals . . . they must win them . . . they must fight, sacrifice, suffer, go to jail, and, if need be, die for them. These rights will not be given. They must be taken."[63]

For some African Americans, the work of the FEPC seemed comparable to a second emancipation. African Americans during the 1940s were granted access to jobs that under some circumstances would have remained closed to them. The FEPC, African American militancy, and the stated aims of the war provided an avenue through which much of the African American working class could escape the Depression. However, the truest test of African American gains would come during the return of a peace-time economy. While all of these examples in this chapter highlight the difficulties black workers experienced when attempting to challenge racial discrimination in the workplace, they also tell us how they viewed and articulated their place in wartime industry in very patriotic terms. Indeed, they saw themselves as soldiers of the home front. Their demand for jobs was motivated by a need for income and by the belief that African Americans' role in the fight for democracy could be used to resist being treated as second-class citizens by white employers and coworkers.

In the end, we are left with questions about the long-term impact of World War II labor policy on the African American in the years following the war. Historian Herbert Garfinkel offers a realistic, if not overly pessimistic, assessment of the long-term effects of the FEPC in the United States: "Just as the Emancipation Proclamation by Abraham Lincoln did not bring to a close the struggle for freedom, the Second Emancipation Proclamation (FEPC) did not produce a final victory in the Negro's struggle for equality of economic opportunity."[64] To some degree, Garfinkel was correct. The FEPC was a temporary wartime measure with an unclear fate at the conclusion of the war. Still, African Americans embraced the idea in its mandate to speak out against discrimination.

Despite all of its flaws, the FEPC was important for working-class African Americans as an outlet through which they could articulate their demands for the systematic dismantling of the racial status quo in the workplace during World War II. They used this nondiscrimination policy as a way to demonstrate their patriotism, and they used their patriotism to show how racism ran counter to the ideals of American liberalism. This strategy of speaking up for their rights, coupled with the return of African American GIs to civilian life, would shape the postwar debate for jobs and civil rights in Chicago and would be used to hinder a return to the prewar economic racial hierarchy in American industry. African Americans knew they had to demonstrate that they were both better workers and better citizens and had to do all in their power to show the man at the top that the black worker was just as good as the white worker.

5. FROM FOXHOLES TO RATHOLES
STRUGGLES FOR POSTWAR HOUSING

But we don't want to socialize . . . we don't want to socialize. All we want to do is to live in a house, a good house, and have milk delivered to our door, and to go in and out without causing any trouble to anyone.

—Black veteran to CHA executive
secretary Elizabeth Wood, 1946

THE CONCLUSION of World War II brought thousands of African American men and women home to civilian life from the conflict in Europe, Africa, and Asia to face a number of racial conflicts in a society that was heavily segregated and opposed to any form of neighborhood integration. This struggle by African American servicemen and servicewomen to move their families out of the Black Belt and into cleaner, safer housing became important in the postwar search for articulation of Roosevelt-era liberalism that was already well under way. By the end of the war, not only was there no noticeable improvement in the housing stock available for African American occupancy, but the utter lack of home construction during the war actually made the conditions on the South Side substantially worse. According to the Illinois State Housing Board and the National Housing Agency, the lack of adequate building during the war, especially in African American communities, where an estimated 14,500 veterans would return to the city, contributed to "criminally substandard Negro housing in the city and adjacent areas" and created an environment that "constitute[d] a virtual crisis in the city's development."[1]

Between 1946 and 1955, black-white confrontations over neighborhood integration escalated as African Americans, who were outgrowing the cramped housing of their segregated Bronzeville community, continued to explore housing alternatives in surrounding white communities. The Chicago Housing Authority, armed with its own nondiscrimination charter, continued on a mission to build integrated homes: first for war workers and later for returning GIs and their families. This added to white fears that local government was pushing racial integration. As it became clear that restrictive covenants could not keep African Americans out of white neighborhoods, white protective property associations and political leaders fanned the flames of race hatred by arousing fear. These coalitions of white interests emboldened certain groups and encouraged them to commit acts of racial terrorism against black Chicagoans seeking relief from the slums. Thirty-five acts of arson or attempted arson attacks on African Americans' property occurred in 1946 alone.[2]

Arnold Hirsch's study on housing violence in Chicago pays particular attention to white resistance to integration and details how the "clashes between whites and blacks had merged with economic, political, and ideological conflicts to produce the 'archetypal communal riot.'"[3] The riots Hirsch describes developed primarily out of white homeowners' irrational fear of declining home values if African Americans moved into their neighborhoods and a deep-seated unwillingness to share public spaces with African Americans. As a result, Chicago endured a "pattern of chronic urban guerilla warfare that was related more to ideological currents than to the ebb and flow of the population."[4] While Hirsch's conclusions are sound, throughout most of his work the voices and experiences of African Americans who engaged in these conflicts are largely silent. Their experiences are relegated to that of victims of racial oppression.

As seen in earlier cases, African Americans were far from victims and actively engaged their white neighbors in a continuous struggle over how to best define the meaning of liberalism in regard to housing and over access to the privileges associated with American citizenship. They organized, fought back, and employed a variety of strategies to move their families to better housing. Although not successful in all cases, their postwar activism offers a look at postwar debates about integration and how the politics of space shaped race relations during the late 1940s through the mid-1950s. In the postwar period, housing segregation was challenged by individual African American families and by the CHA. Most of the time, white residents resisted with violence. These challenges to segregation were not necessarily motivated simply by an integrationist agenda. To the contrary, the movement by African American veterans and their families into white neighborhoods was more often than not driven by, first, their frustration over their inability to find clean, safe, and affordable housing within the confines of the segregated South Side and, second, their belief that fighting for freedom overseas had earned them certain material benefits at home.

To get a better idea of scope of this debate, this chapter will examine several cases where African American veterans worked with a number of different groups to challenge segregation during the postwar period. To facilitate this discussion, the chapter focuses on the development of the CHA's emergency veterans' housing program between 1945 and 1948; housing disturbances in Chicago's private housing market following the U.S. Supreme Court's ruling on the unconstitutionality of race restrictive covenants in 1948; and Chicago's longest housing riot (1953–55) and how this incident changed the direction of public housing in the city. In addition to looking at black residents' responses, this chapter also outlines how local government officials reacted to white community violence and how enforcement officials' responded to these disturbances changed throughout the period.

Between 1940 and 1949 the number of nonwhite persons in Chicago swelled from 282,000 to 400,000.[5] While the burdens this influx placed on the already overcrowded conditions in Bronzeville were significant, the general lack of construction during World War II created a situation that prompted the Mayor's Commission on Human Relations to conclude that the housing situation was in worse shape at the end of 1946 than at the end of 1945 and that "the city had actually lost more dwelling units through fire, simple decay and disintegration than it put up during the year."[6] An overall net loss of housing greatly worsened an already tenuous situation. Indeed, considering the estimate made by Chicago's NHA that "only 118 families left Chicago when war production stopped," one finds that housing was one of the most critical issues facing Chicagoans.[7]

Veterans faced a unique set of challenges since overseas deployment had left them at a distinct disadvantage in the search for postwar housing. A report by the Metropolitan Housing Council estimated that there was an 8,000-name waiting list of veterans looking for housing. According to the report, "There are 3,000 current applications [to the NHA] from Negro veterans," and in "a 10 day period in October [1945], of the 2,100 inquires made by the housing center, only 324 persons could be furnished housing of any kind at any price."[8]

In December 1945, the city's major newspapers each published a questionnaire to determine the need for housing in the city. Of the 206 families responding to the survey, 49 reported they were homeless; 16 reported they had been evicted when the building they were living in was sold; 12 had recently moved to the city and were unable to find housing; and 21 had been separated and were living in different locations. In addition to having difficulty finding housing, 95 respondents wrote of the overcrowded conditions they experienced. Also responding to the survey were 2 families that were quartering 10 people in five rooms, 3 families that were housing 9 people in four and a half or six rooms, 4 that had been housing 8 people in four or five rooms, and 5 that reported they were housing 7 persons in five rooms.[9] For African Americans, this problem was especially critical as many of them lived under these conditions at a higher rate (26 percent) than white veterans (6 percent) in the city. The lack of housing forced many veterans to live under less-than-desirable conditions.

A number of initiatives were implemented at the federal, state, and local levels to enact public policy that would provide more housing for veterans. At the federal level, Congress was presented with the Wagner-Ellender-Taft Bill of 1949 that was designed to establish a national housing policy. The bill's primary objective was to eliminate slums and blighted areas and to promote the "goal of a decent home and a suitable living environment for every American family."[10] To achieve this, the legislation called for the construction of 1,250,000 homes per year. The bill also promoted the construction of 125,000 units of public housing, many of which, according to a Chicago Urban League report, were to be occupied by African American families.[11] The *Chicago Defender* praised the bill and argued it would "attack all phases of the housing shortage." "Slums," they claimed, "would be attacked through the concept that everyone is entitled to decent housing."[12] The *Defender* also argued the bill would help stabilize rents by establishing national financing guidelines for dwellings.

The aspect of the Wagner-Ellender-Taft legislation that held the most promise was the bill's homeownership plan. Under this plan, veterans had the opportunity to finance a home costing less than $5,000 with a down payment of as little as $250. This provided the necessary financial resources to enable veterans to purchase their own homes. The public housing provision was also important because many of these projects provided immediate, short-term housing options that were desperately needed to ease the housing burdens of GIs and their families. To address long-term needs, the bill contained mechanisms designed to stimulate homeownership and apartment building construction; provide for lower interest rates and lower loan payment periods; reduce down and monthly payments; and provide resources to enable African American individuals, churches, unions, or other civil or fraternal groups to build housing in their communities with the backing of the federal government.[13]

Although the bill seemed promising, it had a checkered legislative history. In 1946, the U.S. Senate passed the bill only to see it defeated in the House of Representatives. When Congress reconvened the following year, the bill was rewritten and, according to economist Robert Weaver, "so watered down as to render the measure less effective."[14] Neither house voted on this new, rewritten bill. Nonetheless, the mere idea of the Wagner-Ellender-Taft Bill was well received by various groups in Chicago. The Chicago Branch of the NAACP commented on the importance of the bill and issued a statement that declared, "Public housing has been the only real answer to the needs for decent housing on the part of low income groups."[15] The United Negro and Allied Veterans of America saw the bill's potential to address the "iniquitous discriminatory practices in the renting and selling of homes and real estate."[16] The Mayor's Commission on Human Relations approved the principles included in the bill and gave its support.

Even though it failed to pass, Chicago moved forward with its own initiatives to provide housing for its residents. CHA executive secretary Elizabeth Wood recalled, "Mayor Kelly gave us a straight forward directive. . . . He said 'We've got to build this housing and we've got to build it fast.'"[17] The city became the first major metropolitan area in the country to receive federal emergency housing for its returning veterans. In December 1945 the Mayor's Committee on the Chicago Housing Crisis applied for and received use of surplus temporary war housing from the federal government. These units came in such forms as prefabricated homes, frame-type apartment structures, converted military barracks, Quonset huts, and trailers. Each unit contained between two and five rooms and was equipped with heating, plumbing, and cooking facilities.[18] These emergency homes were to be provided to localities where there was a shortage of homes, and only on the condition that the local community provided the land and access to the necessary utilities. In return for this housing, the local government agreed to tear down the temporary homes by 1949, as this was the year that was to be considered the "end of the war emergency."[19]

Shortly after Kelly's office applied for postwar housing, the city council appropriated "hard to find" cash to aid in the construction of the emergency housing. The land for such housing was leased, free of charge, from the Board of Education, the Park District, the Sanitary District, and the Forest Preserve District, most of which was in "predominantly white or lily white areas."[20] The CHA would handle the administrative and oversight responsibilities for the housing. Eligibility was restricted to Chicago residents who were both World War II veterans and married heads of households. The homes were also available to families in which the husband, wife, and children lived apart from each other; families that had been evicted from their homes; overcrowded families; and families suffering from physical or mental hardships. When these homes were opened, the Chicago Housing Center received more than 170,000 applications from veterans, 25,000 of which were referred to the CHA. The CHA would then determine which of these applicants would occupy the 3,200 emergency housing units.

Even while this progressed, African American veterans', civic, and labor organizations continued to call attention to the disparate conditions facing African American veterans. In June 1946 an organization called the Public Housing Association brought together various veterans', civic, housing, labor, welfare, and community groups for a meeting at city hall. The purpose of this meeting was to push passage of the Wagner-Ellender-Taft Bill, promote a change in the building code, and lobby the Illinois General Assembly to adopt a statewide housing program.[21] The CHA was in the best position to address the housing situation and instituted an emergency housing program for veterans and expanded its low-income housing program following the war. On August 8, 1946, the CHA opened one of its first postwar housing projects, Wentworth Gardens, on the South Side. The project, however, failed to fully address the housing needs of the South Side because it offered a very limited amount of space for potential residents. Designed as a 422-unit complex, more than ten thousand people showed up at the rental office at the Allen AME Church to apply for residency. The crush associated with such a large crowd was unimaginable. The scene at the church was so chaotic that one observer, an employee of the CHA, reported that as he attempted to close the facility at the end of business, he was attacked and "had all the buttons torn from his coat."[22]

The opening of Wentworth Gardens failed to address the housing shortage among African American veterans, too. Although they were given first preference in moving into this particular housing project, more housing for them was still needed. Such housing had to be developed outside of the Black Belt, where available land was scarce. The sole option was to introduce housing for African American veterans in white communities. The CHA began to experiment with biracial housing following World War II with mixed results. In March 1946, two African American families moved into a CHA development on Chicago's northwest side. Before the move, the CHA and the Mayor's Commission on Human Relations met with community groups and the project's Tenants' Council and drew up a resolution welcoming the veterans and their families to the project regardless of race, creed, or ethnic origin.[23] Some white residents from outside the project responded by holding a meeting to draft a restrictive covenant to deter any further moves of African Americans. Representatives of the CHA and the Cook County Council of the Veterans of Foreign Wars responded by issuing a statement denouncing the discrimination. In the end, the covenant meeting adjourned without any action being taken.[24] In another veterans' project on the southwest side, African American and white veterans lived together without any obvious racial tensions. The homes in this development opened under the strict adherence to the housing authority's nondiscrimination guidelines. Eleven of the twenty-two original housing projects were occupied on an interracial, nonsegregated basis. In addition, all but one of the housing projects were located in neighborhoods that were entirely or nearly entirely white.[25]

One of the reasons the CHA may have avoided creating any major housing riots was that it introduced neighborhood integration on a very limited basis. In 1937 the CHA officials had issued a policy directive that called for African Americans to be accepted into public housing projects "in the same proportion as they are at present represented in the [given] neighborhood."[26] This neighborhood composition rule drove CHA policy until late 1946, but its vagueness often left the policy open to interpretation, and in some cases the introduction of even a small number of African Americans was too much.

The CHA's interpretation of the neighborhood composition rule was easily blended with its policy of nondiscrimination. Nowhere was this more obvious than in two veterans' housing developments, the Airport Homes and Fernwood Park. At both of these housing projects, the CHA's stance on equal housing would come under attack, both physically and figuratively, by white residents of the community. However, in both cases, the resolve of city officials, labor organizations, and veterans' organizations averted larger racial incidents.

The Airport Homes was a 186-unit veterans' emergency housing project that was constructed on land leased from the Board of Education on the city's southwest side. Construction of the apartment complex occurred in three stages. The initial occupancy took place in September 1946. By October, 127 units of the project were completed and occupied. The remaining apartments were scheduled to be completed and occupied by November 18. In August 1946, members of the Mayor's Commission on Human Relations met with CHA officials to discuss reports of growing tension in the community over the construction of the project and the possibility that African American tenants would move into the buildings. In an effort to deter any escalation of racial hostilities, the Mayor's Commission met with labor leaders to encourage union members living in the area to refrain from conflict. In addition, the members of the commission solicited the aid of veterans' and church groups to help minimize interracial tensions.

In September it appeared that the proactive moves by the commission were successful. On two occasions, Ralph Metcalfe, director of the Department of Civil Rights, met with Captain Charles O'Regan of the Sixteenth Police District. O'Regan reported to Metcalfe that he had received no reports of civil unrest regarding the project and "anticipated no violence as a result of the integration into this project of veterans who were members of minority groups."[27] But the situation changed in October and November 1946 when the Mayor's Commission on Human Relations received reports that several windows had been smashed in the unfinished units. By the end of the month, the commission received word that "considerable tension in the community [existed] and that petitions had been circulated and presented to the Chicago Housing Authority requesting that the apartments in the project be reserved for veterans living in the immediate neighborhood."[28] The CHA refused to accept the demands of the community and maintained its nondiscrimination policy.

On November 4, a number of white residents from the community descended on the office of the project manager and stole the keys to the fifty-nine unoccupied apartments. The next day, these squatter families moved into the project and took over the empty apartments. Meetings between the commission and representatives of the squatters revealed that although there were a number of reasons behind this occupation, many, but not all, of the protesters saw their actions as an "attempt to occupy the available space so the Negroes could not move in."[29] Nonetheless, the CHA remained undeterred in its efforts to integrate the Airport Homes and proceeded with its plans. On November 9, fifty of the veterans chosen to occupy the apartments appeared in order to sign their leases and move into the development. Among this group was a sole African American tenant, Theodore Turner, who had spent three years as an antiaircraft gunner in Europe and North Africa. Before moving into the Airport Homes, Turner, his wife, their three-week-old baby, and their orphaned nephew all lived in a one-room kitchenette next to five other families.[30] Their assignment to the Airport Homes housing development had the potential to mark the end of the housing dilemma for the Turners.

Turner and his family were scheduled to take possession of their apartment on November 16, 1946. The previous night, white members of a group calling itself the Tenants' Council met at the West Lawn Church of God to discuss the family's move. During the meeting, Turner, who was attending the meeting along with Russell Babcock, director of Public Information and Education, part of the Mayor's Commission on Human Relations, stood and inquired "if he would be welcome as a member" of the community.[31] Earnest Masur, who was the temporary chairman of the council and one of the white residents opposed to racial discrimination in the housing complex, replied, "All residents of the project, regardless of race, color, or creed[,] would be welcome" on the Tenants' Council.[32]

Turner demonstrated his resolve to move into the housing project. After his first confrontation with protesters, he addressed members of United Packinghouse Workers of America Local 82. At this meeting he reiterated his intention to stay at the housing project. Turner also made it known that his presence at the project was important for himself and other African American veterans. Turner told the UPWA members of his intention to keep fighting "not only for myself, but for the thousands of Negro vets in this city who need housing so badly as I do."[33] This sentiment was important because it showed how individuals like Turner recognized that civil rights in housing held far-reaching implications that could affect the welfare of thousands of African American veterans throughout the city. This sentiment appeared again and again throughout this period.

Despite Masur's assurances, other factions within the community planned to show Turner and his family that they would not be welcome. Turner arrived at the project on the morning of November 16 as scheduled, accompanied by several other white and African American veterans, to get a feel for the racial situation of the community before moving his family and possessions into the neighborhood. Shortly after his arrival a group of protesters gathered, and as the crowd began to grow in size, Turner and his friends retreated to the home of Earnest Masur. The occupants of the apartment called the police for assistance, but authorities responded slowly. It was not until Kenneth Kennedy, president of the United Negro and Allied Veterans of America, told police dispatchers "that he had a .45 [automatic pistol] and planned to use it" did the police arrive at Masur's home to escort Turner and the other veterans from the building.[34] The next day, Turner returned his apartment key to the CHA and informed it that he would not be moving into the building. Shortly after, the Mayor's Commission learned that another white "squatter" was occupying Turner's apartment. Masur, who publicly supported Turner and offered refuge to him and his colleagues, reported that in the days following November 16, he and his family were victims of continued anti-Semitic insults.

Following the violent events at the Airport Homes, Mayor Kelly issued a public statement condemning the actions of the protesters and reiterating his support of the CHA's nondiscrimination policy. The mayor made it clear that his administration supported the fact that this housing was available to veterans and their families "without regard to race, creed, or color."[35] Furthermore, the mayor proclaimed that "the city of Chicago will support this [nondiscrimination] policy and will provide full police protection to all veterans who are authorized by the Chicago Housing Authority to occupy the Airport Homes or any other public housing project." To protect and provide for the safety of African American veterans scheduled to move into public housing in the future, the mayor and the Chicago Police Department devised new protocols designed to avert more violence. The new policy stated that the Mayor's Commission on Human Relations would "see to it that the Police Department was notified at the time when the Chicago Housing Authority planned to move in white and Negro families who had been selected in line with their standards."[36]

Many white residents in the community believed that the "indiscriminate mixing of white and Negro families [would] not encourage racial tolerance but on the other hand create ill feeling" and predicted violence.[37] To ensure that the city understood their position, three hundred residents of the community stormed the chambers of the city council on December 3, 1946, and staged what some have called "a vicious race hate demonstration."[38] Believing that the city council meeting was adjourning without hearing their petition to keep the Airport Homes all white, the protesters began yelling, "We want a hearing," "Now or never," and "Let's get it over with" in the council chambers.[39] Several of the protesters even attacked an African American news photographer who was recording the demonstration.[40] The mayor continued to take a hard line with the protesters and proclaimed that city hall would do everything in its power to "insure the democratic and impartial handling of all incidents in the future involving racial, religious, and national minorities, so that all law abiding citizens may be assured of their rights to live."[41]

On December 4, 1946, the CHA again moved forward with its plan to move African Americans into the Airport Homes project. That morning, a number of white CHA residents arrived at the complex to move into apartments formerly occupied by the squatters. According to the Mayor's Commission on Human Relations, "A crowd of more than two hundred people gathered on the south end of the project, directly opposite the project office."[42] The commission also reported, "The whole demonstration was clearly anti-racial and rapidly becoming anti-Semitic."[43] Just before noon, several trucks containing the possessions of two African American veterans, John Fort and Letholian Waddles, arrived at the housing project. The protesters immediately attacked these trucks. The Chicago police eventually escorted the trucks into the project to keep Fort and Waddles isolated from the protesters. Under a barrage of stones and sticks, Fort, Waddles, and others began to move furniture into the apartments of the two men.

Like Turner, Fort and Waddles also served in the military during World War II. Fort was an experienced soldier. During the war he saw combat at the Battle of the Bulge and was awarded four combat stars. Waddles was a veteran of the Pacific Theater and spent some time in the Philippines. At the time they moved into the Airport Homes, each was married with children. Fort was employed for the Santa Fe Railroad, and Waddles was enrolled in trade school classes under the GI Bill.[44] After the initial confrontation, Fort and Waddles telephoned their wives and instructed the women not to join them at the new apartments that evening. Unfortunately, Kenneth Kennedy was not informed of the trouble within the community and approached the project by car. When he arrived, protesters attacked his car and succeeded in tipping the vehicle over. The police arrived on the scene, aided Kennedy in righting the car, and sent him on his way, out of the immediate area.[45]

During the next several weeks, violence and protests continued around the project, and much of it targeted property belonging to African Americans, many of whom did not live in the community. On December 5, crowds of white protesters attacked a coal truck driven by African Americans as they drove near the project. Throughout the week, the Chicago police worked to escort African Americans and their friends into and out of the project. However, the police soon found that they, too, needed protection. Following the attack on the coal truck, officers that were patrolling the area surrounding the project attempted use their squad cars to divert a large group of protesters. In response, the crowd surrounded the officers and tried to overturn the police vehicles. To gain some control over this situation, officers, for the first time in these housing disturbances, used their batons to subdue the crowds. Some reports recalled how protesters attacked a fire truck that was stationed at the housing project to guard against arson, and in one instance, a Catholic priest walking through the area in an effort to visit with his parishioners was accosted by two white protesters, spat upon, and told to "go home and tend to his own business."[46]

After the initial incident with Turner, the Chicago Police Department failed to provide adequate protection at the Airport Homes. To supplement the police efforts, members of several local union and veterans' groups helped stem the crowds. On December 10, members of the Chicago Industrial Union (CIU) sent a memo to all affiliated CIO unions denouncing the violence at the Airport Homes. In the statement, Michael Mann, secretary of the CIU, wrote, "Our council is doing everything humanly and organizationally possible to help this local situation. We are working closely (on a day-to-day emergency basis) with all of the major civic organizations including the Catholic, Protestant, Jewish, Negro, and other reputable fraternal, religious, and civic organizations in town."[47] Groups like the UPWA also provided security at the Airport Homes during the controversies. According to historian Rick Halpern, the UPWA "sent teams of packinghouse workers to the Airport project each night to guard the homes of the black families."[48]

By December 27, many of the most serious acts of violent protest had ceased at the Airport Homes. Although some of the African American residents reported they were still subjected to racial slurs, the most substantial problem reported by Fort and Waddles was the difficulty in getting deliveries of ice, milk, and laundry. According to one delivery driver, "he could not serve them because if he did the community would boycott him."[49] This relative calm lasted only until February 1947, when unknown assailants fired four gunshots into Fort's apartment. The bullets narrowly missed hitting Fort's wife and six-week-old baby.[50] The Chicago Police Department failed to apprehend anyone in connection to this incident, and despite Mayor Kelly's orders, police protection soon became more suspect. In fact, some critics of police action at the homes alleged that members of the Chicago Police Department and local Democratic precinct captains initially aided rioters and deserted their post during the shooting.[51] In the end, this proved too much for either the Fort or the Waddle families to bear. After the shooting, both veterans and their families finally moved from the Airport Homes. Still, the events at the housing development did not stop the CHA, African Americans, or city hall from continuing on the path of nondiscrimination in public housing. In fact, the Airport Homes development was "the last of the veteran projects which turned out to be all white."[52]

Several months following the events at the Airport Homes, Chicago experienced more racial violence when racial tensions erupted at the Fernwood Park Emergency Veteran Housing Project on 105th and Union in April 1947. Three months prior to a scheduled move-in, members of the Mayor's Commission on Human Relations met with area community groups, principals and teachers, police, and the CHA's Veterans' Housing Manager to discuss the opening of the Fernwood project and how to avoid further racial disturbances. At the conclusion of this meeting, it was suggested that the Fernwood Park PTA sponsor a canteen for the veterans to "deter hoodlum elements in the community who might otherwise be the cause of demonstrations."[53] But any hopes that this would avert escalating racial tensions were short-lived. Instead of serving as the catalyst for racial tolerance, the PTA instead chose to sponsor a canteen for white veterans only.

Further resistance against the presence of black veterans at Fernwood came from Alderman Reginald DuBois and the Fernwood Civic Association. In the months leading up to the opening of the Fernwood project, DuBois made a public statement claiming, "If the Chicago Housing Authority would stop trying to prove its ideological contentions and would just furnish housing where it was needed, everything would be all right."[54] The Fernwood–Bellevue Civic Association held similar beliefs, and according to its president, W. D. Thomas, he and his organization "were doing all in their power to ensure the continued peace of the community, but if the Chicago Housing Authority persisted in its present course," he could guarantee nothing.[55] DuBois and Thomas may have believed that their comments reflected the will of the community. However, they met with resistance from other groups within their communities.

Local trade union members living in the area attempted to counter white resistance by forming the Community Good Will Council to work "in support of the maintenance of the CHA non-discriminatory policy at the Fernwood Homes."[56] Aside from scheduling programs to educate residents in race relations, the Good Will Council also agreed to sponsor the aforementioned canteen on move-in day, August 9. When veterans assigned to live in the homes reported to CHA headquarters to sign their leases and receive their keys, they, along with members of the Good Will Council, engaged in shouting matches with members of the Fernwood–Bellevue Civic Association and other white residents of the community who protested the move.

The events of Fernwood in many ways mirrored those at the Airport Homes. For example, white residents in the community started their protest at the first sign of the African American tenants. As was the case at the Airport Homes, white residents targeted not only African American veterans living in the area or their friends who were visiting the facilities but also African American bystanders in communities some distance away from the project and liberal whites siding with the CHA. At 10 P.M. on August 9, a group of more than two hundred white protesters threw bricks and bottles at a home owned by an African American at 6341 South Wabash, more than four miles from the Fernwood Park homes. The police arrived and dispersed the crowd but made no arrests. At 2:30 A.M., an African American couple was involved in a drive-by shooting in the all-black section of Morgan Park. In another example, a white member of the Fernwood Park Goodwill Council reported that she and her daughter were attacked by neighborhood youth. This attack reportedly stemmed from the woman's participation in a welcome canteen that was established on the day of the move-in to provide refreshments to both black and white veterans.[57]

The most striking differences between the events of Fernwood and those of the Airport Homes was the effective coordination of police protection and the response of African Americans outside of the community to the violence. The police department addressed the lessons learned from the unrest at the Airport Homes and by mid-1947 was implementing this new strategy. Police officers employed such tactics as making mass arrests during the outbreak of violence; maintaining a large police presence during these disturbances; closing down local bars and taverns in the area during disturbances; and limiting the traffic in the area and discouraging "sightseers" from entering the area.[58]

African American responses to the violence changed significantly between the 1946 and the 1947 disturbances as some demonstrated a willingness to confront and engage rioters—sometimes on their own terms. An African American family returning from vacation and an African American cabdriver were each attacked in separate instances while driving through the area. After the altercations, the family and the cabdriver both proceeded to a South Side gas station frequented by other black cabdrivers. When they arrived, the family informed the people there about the attacks at the Fernwood project, leading some to plot retaliation. Witnesses told city officials that some of the cabdrivers were determined to not be victimized and planned on "going home [to] get their guns, crankshafts, and knives. . . . They were going out to Fernwood as a body, seeking revenge upon the whites."[59] In several South Side taverns, it was suggested that signs be put on the damaged cars and each vehicle should be driven through the African American community as a rallying point that would perhaps motivate "armed expeditions to return to the Fernwood area to be organized."[60] While armed incursions never materialized, black activism sometimes moved past the planning stages, and some white Chicagoans, unfortunate enough to be caught in African American communities at the height of the tensions, became targets. In one case, African American youths threw rocks and other materials at stalled streetcars on Ninety-Sixth and Michigan, injuring several white passengers; in another, black teenagers threw bricks and stones at white motorists driving though a black neighborhood on 111th and Ashland Avenue.

The Airport Homes and Fernwood Park incidents established a dangerous precedent in postwar housing and held long-term political consequences for African Americans who were building coalitions with allies in local government. Edward Kelly, whose support of African American issues had made him unpopular with white voters, failed to secure the Democratic nomination for mayor in 1947, and Martin Kennelly was selected to replace Kelly as the Democratic nominee. As a candidate, Kennelly initially supported public housing initiatives. While campaigning, Kennelly told the *Chicago Bee*, "The housing situation is a crime. It is more than a problem. It is an emergency that must be met. And I pledge that, if elected, the city will do everything within its power and its means to bring about a solution of this desperate situation."[61] Indeed, after the election, Kennelly listed better housing at the top of his plans for a greater, more progressive Chicago. Once in office, though, Kennelly's stance on the housing disturbances differed sharply from that of his predecessor. After the Fernwood Park incident, Kennelly issued no public statement against the violence and told Elizabeth Wood that he could see no sense in a thousand policemen mobilizing for duty at a fantastic rate per day just to protect eight "Negro families."[62] By the end of the decade, groups such as the Conference to End

Mob Violence would call for impeachment of Kennelly for "failure to halt increasing mob violence against Negros and Jews."[63]

Nationally, African American housing searches were aided by the U.S. Supreme Court's ruling on the constitutionality of state-enforced restrictive covenants. In a 1948 case, *Shelley v. Kraemer,* the Court reversed the decision by a Missouri court that barred African Americans from purchasing homes in a St. Louis neighborhood protected by a covenant. Chief Justice Fred Vinson, in reading the opinion of the Court, determined that by supporting covenants, "the States have denied petitioners the equal protection of the law."[64] The Court further argued that individuals' freedom from discrimination was one of the basic goals of the Fourteenth Amendment. This amendment declared that all persons stood equal before the law, and the Court determined that "because of the race or color of the petitioners, they have been denied ownership or occupancy enjoyed as a matter of course by other citizens of a different race or color."[65]

Shortly after the Supreme Court's ruling in the *Shelley* case, Congress passed the Public Housing Act of 1949, which provided federal funding for the construction of 810,000 units of public housing throughout the United States. This act, along with the Court's decision, prompted opponents of neighborhood integration in Chicago to move to limit access of African Americans to white neighborhoods. To help ensure African Americans would have a stake in the construction of this new housing, Third Ward alderman Archibald Carey Jr. proposed an ordinance that would forbid racial or religious discrimination in any housing constructed on public land secured from the Chicago Land Clearance Committee.[66] If passed, the Carey Ordinance, as it became known, could potentially open the door for African Americans to move into newly constructed housing all over the city, breaking free of the confines of the South Side.[67] The ordinance was favorably received during an executive session of the city council's housing committee, but when it came time for the full council to vote, upon the urging of Mayor Kennelly, the ordinance was defeated, 31–13.[68] Kennelly's opposition to the bill was intriguing because it ran counter to the housing reforms sponsored by other Democrats at the federal level. Although Carey was a Republican, the mayor's and council's objection seemed more racially than politically based. Kennelly defended his actions, claiming that passage of this ordinance would cause the city to lose "$125 million in new construction and tax revenues" and was clearly "not in the best interest of the city." However, "given Kennelly's reluctance to openly support efforts to address the housing issues facing African Americans, his critics claimed the actions by the mayor and city council opened the way for further use of public power and money against the rights of Negroes everywhere." They also asserted that "by his words and his actions . . . Mayor Kennelly allied himself with the group of narrow minded, bigoted individuals who tell Chicago it dares not be democratic."[69] While the defeat of the Carey Ordinance was not the only setback for open housing activists, it was clear that, in the words of journalists Adam Cohen and Elizabeth Taylor, "to most white aldermen, the new housing was seen as an invitation to Elizabeth Wood and the CHA to build public housing for blacks in white neighborhoods."[70]

To prevent this, the Chicago City Council persuaded the Illinois State Legislature to give the council the power to approve or disapprove all sites selected by the housing authority.[71] These moves by public housing opponents at the municipal level were potentially devastating to the CHA's nondiscrimination policy. On November 23, 1949, the CHA presented the city council with a proposal to build seven new housing developments. The council approved only two of these proposed sites, which were in predominantly African American communities and in close proximity to existing public housing.[72] Furthermore, the council presented the CHA with its own plan to form a subcommittee on site selection. It soon became obvious that the council's plan "turned out to be no more viable than the CHA's plan."[73]

Two prominent Chicago aldermen, John Duffy and William Lancaster, developed an alternative plan when it became clear that the city council would never approve the CHA's proposal and the council's subcommittee could not adequately address the site selection process. The Duffy–Lancaster Compromise called for eight sites (10,500 units) to be built in established African American communities and for seven sites (2,000 units) to be built outside traditional black enclaves. This compromise was met with disdain by the CHA and its supporters. Elizabeth Wood traveled to Washington to appeal to the federal Public Housing Authority and argued that the compromise violated federal nondiscrimination stipulations and should be overturned. At the same time, the *Chicago Defender* declared that this compromise was "calculated to continue the ghetto and strengthen the spirit of segregation."[74]

In spite of the negative consequences that the Duffy–Lancaster Compromise held for public housing residents, in the wake of *Shelley*, African Americans with the financial resources to move out of the existing Black Belt used this opportunity to move into better neighborhoods. Many of these moves were not into public housing. Instead, African Americans began buying private homes in white communities. One of the earliest post-*Shelley* housing disturbances occurred at 7153 South St. Lawrence Avenue in the community known as Park Manor. This neighborhood was adjacent to Washington Park, the community first integrated by Carl Hansberry in 1940.

On July 25, 1949, Roscoe and Ethel Johnson, an African American couple, moved into a home they purchased in the all-white community. The Johnsons were initially concerned with the idea of moving into the neighborhood as no other African Americans lived in the immediate vicinity, but the real estate agent who sold the home to the Johnsons tried to alleviate their fears by assuring them that "the only trouble they might have would be for someone to throw a brick in the window."[75] Given the events of the Airport Homes and Fernwood Park, though, one could logically assume that the levels of violence could go beyond a simple stone thrown through one's window.

The Johnsons had planned on moving into their new home during the early morning hours of July 25. However, when that day arrived, the moving company hired by the couple to transport their belongings ran behind schedule and did not arrive at the St. Lawrence Street home until 3:30 in the afternoon. As the movers began to unload, a crowd gathered, hoping to catch a glimpse of the new owners. Roscoe Johnson then arrived at the home, accompanied by a coworker, Sylvester Dunn, and began to help the movers unload the delivery truck. After a short while, Dunn left to pick up Mrs. Johnson in order to bring her to the new residence. According to Mr. Johnson, he was "not certain whether or not the crowd thought that he was employed by the moving company, or employed by the new occupants to arrange the furnishings, or was the new occupant."[76]

As the men continued unloading the belongings, one of the movers got into a verbal altercation with an onlooker. Hoping to avoid an escalation of tensions, the movers boarded their truck, without completing the unloading, and drove away. As they were leaving, a mattress fell off the back of the truck and was set on fire by one of the onlookers. Finding himself alone, Johnson entered the house and locked himself in. In the following days, crowds as large as three hundred people gathered to protest against the Johnsons. As was the trend in the previous disturbances, white protesters used force not only against the African American residents but also against liberal whites associated with them. A caseworker for the Cook County Bureau of Public Welfare, Rhea Cox, reported that she encountered virtually no problems going to visit Mr. and Mrs. Johnson, but "as she left she was victim of all kinds of vile name calling and a few stones were thrown at her." Another caseworker, Elta Lanart, reported being "jostled by the crowd as she left the Johnsons' home." She further explained that she was challenged by a police officer who spoke "very roughly" and "suggested that she stay out of the area." William Gremley of the Mayor's Commission on Human Relations recalled that while standing on the other side of the street talking to some policemen, a car drove up to the curb and I noticed several *Chicago Defender* men get out of the car and as the *Chicago Defender* photographer got out, I shook his hand. I was subjected to numerous racial insults from housewives on the corner, who had observed this incident and was informed that I was as black as any Negro. I was called a "nigger lover," and given advice to go home and cut off my hand.[77]

Learning from the mistakes of the past, the Chicago Police Department maintained order fairly well, and by the end of July both the Mayor's Commission on Human Relations and the police department reported that many of the crowds that had been protesting against the Johnsons had subsided. Even so, it would be a mistake to consider that those in the community fully accepted their African American neighbors. A group of white Park Manor residents calling itself the Park Manor Improvement Association held a meeting at a church at Seventieth and South Park. The Park Manor Improvement Association appeared to be one of the most active race-restricting groups in the neighborhood, and according to its bylaws, the primary focus of the organization was to "discourage undesirable people from living and undesirable trades, occupation, and business from being established therein." For this group, the only desirable person welcomed in the community was "any white person of the age of twenty-one years or upwards and of good moral character."[78]

This particular meeting touched on the real estate agent who sold the home to the Johnsons, incidents of police brutality by black officers toward white civilians, and "several rape cases in the district that have been hushed and no action taken."[79] One of the most important resolutions to develop out of this meeting was that the group decided to elect a committee that would approach the Johnsons and ask them to sell their home. The leadership of the association believed that buying the family out of the community was a more viable alternative than mob violence. In fact, the president of the organization even stated that he "had no ill feelings toward any Negro [but] he just does not want them living near him." Moreover, he believed that "he would not want to live in a neighborhood where he was not wanted, [and] he was certain the Johnsons felt the same way."[80]

These activities did little to affect neighborhood change, and sporadic violence flared into 1950 after another African American family, Mr. and Mrs. Leander Griffin, took up residence at 7224 South St. Lawrence Avenue. On the morning of August 16 the Griffins moved into their home without incident. As darkness approached, though, protest activity by some white residents increased, and by 9 P.M. a large number of people began to gather at the scene. Police responded to the buildup by setting up barricades and diverting all vehicular traffic from the area. Two hours later, police moved from home to home along the block telling residents to "get in the house or into the police wagon!"[81] Those who refused were arrested. By 11:45 P.M. the crowds that had developed were dispersed, and no subsequent groups reformed.[82] The action of the police in the area was successful in keeping residual violence from occurring. Throughout the area, there was not a single report of attacks on African Americans, and no crowds gathered in front of the Johnsons' home. After this brief 1950 disturbance, not only did the violence almost completely disappear in this area, but some African Americans were accepted into the community. Following the second St. Lawrence Avenue incident, racial tensions had subsided to such a degree that an African American woman, the wife of Olympic track champion Jesse Owens, was eventually elected president of a local PTA.[83]

The transition that took place in Park Manor was a slow process, and as African Americans gradually moved into this community, white residents sold their homes and moved out. It was during this process that the racial characteristics of the community started to change. But violence against African Americans seeking homeownership in white communities was not limited to Chicago. In the Chicago suburb of Cicero, white residents protested the occupancy of an apartment by an African American veteran and his family in 1951. Unlike in Chicago, African Americans in Cicero could not readily rely on support from law enforcement or the local government to protect them from violence. What African Americans could and did do was find support from the courts in guaranteeing the enforcement of the Supreme Court's decision regarding restrictive covenants.

The disturbances in Cicero started in March 1951 when Harvey Clark and his wife, Johnetta, rented an apartment in a building at 6132–42 West Nineteenth Street.[84] Clark, a World War II veteran, had served as an aviation instructor at the Tuskegee Institute in Alabama. After his discharge in 1945, he attended Fisk University in Nashville, Tennessee. He and his wife, also a Fisk graduate, moved to Chicago in 1949 and eventually settled in Cicero because this apartment afforded Clark a much shorter commute to work.[85] Although the Clarks signed a lease for the apartment in March, they did not move into it immediately, choosing instead to wait until June.

Several days before the Clarks were to take up residence in the building, Camille De Rose, the building's owner, awoke to find several Cicero police officers and other officials stationed outside her door. When De Rose approached the officers to inquire as to why they were there, Cicero town attorney Nicholas Barkos confronted her. Barkos warned De Rose that "[Cicero] would not and could not afford to permit Negroes to be in the neighborhood because it would come to bloodshed and would not and could not be responsible for their safety." Undoubtedly, Cicero officials had witnessed the disturbances that took place in Chicago's neighborhoods over integration. Unlike Chicago's position, Cicero's position that it would not protect black residents moving into the community established a dangerous precedent.

When the Clarks arrived at the apartment building with several friends and associates on June 8, two plainclothes policemen met them and told them that they "could not move into the building without a permit." The officers then ordered Clark and his associates from the building at gunpoint. Charles Edwards, who was with Clark that day, recalled that not only were he and his companions harassed by Cicero officers, but the chief of police himself, Ervin Konovsky, told Clark, "Get out of Cicero and don't come back in town or you'll get a bullet through you."[86]

Clark and Edwards took this matter to the NAACP and decided to file a $200,000 lawsuit against the town for "conspiring to deprive citizens of their right of freedom of movement by force and violence and undue authority."[87] The U.S. district judge, John P. Barnes, ruled on the suit but failed to award punitive damages. Barnes did, however, issue an injunction, warning Cicero officials against any further action against the Clarks and stating, "If you don't obey the order, you're going to be in serious trouble. . . . You're going to exercise the same diligence in seeing that these people move in as you did in trying to keep them out."[88]

Following Barnes's ruling, the Clarks again prepared to move into Cicero. On July 10 the family moved their furniture into the apartment but chose not to stay there that evening. After the Clarks left for the night, a large crowd gathered, and many of the windows in the building were broken. The next day, the nineteen other families in the building moved out, and the tensions in the area began to escalate. An observer for the American Civil Liberties Union stated that "at 7:30 P.M. a crowd of 800–900 people were gathered. By dusk [the crowd] had grown to 4,000–5,000 people. There were people of all ages, many women and children. The most active were the teenagers, some in gangs." Moreover, this same observer reported to have seen undercover police officers walking through the crowd and telling a group of youth to "cut out the [throwing] of firecrackers. We don't care how many rocks you throw, but get rid of the firecrackers."[89]

This escalation of white violence all occurred *before* the Clarks ever lived in the building. All the while, the Cicero Police Department failed to effectively do anything to stop the crowd. The Cicero police were aided in law enforcement efforts by county police and police from neighboring communities. As the situation continued, it became obvious to outside law enforcement departments that they would be unable to maintain order. Again, despite all of these events, Clark maintained that he did not believe that "Cicero residents can afford to deny his civil rights after he made such a sacrifice and helped to win the war and to establish the safety of those who live in Cicero."[90] By July 12, the situation in Cicero continued to overwhelm local police efforts, so the county sheriff contacted Governor Adlai Stevenson and requested the National Guard be dispatched to the town. The National Guard was very effective in controlling the crowd in Cicero and quelled the disturbances by July 13. But this did not stop the housing controversy.

Following the Cicero disturbances, a Cook County grand jury indicted NAACP lawyer George N. Leighton and four other lawyers who defended the rights of the Clarks. Leighton and the others were charged with "conspiring to injure property . . . by causing a depreciation in the real estate market price by renting to Negroes."[91] In addition, the five were charged with inciting the Cicero riot and "bringing force and violence against the personal property . . . of Harvey and Johnetta Clark."[92] However, Leighton and the others were never prosecuted for these crimes. In fact, after the indictments, the U.S. attorney ordered an investigation of the riot and the action of the Cook County grand jury as well.

Until this point, many of the housing disturbances that occurred to protest the presence of African Americans in Chicago and in the surrounding areas had several things in common. First, the disturbances centered on a small number of African Americans moving into each community. In many of these cases, one African American family was enough to spark protests by hundreds or even thousands of white residents. Moreover, many of these protests started before any black family took actual possession of a home in the community. Second, in each incident, law enforcement agencies played a crucial role in quickly restoring lawfulness in areas where these incidents took place. After the events at the Airport Homes, Chicago police became much more efficient in handling crowd control. In Cicero, even though there was massive resistance by local law enforcement to maintain law and order, Cook County police officers and the Illinois National Guard proved more than adequate in cutting down the racial violence in that community. Each of these disturbances lasted from between several weeks to several months. Although there were residual tensions in each of these communities, there is no evidence that suggests any serious incidents of interracial violence. But by 1953, events at the far South Side housing development Trumbull Park challenged many of the established trends in previous disturbances.

The problems began on August 4, 1953, when Edward Greenbaugh, manager at the Trumbull Park Homes, called the Mayor's Commission on Human Relations to report that Donald Howard and his family were moving into the housing project at 10630 South Bensley Avenue. This move came as a total surprise to the CHA and the Mayor's Commission; since the Airport Homes disturbance in 1946, the commission had asked the CHA to report when African American families moved into public housing projects in white communities. No one at the CHA had notified the commission because at the time the CHA was unaware that the Howards were African American. According to CHA employees, Mrs. Howard and the children "were reported to be white in appearance."[93] The Howard family's racial background was further called into question because Mr. Howard's military discharge papers, which were used for priority in housing assignments, stated that he was "white," and the family listed their previous address as 9337 South Park Avenue, a community not immediately known as an African American community.[94] The Howards had originally applied for housing at the "black" projects of the Ida B. Wells Homes and Altgeld Gardens; however, finding no vacancies at either development, Mrs. Howard applied directly to the Trumbull Park project office. As a result, the Mayor's Commission on Human Relations had had no advance warning as to the integration of this housing project. Any confusion as to whether the Howard family was in fact African American was put to rest when Mr. Howard went to the project office to request some repairs for his new apartment and some of the local residents saw for themselves that African Americans had moved into this all-white housing project.

Word of the integration of Trumbull Park spread very quickly, and by the evening of August 5 a small group of twenty-five to thirty people gathered in front of the apartment and began throwing bricks and stones and shouting toward the Howard residence. The Chicago Police Department arrived and dispersed the crowd, but after this first crowd was disbanded, others began to form throughout the development. For the next several days, the level of hostilities toward the presence of the Howards grew. On August 6 stones and bottles were thrown at the Howards' apartment and at the car of the project manager. On August 8 the commission reported that protesters threw burning flares through the rear windows of the apartment. The next day, protesters harassed a friend of the Howards who came to Trumbull to visit the family, and a protester threw a brick through the family's front window. When police arrived for this last incident, they encountered a group of between one and two thousand people.[95]

The CHA, as it had in previous cases, did all that was within its power to protect the Howards. One way they attempted this in Trumbull Park was by installing provisions in CHA apartment leases prohibiting disturbances of the "peaceful enjoyment of the premises by other tenants" and by evicting members of two white families due to their involvement in these actions against the Howards. The CHA also adopted a resolution that reaffirmed its stance on nondiscrimination and publicly condemned "the use of mob violence to protest the occupancy of a home in the Trumbull Park Homes by a Negro family."[96]

In addition to these initiatives, the CHA discussed a plan to move more African American families into Trumbull Park, and on October 3, 1953, it went forward with its decision: three African American families were assigned to the homes. As expected, there was a considerable amount of resistance from the white residents. For this second move-in, the CHA, the Mayor's Commission, and the Chicago Police Department arranged to caravan the new families into the homes. As these groups arrived at Trumbull Park, according to the *Chicago Reporter*, "several women literally hurled themselves, first at the trucks loaded with the newcomers' furniture and later at a new car driven by the head of the Negro family."[97]

The *Daily Calumet* reported, "Angry crowds lined the walks of the project and loudly declared their displeasure. Scores of police were forced to wield clubs to hold back the surging masses of the glass-slinging and vegetable-throwing mob."[98] The inclusion of more African American families appeared to achieve nothing but escalated violence. Granted, the Howards were no longer isolated in the project, but by introducing more black families into an already contentious scene, the CHA exacerbated a situation that the police were already reluctant to get into. Following the move-in, African Americans living inside the project as well as those living in other parts of the city became very critical of police protection and the inaction of Mayor Kennelly. This was especially true as African Americans saw an increase in police apathy and the police department's continued failures to catch or pursue white residents who were breaking the law and as the police became more verbally abusive to African Americans living in Trumbull Park. In some cases, police officers' attitudes toward the black residents mimicked those of the white protesters in Trumbull Park. CHA employee Albert Rosenberg overheard an officer at Trumbull Park remark, "These damn Polacks, why are they picking on us. They should go down to the City Hall where they can do some good, and go after the Urban League." According to Rosenberg, another officer said he believed that families who moved into Trumbull Park should be arrested for making a riot.[99]

Opponents of the mayor were especially critical because he continued to take such a weak stance on housing violence. On March 18, for instance, the mayor declared that his administration would "prevent violence no matter where it may arise or from whatever cause. The rights of individuals with respect to their homes and property must and will be protected against any violence of their lawful right."[100] He continued by appealing to "all religious faiths, races, and backgrounds to join with [him] in the effort to maintain the peace and good order of the city and to build understanding."[101] By issuing such a vague statement, the mayor avoided either fully supporting integration or supporting white efforts to move African Americans from their neighborhoods.[102] This vagueness signaled to African Americans that city hall would not fully protect their housing interests as Mayor Kelly had done in previous years.

African Americans continued to move into the Trumbull Park project. By April 1954, Frank L. Brown and his family became the tenth African American family to take up residence in the housing project. Brown, who later penned the novel *Trumbull Park*, based on his experiences at the development, found that some of the racial tensions had faded but not disappeared. According to the Mayor's Commission on Human Relations, the area was "quiet for some weeks and there had been a decline in the number and size of the crowd gathering."[103] The commission also reported that "the incidents that did occur seemed to have been lacking purposefulness of the earlier demonstrations and were spasmodic and not focused."[104] Nonetheless, it was still there. The Howards, who over time came to symbolize racial hostilities in the area, moved out of the homes in May 1954. Violence at the development continued into May 1955 and did not completely subside until well into the 1960s. By that time, twenty-nine African Americans were living in the projects. For the rest of the decade, African Americans and white residents inside the project and the surrounding community challenged the practice of segregation over housing and access to public facilities.

The housing disturbance and the city's inability to handle the violence led to the downfall of the CHA's executive secretary, Elizabeth Wood, and Mayor Kennelly. Wood's dismissal from the housing authority grew out of her insistence on maintaining the CHA's nondiscrimination policy and her unwillingness to allow the CHA to become a bastion of political patronage. In 1952 the CHA continued to publicly push a nondiscrimination policy in regard to public housing. However, a secret CHA executive board directive ordered a systematic effort to exclude African Americans from all-white housing projects.[105] While Wood resisted this policy, some of her critics, like Tenth Ward Alderman Emil Pacini, called for her removal in favor of "someone who would not subject people, either Negro or others, to insults and indignities."[106]

Wood's replacement was William Kean. Kean, a retired army general, was hired as the executive director of the CHA despite his complete lack of previous experience in civilian housing. The *Defender* reported, "Kean was chosen because of his outstanding administrative ability."[107] Wood's supporters, expectedly, resisted and argued that this politically charged move held potentially dire consequences in regard to race and public housing in the city. Morton Berman, of the Temple Isaiah Israel, saw the move as a "serious blow to civic integrity." Alderman Archibald Carey argued that Wood was replaced because she "protected minorities and secured for them unsegregated housing and accommodations." The Chicago Negro Chamber of Commerce voted unanimously to condemn the action, claiming Wood was removed because "she has tried to carry out the avowed policy of the Authority in admitting tenants on the basis of need and qualifications, without regard to race or color."[108]

During Kean's administration, the CHA enacted policies that reversed Wood's system of proportional representation of African Americans in public housing and thereby ended any significant integration efforts in such projects as Trumbull Park.[109] The housing authority created new policies that assured that Chicago public housing would remain overwhelming African American. According to historian Arnold Hirsch, Kennelly was left "shell-shocked and alienated from whites who blamed him for the disruption of their neighborhoods as well as from embattled blacks who vainly sought his protection."[110] In addition, Kennelly lost the support of the Democratic Party in Cook County. Without such support, Kennelly's aspirations for a third term as mayor of Chicago quickly faded.

Richard J. Daley declared himself the Democratic nominee for mayor in December 1954 and eventually won the office in 1955. The election of Daley signaled the end of New Deal liberalism in housing that had flourished under the Kelly administration and managed to survive eight years under Kennelly. In 1957 William Kean resigned and was replaced by Alvin Rose. Under Rose, the CHA's plan for integration was completely abandoned. An illustrative episode occurred in January 1958 at a meeting at the City Club of Chicago on the city's North Side. During the meeting, a white resident of the community asked Rose why there was no public housing being built in his predominantly white community. Rose explained that if the CHA built public housing in the man's neighborhood, it could not guarantee African Americans would not move in. Journalists Adam Cohen and Elizabeth Taylor, in their biography of Richard J. Daley, comment on this exchange, describing it as if Rose was asking the man who questioned him, "Do you really want a project out here, because if we put a project here some Negroes are going to move into Uptown."[111]

By the beginning of the 1960s, much of the momentum that housing activists had developed during the previous thirty years had faded. With the election of Daley as mayor, hopes of integrating the communities of Chicago through the actions of the city government ceased. The shift in

CHA policy moved from one that publicly supported nondiscrimination to one that concentrated African Americans, especially in public housing, in all-black communities. In the private housing market, not even the activities of Martin Luther King Jr. and the Southern Christian Leadership Conference could effectively dismantle the patterns of residential segregation that existed in Chicago during the 1960 and early 1970s.[112]

There were some victories. In *Gautreaux v. Chicago Housing Authority* (1968), the courts found that Chicago had discriminated against African Americans in the placement and tenancy of public housing. However, the uncovering of discrimination did little to change the patterns of segregation in Chicago. In other words, as more African Americans moved into white communities, more and more whites fled. Neighborhood segregation, along race and class lines, reinforced the cycles of poverty that already existed in poor African American communities. White flight left in its wake high rates of crime, drugs, and hopelessness for those without the resources to move into better conditions. In addition to white flight, the lack of capital investments in black communities eventually meant that the possibility of finding adequate employment was more difficult. However, to completely indict white residents in Chicago for the condition in many areas would neglect half the story. In the post-*Shelley* age, the exodus of middle-class African Americans from places like Bronzeville contributed to the general decline of neighborhoods as African Americans who had the financial resources to move out of the black community sought better housing in communities that were undergoing their own racial transition.

6. PICKET LINES WERE THE FRONT LINES FOR DEMOCRACY
BLACK VETERANS' LABOR ACTIVISM IN POST-WORLD WAR II CHICAGO

The economic fate of the Negro has never been and will never be disassociated from that of all labor of the nation. As with all workers, the volume of total employment in the nation is the key to the Negro worker's future.

—Robert C. Weaver, February 23, 1946

IN 1946, thirty thousand members of the United Packinghouse Workers of America went on strike in Chicago in an attempt to cripple the meat processing industry. More than fifteen thousand of the strikers were African American. The strike arose from growing fears of a postwar rollback of gains made during the war. Willie Johnson, a striker who started working at the packinghouses after serving in the Marine Corps, commented that the strike was important to him because it "was the only way to get what's coming to us and now was the time." In a *Chicago Defender* article in 1946, navy veteran Archie Knuckles, who did not work in the stockyards but came to the picket lines to support the strikers, claimed he was picketing because he knew the strikers had a legitimate grievance. Knuckles told the *Defender* that he "heard [the meatpacking] companies made 154 per cent profit during '45. They [company owners] don't need to raise prices to raise wages."[1] For Johnson and Knuckles, the goal of maintaining the economic leverage gained during the war was central to the postwar experiences of black war workers and black veterans.

Many of the labor conflicts that occurred after the war stemmed from labor and management's divergent visions of the postwar economy. The UPWA strike was symbolic of this divergence because it underscored a national movement by organized labor to demand an increase in wages in return for members' "no-strike" pledges signed during the war. For many within the working-class African American community, a better wage, along with better housing, was synonymous with the "American dream." Some felt that picket lines all over the country were the front lines for democracy. World War II veteran Jessie Walls admitted in 1946, "When I was in the Army, I thought folks who struck were falling down on the job. But since I came back and found out what it is all about, that they're standing for a half-way decent wage, I'm right there with them."[2]

In his study on Chicago's meatpacking history, historian Rick Halpern found that the "elimination of overtime hours meant a sharp reduction in take-home pay—in meatpacking, where there had not been a wage increase since before Pearl Harbor, this cut was as deep as 30%—and postwar inflation was expected to make this problem more acute."[3] Historian Elizabeth Fones-Wolf found that following the war, "labor, particularly the CIO, had an aggressive program for postwar reconstruction," which included tax reform and restructuring the minimum wage.[4] The centerpiece of organized labor's program lay in a Fair Employment Bill that was being debated in Congress.[5] Business leaders objected to added government intervention on the behalf of labor rights just as they had during the war period. Managers responded by pressuring conservative politicians to limit any fair employment legislation and launched public campaigns to label labor activism as Communistic. Thomas Sugrue notes that the demands made by the working class also came at a time when "firms reduced employment in center-city plants, replaced workers with new automated technologies, and constructed new facilities in suburban and semi-rural areas."[6] The fact that half of the UPWA strikers were African American underscores that this strike held serious stakes for Chicago's black population.

President Truman's eventual intervention in the packinghouse workers' strike highlighted some of the challenges that confronted both black workers and black vets in this struggle for postwar industrial equality. Unlike in the war years, when the federal government initiated measures designed to protect the rights of workers, after 1945 the powerful interests within the federal government seemed more concerned with bringing the nation's economy to peacetime levels and returning control to private interests than with addressing workers' grievances. Nonetheless, African American union men and women, churches, and community leaders lent their strong support for the strikes as the packinghouse workers walked out on their jobs in Chicago. In the wake of the packinghouse workers' strike, other veterans also struggled to make sense of the postwar conditions for laborers.

The comments made during the packinghouse workers' strike (as seen above) reflected the battles against the postwar industrial reconversion that were being waged between labor and employers following World War II. For those strikers who had served in the military during the war, the connection between their status as veterans and their positions as workers was especially clear. Many of the strikers and their supporters saw the strike as an extension of many of the gains made during the war in military and civilian life and a refusal to return to their prewar status. In turn, they called upon their veterans' status to bring about fundamental changes in their economic realities and to force the nation to live up to its democratic principles. According to St. Clair Drake and Horace Cayton, veterans' linking of their self-interests to the patriotic ideals of the era not only aided in the overall goal of "racial advancement" and integration but also was a crucial element in the fight for democracy.[7]

Of course, there were many more incidents that failed to gain as much national attention as the UPWA strike, several of which were led by African American World War II veterans. Black servicemen and servicewomen returning to civilian life across the United States found a society still heavily racialized and hostile to any level of social equality or integration. This chapter examines the racial dynamics shaped by the return of black veterans to Chicago during the immediate postwar period. For many of these veterans, the activities they participated in during the years following World War II demonstrated their refusal to return from the foxholes of Europe and the Pacific to the ratholes in the African American community of Chicago's South Side. To understand these issues, three questions must be answered. First, how did segments of the black community in Chicago attempt to control when, where, and how they worked? Next, how did their status as veterans shape the action they took? Finally, how did black militancy within the working class shape the relationship between labor, business, and the state?

Hilton Joseph, veteran of the Ninety-Second Artillery Division, believed that the return to civilian life would bring "increased recognition for his service and that his service could allow him access to more opportunities."[8] Like Joseph, army veteran Timuel Black, who served with the "Red Ball Express" in Europe, recalled that he and other vets often came back to civilian life with "the determination that they were going to make a difference."[9] Joseph and Black reflected on the idea of entitlement that was articulated by a number of veterans. Their status as servicemen could be used to make claims for increased federal protection and to speak out against racial injustice. This idea was important in shaping the direction of postwar militancy among veterans and was vital to the shaping of postwar policy in regard to veterans in Chicago. As World War II drew to a close, policy makers, organized labor, veterans' groups, and civil rights activists all worked to address ways to lessen the negative effects of postwar industrial reconversion from a wartime economy to a peacetime economy. African Americans stood to be the biggest losers during this transition. According to Robert Weaver,

> Any type of re-conversion will present serious problems to the black worker; he will suffer much higher incidences of unemployment than the white worker. The Negro worker will often be displaced from the better jobs he held during the war, and the Negro woman will, for the most part, leave industrial employment. The intensity of these losses and their influences upon black workers' permanent status in the economy will be determined chiefly by the timing and smoothness of our shift from a war to a peace economy.[10]

In Chicago, the pressures associated with reconversion were especially acute because of the large numbers of workers who had moved to Chicago in search of wartime jobs. According to the U.S. census, 550,000 people were employed in manufacturing in the Chicago area in 1940. By 1944, this number had increased to 875,000. By the end of the war, the employment situation in the city faced greater challenges as more than 425,000 men and women veterans returned to the Chicago area to either secure new jobs or seek to reclaim the jobs they held before their induction into the armed forces.[11]

For African American veterans, this push to dismantle old racial and industrial hierarchies in places like Chicago was stimulated by many of the same liberal ideas that had prompted arguments for better jobs and housing during the Depression and the war. Black servicemen and servicewomen believed the ideas of the Four Freedoms were, according to scholar Rufus E. Clement, "accepted literally and by almost the entire [African American] population of this country."[12] Clement, writing in 1943, further stated that "the group knows that it might be difficult to establish these freedoms in America, but is willing to accept the word of the leader that these are things for which [they] strive."[13] Indeed, African Americans had reasons to believe, at least in principle, that the federal government would support the promises enunciated in the Four Freedoms.

This belief, discussed in a previous chapter, was sparked by the creation of the Fair Employment Practices Committee. Although there is still debate over the effectiveness of the committee, for many black workers it provided an outlet to voice concerns over workplace discrimination. African Americans in Chicago viewed the FEPC as a way to secure improvements in their economic conditions during the war. Black churches and organizations held rallies throughout the war, and for many, the creation of the FEPC was vital and "absolutely essential with more than 40% of the black workforce engaged in economic activities outside of domestic and service fields."[14]

When the war ended, American businesses began to roll back many wartime gains made by African American men and women. Reconversion to a peacetime economy signaled a potential return to the prewar racial hierarchies in the labor market. By the end of the Second World War, Congress began to dismantle the FEPC. When President Roosevelt died in April 1945, the FEPC lost one of its most ardent supporters. The House Appropriations Subcommittee then voted to cut the proposed FEPC budget and omitted any funding for the 1946 fiscal year.[15] With the fall of the FEPC, African American veterans discovered that access to the educational and financial benefits of the GI Bill, irrespective of its presumed color blindness, remained "For White Veterans Only," and the administration of the GI Bill more often than not widened the country's racial gap.[16] Unfortunately for FEPC supporters, a permanent FEPC office never materialized. On June 27, 1945, Senator Theodore Bilbo of Mississippi, himself a longtime opponent of the FEPC, took the floor of the Senate and launched a virtual filibuster to prevent any debate about FEPC funding. Bilbo's actions prompted FEPC supporters to offer a compromise rather than risk the dismantling of the office altogether. In the end, no level of compromise would save the doomed committee. In May 1946, the committee issued its final report to President Harry S. Truman along with the resignations of the entire FEPC staff.[17]

The demise of the FEPC presented serious impediments to the struggle for economic equality for African Americans in Chicago. Historian Louis Ruchames found discrimination was more prevalent in Chicago than anywhere else in Illinois. His 1953 study on the FEPC cited an Illinois Interracial Commission report that found that "85 percent of the firms that contract to the city use discriminatory application forms."[18] Still, the psychological impact the office had on civil rights advocates was substantial. Historian Andrew Kersten reports that although the committee failed to fully end job discrimination, it did make some positive strides in increasing employment opportunities in the midwestern states between 1941 and 1944: "The FEPC handled over 1,400 complaints of discrimination . . . [and] was able to close over 60 percent and settle satisfactorily about 35 percent of its Midwestern cases."[19]

Sadly, as the FEPC died, the number of cases of discrimination against black workers in Illinois grew. According to a survey done by the U.S. Employment Service, "More than one-third of employers discriminate against the Negro workers[;] current services of commercial employment agencies show an overpowering majority in requesting job applicants to state race, religion and national origin."[20] Without some legislation, employment opportunities for African Americans living in Chicago stood to worsen. Furthermore, city officials and civil rights activists each feared a repeat of the labor and racial violence that had unfolded during the summer following World War I.

Local municipal ordinances and some local politicians supported efforts to ease tensions during the transition from a wartime economy. Although

Chicago would not be the only major metropolitan area to enact such legislation, part of what set the politics in the city apart was the role played by the administration of Mayor Edward J. Kelly in postwar employment. The Kelly administration realized the long-term political and social implications of instituting fair employment legislation and proposed the passage of a Chicago fair employment practices (FEP) ordinance. On August 21, 1945, the Chicago City Council passed the nation's first municipal FEP ordinance that outlawed discrimination based on race, color, or creed in city agencies, private firms with municipal contracts, and private companies operating within the city. Violation of the FEP ordinance would be punishable by a fine of up to $200. This ordinance was unique because it not only assigned a monetary penalty to companies that violated the order, something Roosevelt's FEPC failed to do, but also was the first fair employment legislation enacted in the entire state of Illinois. The Illinois legislature would not enact a state FEP law until 1947.

The first challenge to this ordinance occurred shortly after its passage when Helen Wideman, twenty-nine years old, answered an advertisement seeking a temporary typist with the Pepsodent Company. Upon applying for the job, she was informed by a representative of the company that "the position was not open to Negroes."[21] Wideman filed suit against the company, citing a clear violation of the city's FEP law. The judge presiding over the case strongly suggested that Pepsodent hire Wideman "under the same conditions and at the same salary as all other employees in the same category."[22] The company chose not to appeal the court's decision and eventually hired Wideman.

In addition to the ordinance, the Mayor's Commission on Human Relations also established a Subcommittee on Post-War Employment of Minority Groups in Wartime in 1945. This group was made up of thirteen representatives from management, organized labor, and the communities of Chicago. The work of the subcommittee was concentrated in two areas. The first dealt with the problems of employment "on the ground floor" by working with personnel and industrial relations directors, leaders of organized labor, and representatives of the community to encourage nondiscriminatory hiring practices. The second area was a technical advisory section that collected and analyzed data on the unemployment of different minority groups.[23]

The subcommittee submitted its first report to the mayor in September 1945 and found that at the conclusion of the war, the percentage of nonwhite workers declined by only 0.2 percent, from 11.4 percent to 11.2 percent. By November 1945, this number dipped another 0.2 percent to 11 percent. At the outset, these numbers seemed very promising and suggested something of a stabilizing trend in the employment of African Americans. This stabilization, however, was short lived. Between January 1945 and September 1946, the number of nonwhite factory workers in and around Chicago fell from 114,400 to 95,600. Many of the heaviest job losses occurred in such fields as transportation equipment, ordnance production, food processing, and printing and publishing.[24] These losses were worsened by the in-migration of approximately 25,000 African American civilian residents during this same period. Layoffs in manufacturing seemed less racially motivated than a function of a postwar reconversion to a peacetime economy. However, the commission found that there were distinct patterns of discrimination in the rehiring of unemployed workers. In an effort to assist veterans, the Mayor's Commission on Human Relations and USES developed strategies to ensure that job placements adhered to the city's nondiscrimination ordinance.

Campbell C. Johnson, executive assistant to the director of the Selective Service, commented on the significant obstacles facing African American veterans and how USES played an important role in developing policy aimed at deterring the discriminatory hiring practices that confronted African American veterans following the war. In a 1945 conference paper, Johnson stated, "It would be unfortunate if the United States Employment Service, which is the principal agency through which the Selective Service System works in securing new jobs for veterans, should return to its order taking and referral policy as in effect prior to the war when under state control."[25]

The Illinois USES office attempted to institute Johnson's vision and worked at securing more job opportunities for World War II veterans. Charles P. Casey, director of the Illinois office of USES, proposed a 1946 job development program to "build a back-log of jobs to the excess of the 37,000 now in the files of the agency in Illinois" and urged all Chicago area employers to participate.[26] The need for such a program was high due to the popularity of the educational benefits of the GI Bill that filled many educational facilities to capacity very quickly. As a result, many veterans had to postpone their educational ambitions. They often turned to USES to find suitable employment. It is unclear what impact Casey's plan had on creating more jobs during the early postwar period. It became obvious to many observers, however, that despite Johnson's assertions that the job placement activities would operate in a nondiscriminatory manner, the employment program often did little to make sure this happened. Representatives of the city and USES met twice in 1946, the first time in May. During this meeting, representatives of the commission and USES officials from the Chicago office developed strategies to coordinate the inclusion of a nondiscrimination clause in all job requests processed through local employment service offices.

Initially, the two sides reached an impasse regarding this issue. USES opted not to institute any nondiscrimination clause and instead chose to defer taking any action against job discrimination without first consulting with its Washington, D.C., office. USES stated that "the agency was then undergoing reformulation to meet situations where local FEP ordinances and statutes were in force, but that pending clarification of that policy, they would continue to accept orders with discriminatory specifications."[27] During a second meeting held in July 1946, the employment service seemingly wavered on its initial position of allowing these discriminatory practices to continue.

USES officials working in Chicago eventually submitted to the Washington office for final approval a draft of a nondiscrimination clause that was to be included in all job orders. However, no further action was taken on this draft as the employment service was returned to state control in November 1946. The inability to reach any workable agreement with the federal government highlights the difficulty facing advocates of equal opportunity in postwar employment. Moreover, this impasse underscored the federal government's inability to enact any substantial policy regarding nondiscrimination and full employment in American industry following the collapse of the FEPC.

Along with their work with the employment service, city planners also discussed new policies to help secure jobs during the postwar period. The Kelly administration planned massive public works projects similar to those put in place by President Roosevelt during the Depression. Philip Harrington of the Chicago Plan Commission outlined a plan for postwar employment before the Congressional Committee of Public Buildings and Grounds in 1944, testifying that Chicago planned more than $860,082,000 in public projects that were to take place after the war. The projects constituted 595,823,000 man-hours of work and included "rehabilitation and modernization of Chicago's mass transportation system, a comprehensive study that will define Chicago's future airport needs, [and] a comprehensive system of limited access expressways to serve its heavily populated areas."[28]

African Americans often initiated their own grassroots campaigns for jobs. Many of these endeavors resembled similar campaigns that took place during the Depression period and during the war. For example, in March 1946 the *Chicago Bee* reported that the Chicago Motor Coach Company had discharged forty-nine of the sixty-eight African American drivers they hired in 1943. This move almost completely reversed an important victory won in 1943 that forced Chicago's public transportation companies to integrate their workforce. In response, the Second Ward Young Democratic Organization issued a formal protest resolution to the Motor Coach

Company and formed a grievance committee to meet with the president of the company, Benjamin Westraub.[29]

The pressure from within the African American community eventually forced the Chicago Motor Coach Company to issue a statement that assured the Second Ward Young Democratic Organization of its plan to "abolish its discriminatory employment policies."[30] Moreover, the company promised to end such practices of "designating Negro employees by a special number on their caps" and also agreed to "investigate allegations that black driver trainees were solely assigned to South Side Jim-crow [bus] barns."[31] In another example, members of the Negro Labor Relations League concluded a two-year fight with the bakers of Wonder Bread, the Continental Baking Company, over the hiring of African American deliverymen in March 1947. This situation was resolved only after the league led a community-wide boycott of Continental Baking and the company agreed to "try out" five African American delivery people.[32]

In the end, no matter how ambitious the city's proposal was, public works alone could not solve all of the employment deficiencies. Furthermore, the campaigns of the Second Ward Young Democratic Organization and the Negro Labor Relations League demonstrated that some of the struggles to overcome discrimination in the private sector were far from over. By examining the activities of African American veterans, one can better understand the lasting impact working-class jobs campaigns had in securing job opportunities during the postwar period.

African American veterans found themselves in a unique position following the Second World War. On the one hand, because of their military status, many believed they were part of a protected class of American citizens. This status would bring with it preferential access to jobs, service benefits, and education. On the other hand, racial discrimination still severely limited African American servicemen's and servicewomen's access to many of the opportunities that were being enjoyed by white vets.

Despite the best efforts of city government to guarantee, protect, and create jobs, unemployment and underemployment were still prevalent among African American veterans. According to the Mayor's Commission on Human Relations, African American GIs were more likely to receive unemployment compensation in the form of federal Servicemen's Readjustment Allowances than were white veterans in Chicago. Between March 1946 and October 1946, the percentage of nonwhite workers receiving unemployment compensation rose from 22 percent to 35 percent. Comparatively, the number of nonwhite GIs receiving veterans' benefits rose from 14 percent in March of 1946 to 27 percent in October 1946. This data, however, still does not fully reflect the depths of unemployment among African American veterans because they fail to take into account the problems facing "hard-to-place" workers; unemployment among such a group ran as high as 42 percent during this same period.[33]

For discharged black veterans, the training they received in the armed forces often left them unprepared for civilian work. Journalist Trezzvant W. Anderson, in assessing the postwar problems facing African American and white veterans, wrote that while "white engineers learned skills such as a drafting, surveying, and other skills that could benefit them in civilian life, black soldiers learned one thing—how to kill."[34] Anderson's assertion as to the limited job skills attained by African American GIs was perhaps a bit simplistic. Many African American veterans did learn valuable technical skills and training they otherwise would not have received. The problem was that black GIs often found it difficult to utilize these new skills in civilian life due to discrimination in the workplace. For example, Mary McBride, a former member of the Women's Army Corps who was assigned to the 688th Postal Battalion, returned to Chicago from France in 1946. While overseas, McBride took several clothing design classes during which an instructor, realizing her talent, sent a letter recommending McBride's admittance to the Vogue School of Design in Chicago. Vogue accepted the recommendation and invited McBride to enroll. But when McBride arrived at the school and school officials saw she was African American, she was told that she was mistaken and that there were no openings at the school.[35]

Discrimination against African American veterans continued despite the introduction of two policies designed to promote, at least in theory, equality: the Selective Training and Service Act (1940) and the GI Bill of Rights (1944). Taken together, these measures established uniform codes as to the benefits all World War II vets were to receive. The Selective Training and Service Act not only authorized the induction of men into the armed services but also guaranteed veterans' rights for reemployment in their former occupations or assisted them in finding new job opportunities following the war. Upon separation from active duty, it was the responsibility of the vets to report to their local selective service system and be advised of their rights to work.[36] Under this act, veterans had ninety days after their discharge date to apply for reinstatement to prewar occupations or to apply for a new job.

The enforcement of this act and its effectiveness depended on the type of employment each veteran held before entering the military. For example, if soldiers were employed in an office or agency of the federal government, that office or agency was required by law to reinstate veterans to their prewar positions with full seniority benefits. However, if veterans were employed in private industry and at the conclusion of the war were refused reemployment, they could petition the court for a remedy: "The veteran himself may file suit in the United States District Court for the district in which his former employer maintained a place of business. He [the veteran] may employ his own attorney, or he may request a United States Attorney or comparable official to represent him without cost."[37]

President Roosevelt signed the Servicemen Readjustment Act, also known as the GI Bill of Rights, into law on June 22, 1944. The bill included six basic provisions: access to education and job training; guaranteed loans for the purchase of a home, farm, or business; unemployment pay of twenty dollars per day for up to one year; assistance in securing new employment; resources for the construction of Veterans' Administration hospitals; and a reevaluation of dishonorable discharges. Some African American civic and political leaders, such as war veteran Campbell C. Johnson, praised the potential in the GI Bill and wrote in the pages of *Opportunity* that the bill promised each veteran, regardless of color, the status of an "unforgotten man."[38]

But despite all of the provisions and guarantees of the Selective Training and Service Act and the GI Bill, African American veterans still faced difficulties securing employment in the postwar economy. Although the Selective Training and Service Act stated that servicemen and servicewomen were entitled to return to their jobs after the war, a large number of African Americans had been unemployed before the war and thus had no job to return to. For those who were fortunate enough to have had a job before their induction, many worked in dirty, unskilled, or semiskilled positions.

Another challenge that confronted returning black veterans was the problem of job seniority. Discharged black veterans were commonly among the throngs of war workers from relatively low-paying jobs who had sought more lucrative war jobs prior to their military service and during the country's peak production years. As a result of these moves, much of the seniority African Americans may have accumulated was lost as "eighty-one percent of those in manufacturing industries and 61 percent in all lines held jobs less than three years."[39] During postwar reconversion, many of these workers faced displacement by later waves of returning veterans or as plants, which once manufactured weapons and munitions for war, closed their doors.

In addition, African American veterans in the workplace began to realize that members of their race would seldom enjoy the full benefits of the GI Bill. Under the law, veterans' benefits were to be administered through the Veterans Administration (VA). As a federal agency, the VA was required to administer all of its programs on a nondiscriminatory basis. The reality, however, was that legalized and institutionalized racism hindered African Americans' access to the GI Bill because VA administrators did not seem overly concerned with addressing discrimination in local offices.

The extent of the racial complacency reached into the upper echelons of the VA itself. In 1947 General Omar N. Bradley, chief administrator of the VA, sent a letter to Robert K. Carr, executive secretary of President Truman's Committee on Civil Rights, in which he suggested that racism and segregation within the facilities of the VA could be and should be tolerated so as not to create any undue tension among staff and clients. It was Bradley's position to support discrimination within the VA because the administration believed that "the need for supplying the best medical treatment for all veterans makes it necessary for the VA to recognize and accept local customs wherever ignoring them would cause mental unrest, unhappiness, or discontent which would interfere with the recovery of the patients."[40]

Furthermore, Bradley went as far as to reject the idea of including a nondiscrimination clause in the mission of the VA. He believed this to be the best course of action in order to avoid highlighting "the possibility of discrimination where none exists except through faulty execution."[41] But the de facto acceptance of racist practices within the day-to-day operations of the VA was by no means the only reason African American veterans remained wary of the office. Restrictive covenants hampered African Americans' abilities to fully utilize low-interest federal housing loans; educational segregation kept them from entering many universities and professional schools; and racial discrimination limited postwar employment opportunities for them. All the while, the VA did little to address their concerns.

Along with institutional obstacles from within the VA itself, African American GIs also faced challenges from white veterans' groups, a strong lobbying force that operated closely with the VA. Following the war, African American and white veterans used whatever influence they possessed to lobby for protection through military service organizations. The Veterans of Foreign Wars (VFW), the Foreign Legion, and AMVETS were all active during the postwar period as servicemen, servicewomen, and their families sought to gain access to provisions guaranteed by the GI Bill and other benefits through the VA.

For African Americans, membership in these organizations could not overcome racial discrimination and did not guarantee access to benefits. In fact, African Americans faced racial discrimination even as they attempted to join these organizations. Critics of these veteran groups often denounced the VFW and other white groups because they segregated African American veterans into separate posts. Black veterans often found that "the legion and VFW endorse[d] and encourage[d] segregation and discrimination against [African American] veterans. Their policy [was] lily-white and anti-Negro, both in the North and in the South, from post level up to the king makers."[42] There were, of course, all-black VFW posts in Chicago.

However, these were often not segregated by choice but rather by rule as many posts that accepted African Americans were located in mostly black communities. As a result, racial discrimination within these white veterans' organizations was often very effective in frustrating African Americans.

Even though racial discrimination presented severe impediments to achieving full veterans' benefits, and rhetoric alone would not end discrimination, African American GIs possessed mechanisms that would help them in their fight for postwar opportunities. At the local level, African Americans in a number of cities engaged in various coalition building activities with progressive organizations and local government officials to advocate for their rights.[43] Two of these groups in particular, the United Negro and Allied Veterans of America (UNAVA) and the American Veterans Committee (AVC), took the lead in advancing the call for equal rights for African American veterans. These organizations offered African Americans an alternative to the segregated veteran groups they were relegated to.

Founded in 1946 at DuSable High School on Chicago's South Side, UNAVA's activism focused squarely on the concerns of the African American veteran who "grappled physically with fascism and knows exactly what it means" and who faced rampant "job discrimination, quota systems in education, denial of loans, and restrictive covenants in housing."[44] The organization developed out of a biracial, national organizing campaign of the Committee for a National Veterans' Organization and united three hundred delegates from thirty-one states and included representatives from such groups as the Georgia Veterans' League, the 93rd Division Association, and the Global War Veterans of Columbia, Tennessee. The interracial composition of groups like UNAVA demonstrated that some black and white veterans realized their futures in a postwar America were linked and that a postwar economy put all in an extremely tenuous predicament. In spite of its interracial origins, African Americans dominated leadership positions; Kenneth Kennedy served as UNAVA's first national commander, and African Americans slowly made up the majority of the group's membership.

While it is undeniable that UNAVA worked for the rights of African American veterans, critics questioned the underlying political motives of the group. The NAACP, whose Veterans Affairs Office competed with UNAVA for membership, alleged that UNAVA was a Communist-front organization that used the offer of assistance in securing employment as a recruitment tool to attract African Americans to the Communist Party. UNAVA, of course, denied these charges. Instead, it claimed that the accusations were no more than a "clever means of creating ill-will and confusion by those who do not want Negro veterans organized and would destroy the unity created during the war between Negro and white servicemen."[45] If groups like UNAVA were indeed recruitment tools for the Communist Party, their efforts proved ineffectual. At its peak, UNAVA attracted a modest ten thousand members nationwide—mostly located in southern states—and during that period only approximately five hundred African American Communists lived in Chicago.[46] No matter the extent of Communist leanings, though, scholar Wilson Record found that UNAVA still "received some support from non-Communist groups [and] was endorsed by a number of religious and fraternal organizations, and included non-Communist veterans" such as boxer Joe Louis and Jackie Robinson, who served as honorary national commander and a member of the National Advisory Board, respectively, even though neither was openly Left-leaning.[47]

The AVC was created in 1944 with a mission to safeguard a "democratic and prosperous America and a more stable world."[48] To this end, membership was open to all U.S. World War II veterans regardless of race, class, creed, or national origin. Many of their activities centered on issues of housing, education, voting rights, employment, and equal access to the GI Bill of Rights. The AVC was somewhat less confrontational in its tactics than UNAVA. The reason for this may have been found in their own internal battle with radical Communists, but these internal conflicts did not keep the organization from taking a strong stance in defending the rights of African American veterans. On June 10, 1945, the AVC met with representatives of the American Legion, the VFW, USES, the VA, and the Mayor's Commission on Human Relations to address how to increase opportunities for all veterans regardless of race or creed. At the conclusion of the meeting, these groups presented several recommendations, including "joint support of legislation prohibiting state support (e.g. certification or tax exemptions) if discriminatory practices are followed, and pooling of information in order to generate understanding and awareness of the problem of discrimination."[49] This joint action was also successful in exerting pressure on vocational and trade schools in Chicago. The AVC was influential in eliminating discrimination in postwar job training in the city, and the Mayor's Commission detailed how the AVC was influential in working with city officials to open more positions in one of the "large technical schools, which had heretofore barred Negroes." Pressure brought by the AVC and the city forced the school to agree to "enroll qualified students of any race where their present application for enrollment had been cared for."[50]

The activities of veterans' organizations demonstrated how African American veterans were engaged in constant conflicts over access to benefits many believed they were entitled to. The efforts of the mayor's office and liberal veterans' service organizations notwithstanding, job prospects for African American veterans were still subject to constant negotiation. To combat incidents of discrimination, groups of veterans sometimes formed ad hoc labor organizations through which to argue for better treatment in employment. For example, for one group of cabdrivers in Chicago, the transition back to civilian life proved to be very difficult. Corruption, legal battles, and memories of the 1932 "Bonus Army" highlight the quest of the Illinois Cab Drivers' Association for Discharged Veterans (ICDADV) for licenses.

Historically, operating a cab afforded African American workers a degree of economic independence and became an ideal profession. Ownership of one's vehicle provided a livelihood and offered relief from some repressive Black Codes. Prior to 1915, anyone with a vehicle could enter this industry, as there were few local ordinances that regulated the taxicab industry or limited the number of licensed taxicabs in any given location. As more cities began to regulate the industry following World War I, larger companies, such as Yellow and Checker, were able to monopolize cab medallions (licenses required to legally operate a cab), and African Americans found it increasingly difficult to operate in this field, since many white-owned companies refused to hire black drivers.

During the 1930s, groups of African American cabdrivers in Chicago organized to protect themselves and their profession from harassment by Chicago Park District Police. In 1935 two African American cab company owners, Jackie Reynolds of Jackie Cab Company and Montell Stewart of the Montell Stewart Cab Company, filed a lawsuit to halt the "alleged discriminatory and wholesale arrest of Race cab drivers on the South Side boulevards."[51] According to their suit, a city ordinance that prohibited the solicitation of passengers on Chicago's boulevards was primarily enforced against African American drivers and the companies that were owned by African Americans. In July 1935 more than 150 African American drivers were arrested for soliciting business, though no white drivers were arrested during this same period. These jitneys were very popular and made for lucrative enterprises in Bronzeville, and due this success African American drivers and black-owned cab companies were in direct competition with the chauffeurs of the Chicago Motor Coach Company and drivers of the Yellow Cab Company of Chicago. African Americans were drawn to the jitneys because they offered services that white-owned buses and cabs could (or would) not. African Americans could travel between downtown Chicago and Bronzeville along the boulevards for as little as ten cents, and for a nominal fee some drivers would take a passenger's bags to his or her front door.

This "squeeze play" by the Chicago Motor Coach Company, Yellow Cab, and the Chicago Park District—along with the limited protection from organized labor—prompted these owners to organize themselves into the Southside Taxicab Owners Protective Association. Its purpose was to fight harassment from the police and white-owned transportation companies. In the end, though, even this was not enough to save the jitney. In September 1936 the courts ruled that no more passengers would be picked up by jitneys on the boulevards unless by special calls. This severely limited the operation of the jitney services. If black cabdrivers could no longer solicit riders like the white cab companies did, their ability to make a living would be hampered. The action taken by the Southside Taxicab Owners Protective Association did, however, bring improved service to Bronzeville. The Chicago Motor Coach Company was forced to replace its old, dilapidated buses with new, modernized buses and end the practice of running express, nonstop buses through the black community.

Although the fight by the Southside Taxicab Owners Protective Association had a direct impact on African Americans' ability to travel within the community, the group was not without its own set of controversies. In 1940 the group, which changed its name to the United Taxicab Owners Association, found itself engaged in a legal battle against another African American cabdrivers' group, the Bronzeville Chauffeurs Safety Union, over increasing cab rental fees. While the argument could be made that cab operators occupied a space between owners and workers, the Safety Union clearly viewed itself as part of the latter group, especially after the group asked for and was granted CIO affiliation as Local 201 of the Transport Workers Union of America. With that support, the union launched a strike against the Southside Taxicab Owners Protective Organization. During the strike, the chauffeurs carried out a variety of actions against their managers ranging from court challenges to several physical confrontations with other African American drivers working as strikebreakers.[52] The strike ended in mid-December when eighteen companies agreed to the strikers' demands: as part of the victory, drivers won a closed union shop contract within the industry, a reduction in the cost of gasoline and oil, lower cab rentals and deposits, a general increase in weekly wages, and seniority and other job protection rights.[53]

Regardless of the internal conflicts between owners and drivers that existed within the cab industry on the South Side, it is undeniable that black drivers provided valuable services to the African American community. White-owned taxicabs and public transportation provided either limited or no service to black neighborhoods. Some African American taxi operators managed to find employment in the small number of African American–owned companies or chose to operate unregulated (and illegal) jitney services. In 1942 the Office of Defense Transportation (OTD) imposed limits on the number of taxicabs in operation as well as rationed fuel and parts to most drivers except for those holding special "certificate of war necessity" documents. By 1945 the OTD eased these restrictions by issuing General Order 50 and a public policy statement regarding the taxicab industry and veterans. The order and statement declared that unlicensed taxi operators could enter the field without the requisite certificates if they had owned and operated a taxicab before their induction into the armed forces. At the conclusion of the wartime emergency, however, large companies resisted these provisions and, perhaps in efforts to hinder competition, coerced local governments to again place limits on independent taxi drivers and their ability to work.[54]

In January 1946, twenty-five independent cabdrivers filed briefs in the First District Appellate Court of Illinois claiming that ordinances of Chicago's Taxicab Board were unconstitutional and granted Yellow, Checker, and several other large companies 80 percent of the cabstand licenses issued by the city.[55] This, they argued, created a virtual monopoly in the industry that barred virtually any citizen of Chicago from operating a cab except the three cab corporations and about three hundred other independent cab companies and independent cab owner/operators. The cabdrivers also charged that their inability to secure licenses "flouted the reemployment provisions of the Selective Service Act of 1940" and that many of the veteran cabdrivers were without any unemployment compensation, since many of their social security accounts were in arrears.[56]

At first glance, it would seem that this refusal to hire black drivers violated the city's FEP ordinance. However, the major white-owned companies managed to circumvent the law by hiring African Americans in lower-paying positions such as mechanics and garage help. The group argued that Mayor Edward Kelly, Police Commissioner James Allman, and Public Vehicle License Commissioner Edward J. Gorman, among others, created an environment hostile to former GIs.[57] Furthermore, the cabdrivers claimed the city had no authority to limit taxi stand licenses and that the creation of a public vehicle license commissioner gave Gorman almost complete dictatorial authority. This, they believed, ran counter to "public policy of the state of Illinois, the Illinois and federal constitutions, and that it was in excess of the power granted to the city of Chicago by the legislature."[58]

In light of the public vehicle license commissioner's refusal to grant cabstand permits, many drivers used their personal vehicles to enter into the livery cab business, since livery services were not regulated by any of the same city ordinances that limited operators' access to passenger cabs. By December 1946, under pressure from cab companies, the city council passed an ordinance placing livery cabs under similar licensing restrictions and regulations as the taxicabs.[59] After the institution of these new rules, Gorman reversed his position and immediately granted 250 special permits for the operation of veterans' cabs.[60] But Cook County Circuit Court judge Michael Feinberg issued an injunction that blocked the city from issuing any such permits and prohibited the city from carrying out a plan to cancel 321 licenses belonging to Yellow and Checker cabs not in operation and to redistribute these licenses. This ruling by the judge left the city with no further recourse but to order mass arrests of unlicensed cabdrivers. And officers of the Chicago and Park District police began arrests of any cabbies found operating without licenses.

The court ruling and the arrests did not deter members of the city council from debating cabdrivers' rights. Two Chicago aldermen, James B. Waller and T. W. Merryman, made public promises to continue fighting for more licenses during a special city council meeting scheduled for February 1946. As that meeting approached, Waller and Merryman picked up support from another white alderman, Frank Keenan. During the meeting, Keenan motioned to remove restrictions on cab operation in the city. He introduced an ordinance to further release 1,508 new licenses. Of these, 1,008 would be made available to Yellow and Checker.[61] This effort to aid veterans and stem resistance from the larger cab companies still failed to resolve the problem. The measure further angered members of the ICDADV because they claimed that "while they were overseas fighting for democracy, the right to engage in the occupation of taxicab drivers for which they have been trained before the war was denied them after the war."[62] For one driver, the inability to find a job following his military service both violated the job protection guarantees outlined within the GI Bill and ran counter to the belief that military service afforded African American veterans access to adequate employment.

In mid-February 1946, a 150-car taxi caravan from Chicago drove to Washington, D.C., in an effort to meet with officials of the Department of Justice, the Social Security Board, and the Department of Internal Revenue and even President Truman. The former GIs of the ICDADV were soon joined in this campaign by more than three hundred members of another organization—the all-white American Cab Drivers' Association for Discharged Veterans (ACDADV).[63] The caravan of taxi drivers drove across the country in an effort to highlight their plight in Chicago.[64] Along the way, John Patrick and H. G. Hardy spoke about their inability to gain licenses and the mass arrests of vets operating without licenses in Chicago. To further call attention to the labor conditions of vets across the United States, Patrick and Hardy stated their intention to organize taxicab driver veterans along the motorcade route to the Capitol and worked with groups like the Veterans Taxicab Association, in Philadelphia, and the Deluxe Cab Company, in Baltimore. Like the ICDADV, these organizations also formed coalitions with local institutions to aid them in their fight.[65] If successful, the attention garnered by these activities could turn this local issue into a national test case for veterans' rights.

Since the courts barred city hall from providing additional cab permits, the city's traffic court division returned $2,500 in cabdrivers' fines because the veterans would need the money for "food, shelter, banners and other expenses in the capital" and delayed the trials of drivers caught driving without the needed licenses.[66] Even after Patrick did acknowledge in the press that there were "implications in the fight which rightly should come under the jurisdiction of the Federal Government," he and Hardy readily conceded that their battle was to be waged in Chicago and not Washington.[67] Unfortunately for the ICDADV and the ACDADV, they were unsuccessful in stating their case to President Truman, but they did win a brief meeting with the assistant attorney general at the Justice Department. The publicity their march garnered drew enough attention and public support that governmental action in their defense did occur.

In response to this public campaign, the Justice Department conducted an investigation into the allegations of a monopoly in Chicago. The government's investigation did not uncover a "traditional" monopoly, but Justice Department investigators, working alongside the U.S. Attorney General's office, concluded that Morris Markin, a former Chicago businessman, limited access to the industry through his ownership of the Yellow, Checker, and Parmelee Transportation companies and through his financial interests in companies that manufactured parts and supplies in various other cab companies.[68] Although not a violation of any antitrust legislation per se, Markin's control of these companies unreasonably hindered veteran cabdrivers' ability to secure licenses from the city and work in this field. This ruling soon opened the door for other drivers. After several legal defeats in the courts and city government, the cab-driving vets finally achieved victory: the city council approved the release of 275 licenses for veteran taxicab drivers.[69] By 1952 a total of 761 veterans' licenses was available. Yellow and Checker were forced to allow the veteran cabbies to work, and in a move that reaffirmed this public-private relationship, the city council quickly revised the city taxicab ordinances.

As uncovered in this episode, African American veterans believed their military service entitled them to certain legal and societal protections and thus made them, in their view, a *protected class* of citizen. This was especially evident after Patrick and Hardy called for increased public awareness of the plight of veterans, based not on race but on the belief that their military status would bring about greater opportunities. This story demonstrates the effectiveness of collective action and public protest to bring national attention to local problems—a strategy that would be employed by a number of civil rights activists around the country. The likelihood of the Justice Department stepping into a local labor dispute would have been slim, but because of the national exposure garnered by the ICDADV's march, the Justice Department was pressured to investigate the antitrust allegations.

Despite some of the successes civil rights advocates enjoyed during the early postwar period, by the 1950s many of the gains they achieved began to disappear. This occurred for two reasons. The first was that civil rights groups lost their most influential supporter, Ed Kelly. By 1946 Mayor Kelly began to lose much of his control over Democratic Party politics in Cook County and over the Democratic voters within the city itself. Within party circles, the mayor's failure to produce a strong list of candidates in the 1946 elections cost the Democrats control of several important county positions. Furthermore, Kelly's stance on such controversial issues as school integration, his open tolerance of organized crime, cases of corruption within the police force, and public dissatisfaction with public services cost him valuable support from white Democrats. However, according to Kelly biographer Roger Biles, the most important issue that brought down the Kelly administration was "the mayor's repeated pledges to guarantee the availability of housing city-wide to blacks."[70] Without the support of party leaders and with waning support among whites in the city, Kelly was eventually forced into semi-retirement. Martin Kennelly became the Democratic candidate for mayor and served two terms before the ascension of Mayor Richard J. Daley in 1955.

The second issue that stifled African American militancy in Chicago was America's reactionary posturing and growing fear of American Communism during the Cold War. Labor militancy and civil rights activism that challenged discrimination were especially hard hit by the anti-Communists' activities. This was especially true as the lines between workers' protests and civil rights protest became more skewed. Thomas Sugrue's discussion of Detroit notes that fact when he writes, "Civil rights organizations in the North expended tremendous political energy deflecting accusations of communism."[71] Historian Christopher Reed points out that during the late 1940s, the Chicago NAACP was wary of the level of militancy and influence of radicals in its civil rights activism and of the consequences this influence held for the public standing of the organization. Reed concludes that the "added liability of Communist meddling in the branch's affairs made [the NAACP] look especially militant to the city's respectable and very conservative white civic leadership."[72]

In 1947 Congress passed the Taft-Hartley Act. This legislation worked to limit the power of organized labor by outlawing the closed shop and secondary strikes, mandating a sixty-day "cooling off" period before certain workers could go out on strike, and forcing militant union leadership to sign statements denying Communist ties. Although this act alone would not destroy civil rights activism in organized labor, it could be used to deter mass public support, such as was the case in the UPWA strike in 1946. Opponents of organized labor perhaps hoped that by limiting labor activism and weeding out radicals in unions, they could better control the unions.

To further this anti-Communist program, President Truman signed Executive Order 9835. The order established strict definitions of what groups the government believed posed a threat to national security. It further stated that federal investigators would target individuals they found to have "membership in, affiliation with or association with" any group deemed to be a Communist or Communist-front organization. This order worked by forcing individuals to sign loyalty oaths and subjecting them to public "loyalty tests" to prove they were not Communists. These investigations were unscientific, to say the least, and in some cases relied on rumor and innuendo as evidence in order to out Communists. Many of those suspected of being Communists were guilty of nothing more than being political liberals. However, during the Cold War, as one military official explained, "A liberal is only a hop, skip, and a jump from a Communist. A Communist starts as a liberal."[73] The tests had drastic effects on African Americans who spoke out against racism. One of the most publicized examples occurred in 1950 when an African American woman, Dorothy Bailey, was called before the Loyalty Review Board to explain a letter she had written to the Red Cross objecting to the practice of segregating the blood supply. Investigators questioned Bailey and concluded that her "objection to blood segregation is a recognized 'party line' tactic"; they wanted to know "if she was following that line when she wrote the letter."[74]

The Chicago Housing Authority found itself in the middle of this debate during its meeting in December 1952 as the CHA Board met to implement a rigorous loyalty oath program for CHA residents in accordance with the guidelines prescribed by the federal government.[75] During this same meeting, CHA commissioner William Henry Kruse, also secretary-treasurer of Local 1, AFL Flat Janitors Union, charged that "Communists had infiltrated the Housing Authority staff."[76] The accusations of Kruse, backed by his fellow commissioner William Sykes of the Inland Steel Company, alone were not enough to compel their colleagues to implement a similar loyalty oath policy for employees. This decision was short lived. In the wake of the decision, the Chicago City Council, which had no jurisdiction over the CHA, objected to the board's decision and unanimously approved a resolution urging the CHA to reconsider implementing an employee loyalty oath. Mayor Kennelly voiced his support for an employee program and declared that "he believed employees of the Chicago Housing Authority should be required to take some type of loyalty oath."[77]

In January 1953, over the objections of groups such as the American Civil Liberties Union, the American Friends Service Committee, the AVC, and labor unions, the CHA approved a compromise program. While the oath for public housing residents required them to affirm they were not members of any of the two hundred organizations listed as subversive by the U.S. Attorney General's office, the employee oath required individuals to swear that they were "not a member of any organization which 'to my knowledge' advocates the overthrow of the United States by force of violence."[78] In the aftermath of the compromise, neither the groups who opposed nor those who supported the program claimed victory. Elizabeth Wood argued that the oath would jeopardize the morale of the CHA staff. Edward Clamage of the Cook County Council of the American Legion said "the oath had been so 'watered down' to the point where it is virtually meaningless in comparison with the original [stricter] proposal."[79] In March, Robert Wells, an African American messenger, became the only employee of the CHA who refused to sign the oath and quit his job because he was "opposed to the principle" of the oath.[80] While Wells was the only African American employee to quit in the wake of the implementation of a loyalty program, some African American public housing residents, like Major and Ora Fitch from the Altgeld Gardens development, unsuccessfully challenged the legality of the loyalty program in the courts. The overwhelming majority of residents signed the oaths. A small number of residents—for example, Mary Thompson and her family and Edith Roberson and her family, also Altgeld residents—instead chose eviction rather than capitulation. Eventually, the Illinois Supreme Court ruled against mandatory oaths for public housing residents and made taking such oaths voluntary in 1954. By 1956, the U.S. Supreme Court refused to overturn the Wisconsin Supreme Court's ruling against the practice, and that year the CHA eliminated the loyalty oath program.[81]

African American protest groups in Chicago also felt the effects of loyalty investigations. In the early 1950s, African Americans in the Chicago Post Office found themselves prominent targets of loyalty investigations. Following the war, hundreds of African American veterans gained employment at the post office. While there, black postal workers drew on their status as federal employees to continue to push for equal rights inside and outside the postal service. This made them easy targets for anti-Communist forces in the agency, as they believed that any challenge to the status quo (such as civil rights activism) was dangerous.

The National Alliance of Postal Employees in Chicago spoke out against the oaths. Ashby B. Carter, national president of the organization, issued a statement saying that when a government finds disloyalty in criticisms of the government, "then, by such decree[,] the Government of the United States ceases to be a government of, by, and for the American people."[82] In essence, the fear that the loyalty program had the potential to "permit the Post Office Department [to investigate] its Negro employees" or any employee considered by the department to be "undesirable" was indeed well founded.[83] For NAPE, this was an overt effort to silence those taking "potshots" at Jim Crow. For those individuals, agitation for change was not a sign of disloyalty. In fact, one could argue that it was the duty of the informed citizen to speak out against injustice—including racism. But by the 1950s, the liberal ideas of the New Deal fell out of favor with the more conservative elements in American society. Activists with the postal service saw the post office's use of the loyalty program as nothing more than a "diabolical weapon to frighten them into a state of inaction."[84]

Anti-Communism affected not only federal employees but veterans' groups as well. Historian Robert Jefferson writes, "UNAVA members found it increasingly difficult to carry out its program with respect to housing, full employment, medical care, and training and education for black veterans."[85] By 1949, the organization ceased all operations. The AVC, on the other hand, was so concerned with fighting Communists within its own organization that much of its civil rights radicalism was tempered to avoid the speculation of being a Communist-front organization. For example, the representatives from the AVC protested the investigation of Communist influence on Hollywood by the House Un-American Activities Committee. Despite its protest, the organization's public position was one that, according to one official, "disclaimed, of course, any sympathy for the tortuous doctrines of communism."[86]

While attempting to avoid red-baiting, labor activists fighting to secure civil rights for African Americans in Chicago had to struggle to hold together much of the spirit of cooperation that had developed during the war years. The best example of this was seen in the difficulties faced by the UPWA. The union had been very active in trying to secure equal housing and civil rights for African Americans following the war. To this end, by the early 1950s the union moved its headquarters from the white Back of the Yards community to Bronzeville. But this move severely weakened the interracial support for the organization's program as white unionists refused to travel to the black neighborhood for meetings. As a result, the unions were, in the words of Rick Halpern and Roger Horowitz, "transformed from an interracial alliance to an organization headed and directed by blacks. It enjoyed and benefitted from white support in the plants, but this support was increasingly passive."[87]

The events in this chapter highlight how African American veterans understood that their military service entitled them to certain legal and societal protections. They used their status as veterans as a way of pushing forward a civil rights agenda they hoped would reach into the entire black community. The failure of much of the GI Bill for African Americans and the fact that the United States was a world superpower helped these vets realize that they had earned and were "entitled" to better treatment than many of them were receiving. African American servicemen and servicewomen demonstrated the power of collective action to bring national attention to local problems. In the case of the ICDADV, the likelihood of the Justice Department stepping into a local labor dispute would have been slim. But, because of the national exposure the cabdrivers' march received, the Justice Department was urged to investigate the antitrust allegations.

The cabdrivers' march to Washington highlights the potential for African American militancy in the immediate postwar period. Unfortunately by 1947, neither they nor their allies possessed the necessary political capital to sustain such high levels of agitation. Within city government, Edward Kelly's "forced retirement" in 1946 was attributed, in part, to allegations of unchecked corruption and his support for open housing for African Americans. But it is reasonable to conclude that his ouster was hastened, at least in part, due to his unapologetic support of racial integration. The fleeting opportunity to build on these successes was also hindered by the postwar posturing and developing Cold War ideology at the national level. Moreover, a simultaneous shift in political priorities that deemphasized the interracial private/public coalitions and activists' weariness of being labeled Communist made sustained progress in challenging discrimination against African American veterans and workers at the local level difficult.

Anti-Communist activism was stimulated after the passage of the Taft-Hartley Act, which forced labor militants to deny Communist ties, and President Truman's Executive Order 9835, which established strict definitions of what groups the government believed posed a threat to national security in 1947. Under this governmental pressure, Left-led groups like the UNAVA found it difficult to carry out its veterans' rights program. In 1949 the organization ceased all operations, and by the early 1950s African Americans in the Chicago Post Office, one of the largest employers of veterans and center of GI organizing in the city, became prominent targets of loyalty investigations. Thus, as black postal workers drew on their status as federal employees and veterans to challenge discrimination at work and in the community, historian Ellen Schrecker finds that "many loyalty boards imposed racially discriminatory litmus tests that were strongly biased against civil rights activists, especially in departments like the Post Office."[88]

One is left to wonder about the long-term effects of these missed opportunities and what political pressure says about African American veterans' activism in the early years of the freedom struggle. Despite their ultimate inability to circumnavigate racial discrimination and the fact that Cold War rhetoric pushed many of the more militant actions underground and stymied immediate racial change, this examination demonstrates that African American veterans and their allies knew that the period held important racial and political implications and shows how they actively worked to bring these changes to fruition. It also shows how these veterans were willing and able to develop strategies to address their economic livelihoods by reaching across the racial divide and working with white veterans dealing with similar economic realities. Unfortunately for African Americans, many of their wartime gains were either reversed or constantly attacked, and veterans, alongside their allies, realized local government no longer possessed the political capital to take an active role in people's private lives. Even in light of this realization, the "protected class" argument forced the nation to reconsider, at least for this brief window, its responsibility in enforcing constitutional guarantees.

This militancy eventually fostered a renewed political activism firmly rooted in a coalition building model that would continue to be employed by black World War II veterans into the 1950s and 1960s.[89] Like their predecessors, these individuals would continue to express their demands in both race- and class-based terms by evoking the rhetoric of universal citizenship rights at the local and national level. However, unlike in the immediate postwar period, these future activists, some of them World War II veterans, would diversify these coalitions and incorporate forces from the Left and from other ethnicities in Chicago. A prime example lay in the 1983 election of Harold Washington as Chicago's first African American mayor. Washington, himself a World War II veteran, and others have commonly attributed election success to the Washington campaign ability to form an effective coalition among African American, white lakefront liberals, and Latinos.[90] By focusing on the experiences of military personnel, this examination of the intricate milieu of race, citizenship, politics, and war helps develop a better understanding of how black soldiers, sailors, and marines used their activities to stake their own claims for inclusion into the postwar state and demonstrates how such activism helped shape a social and political agenda for civil rights activism in the coming decades.

CONCLUSION

America feels itself to be humanity in miniature. When in this crucial time the international leadership passes to America, the great reason for hope is that this country has a national experience of uniting racial and cultural diversities and a national theory, if not a consistent practice, of freedom and liberty for all. What America is constantly reaching for is democracy at home and abroad. The main trend in its history is the gradual realization of the American Creed.

—Gunnar Myrdal, *An American Dilemma*, 1940

FOR MORE than twenty years, African American working-class Chicagoans challenged convention by advocating for access to jobs within their communities. From their participation in the "Don't Buy Where You Can't Work" campaigns to agitation for increased inclusion in the New Deal state, they continuously demonstrated a willingness to speak up for their rights and to advocate for their fair share of opportunity. In the housing arena, black Chicagoans showed time and again that they fully understood the politics of both public and open housing and were able to use this knowledge to negotiate access to political powers in the city. In employment, African Americans in the city took advantage of the expansion of the wartime economy, which created unprecedented access to jobs during and immediately following World War II. Taken together, African Americans' demands for homes and jobs and the political acumen developed during these years provided the necessary conditions for an early civil rights movement in the North, in general, and in Chicago, in particular. These developments had the potential to reshape the political and racial landscape of the nation.

African Americans would, no doubt, share in these benefits as their collective wartime experiences would allow them to, in the words of Robert

Weaver, "develop a greater sense of belonging since [they] would have a chance to earn a living and an opportunity to benefit from a larger total supply of housing, education, health services, and recreational and leisure-time facilities."[1] To accomplish this, they showed an uncanny willingness to engage in political coalition building with black and white labor, radical, veterans', and political organizations throughout the city as a means to achieve their goals. The exposure to the political programs of these allied groups strengthened their existing political agenda and provided an outlet through which those within the community could negotiate and shape their experiences during the Roosevelt era. Self-aware African American activists in Chicago employed the language of entitlement, which grew from their wartime sacrifices and military service, the constitutional guarantees of citizenship rights, and the freedoms that were central to the wartime rhetoric of the federal government, and quite often they seized upon opportunities to cultivate an environment from which they could use federal policy to define such issues as better access to education, health care, and ending police brutality. Their embrace of these strategies, in turn, provided the necessary tools with which to best stake claims for access to the benefits of true American citizenship and to argue for equanimity in employment and housing (even though it looks as if the gains they won quickly faded.) In doing so, black Chicagoans combined their own political issues with the rhetoric of New Deal ideology and used wartime rhetoric and programs to engage in physical and legal battles against obvious enemies (individual and institutional racism) and not-so-obvious enemies (U.S. Cold War polices) to demand equal protection of their rights.

Disillusioned by the Republican Party's response to the Depression, African Americans slowly began to align themselves with the Democratic Party, the party of Roosevelt—and, more important, of the New Deal—and to move away from the Republican Party, the party of Abraham Lincoln. In some northern, urban areas like Chicago, the switch occurred because the Democratic Party offered increased opportunities for economic recovery and presented African American voters and politicians alternative avenues through which to seek political power. African Americans in Chicago in particular exemplified this trend as black voters in the city moved in ever-growing numbers to the Democratic Party. Chicago was a special case, however, because African Americans there changed party affiliation well in advance of a national party shift. This was primarily stimulated by the election of Mayor Edward Kelly, whom many saw as a race liberal, and continued as Kelly moved to advance civil rights for his African American allies and their constituents and as the Kelly administration continued to provide access to city services.

Conclusion

Unfortunately, by the mid-1950s many of the allies African Americans had in Chicago politics (at least those with any significant political power) had nearly vanished, diminishing many opportunities for African Americans to press local government on matters of race relations. Nowhere was this more evident than when Richard J. Daley became the thirty-ninth mayor of Chicago on April 5, 1955. The victory over then-mayor Martin Kennelly and Republican alderman Robert Merriman was not only a political victory for Daley but also a victory for the Cook County Democratic machine. Both Kennelly and Merriman had entered the election as reform candidates, and each championed an anti-machine platform. Still, neither candidate was able to garner enough support to overcome Daley's Democratic Party connections. As in other Democratic mayoral victories in city elections since 1933, African American voters and politicians overwhelmingly supported the Democratic Party's candidate. Daley's margin of victory over his opponents, in which the winning plurality was 126,967, came as a result of the 103,320 votes from traditionally black wards. But in spite of the support he received from African Americans, Daley's victory eventually proved what Alderman Paddy Bauler quipped at a Daley victory party, "Chicago ain't ready for reform yet!" African Americans realized the new mayoral administration would move away from and summarily overturn existing Roosevelt-era liberal reforms, and they suspected the mayor would, according to Roger Biles, "redirect the [Democratic] machine's support from the increasingly black river wards to the peripheral [white] bungalow belt"—which he eventually did. By 1964 Mayor Daley went so far as to tell the *Chicago Defender* that he did not "think it [civil rights] was a political issue" and argued "people who try to make it a political issue are making a sad mistake."[2]

Daley's ascension helped dismantle African American political power by essentially silencing the most prominent Roosevelt ally in the city—William Dawson. Dawson's and Kennelly's relationship had been extremely contentious throughout Kennelly's two terms as mayor. When it came time to slate candidates for mayor and Dawson used his influence to deliver votes from the African American wards of the city, he did so—for Richard Daley. By successfully delivering votes from the black wards, Dawson proved, to Kennelly and to his own political enemies, that he was the leader of a powerful Chicago Democratic "submachine" and brandished a considerable amount of political power that made him a major figure in Chicago politics.

Dawson may have believed his antireform/anti-Kennelly alliance with Mayor Daley further strengthened his position within the Democratic machine. But instead, Dawson's control of the black vote turned out to be his ultimate undoing. To the Daley administration, Dawson wielded too much power and was viewed as a threat. Daley undertook several initiatives that removed much of Dawson's control over Chicago's African American aldermen and consolidated this control in the mayor's office. These moves ushered in a period of "plantation politics" whereby black communities throughout the city were brought under the control of either white aldermen or African American aldermen who were themselves under the control of city hall and the Cook County Democratic Organization.

In addition to curtailing the authority of black politicians, Daley ended the race-liberal housing policies of the Chicago Housing Authority and helped finalize plans for constructing large-scale public housing, including the infamous South Side high-rises. In 1955 approximately two-thirds of the residents in Chicago's public housing were African American; four short years later, African Americans constituted 85 percent of public housing residents. By the mid-1960s, forty-nine of the fifty-one proposed public housing projects were situated in economically depressed African American communities in the city and isolated in vertical ghettos, or, in the words of journalists Adam Cohen and Elizabeth Taylor, "public aid penitentiaries."[3]

On the labor front, the Daley administration was very adept at negotiating favorable contracts with organized labor during his tenure, and as a result, there were relatively few major instances of labor unrest. Much of this was due to the fact that the mayor successfully "deflected the call of collective action" made by organized labor, and even organizations like the Chicago Federation of Labor and the Cook County Industrial Union Committee, over time, became "appendage[s] of the Democratic machine."[4] For African Americans, their Daley-era labor experiences were shaped by the quest to secure fair employment policy at the state level. In 1960 the American Jewish Congress called the decade of the 1950s the "lost decade" and issued a booklet that said, "Illinois remains the only non-Southern industrial state which has failed to enact basic legislation prohibiting discrimination in private employment."[5] The house of the Illinois State Legislature voted in favor of a state fair employment practices commission in 1947, 1951, 1953, 1955, 1957, and 1960, only to see the bill voted down in the Illinois State Senate. Although a state FEPC was eventually approved in 1961, it was unsuccessful in reversing either the trend of African American underemployment or addressing racial economic disparities. According to St. Clair Drake and Horace Cayton, the ultimate failure of the FEPC to adequately address these issues actually perpetuated the stereotype of African American inferiority and, in turn, made securing necessary community and economic resources extremely difficult.[6]

The question that remains is this: how did the collapse of the New Deal coalition between African Americans and their allies impact the thoughts and actions of working-class activists for social and economic rights of the

1930s, 1940s, and 1950s? A convenient, albeit ultimately incorrect, answer is that the majority of the momentum garnered by New Deal liberals in Chicago was summarily dismissed as city officials worked to limit reform and reestablish a sense of racial normalcy where agitation and public dissent were discouraged and militant elements within the community were effectively silenced. On the contrary, black militancy was far from silenced, and community activists in later periods continued to organize, albeit often silently and hidden from the prying eyes of racially conservative elements within city government, in the press, union halls, pulpits, and living rooms throughout Bronzeville and other emerging black enclaves in Chicago. As seen throughout this examination, the African American working class was very adept at charting an independent course in the political discourse of the day. This held true even as the New Deal coalition failed. In the following decades, remnants of the New Deal coalition would occasionally reappear to challenge discrimination. More recently, scholars have begun a more intensive study of grassroots civil rights organizing and of the New Deal/World War II–era roots of the modern civil rights movement.[7] An exploration of black protest during the 1950s and 1960s shows that African Americans in Chicago continued to organize and work to advance a civil rights agenda in housing and employment. The most significant difference was that they could no longer rely either on white political allies in city hall or, in some cases, on African American politicians, as they had under the administrations of Edward Kelly and, to a lesser degree, Martin Kennelly. In the final analysis, the organizing efforts that African Americans developed during the 1930s, 1940s, and 1950s helped black citizens develop a political culture that would demonstrate the kinds of possibilities that broad-based support from African Americans and liberal whites could bring to this city of divided neighborhoods. By understanding these issues, scholars will come to better understand both the direction of civil rights activism in Chicago and politics as it occurs at the grassroots level.

NOTES

BIBLIOGRAPHY

INDEX

NOTES

Introduction

1. Myrdal, *American Dilemma*.
2. See ibid., 997; and Dalfiume, "'Forgotten Years,'" 96. Also see Wynn, "War and Racial Progress."
3. Sugrue, *Origins of the Urban Crisis*, 59.
4. Biondi, *To Stand and Fight*, 50. Also see Mettler, *Soldiers to Citizens*, 136–43.
5. A number of scholars have examined the impact and extent of coalition building regarding various aspects of black life and culture in Chicago during this period, which has become known as the Chicago Black Renaissance. See Mullen, *Popular Fronts*; Green, *Selling the Race*; and Knupfer, *Chicago Black Renaissance*.
6. Similar examinations can be found in Biondi, *To Stand and Fight*; Korstad, *Civil Rights Unionism*; Denning, *Cultural Front*; and Sitkoff, *New Deal for Blacks*.
7. Brown and Leighton, *Negro and the War*, 4.
8. Contributors to Logan's book include Mary McLeod Bethune, Langston Hughes, A. Philip Randolph, W. E. B. DuBois, and Willard Townsend.
9. See Patterson, "The Negro Wants Full Participation in the American Democracy," in Logan, *What the Negro Wants*, 264.
10. T. Reed, *Not Alms but Opportunity*, 6.
11. Drake and Cayton, *Black Metropolis*, 507.
12. *Chicago Defender*, March 2, 1946.
13. This information was included in a telegram sent to President Truman by members of the ICDADV and the all-white American Cab Drivers' Association for Discharged Veterans. *Chicago Tribune*, February 7, 1946.
14. Drake and Cayton, *Black Metropolis*, 750.
15. Timuel Black interview, Chicago, December 20, 2000, and Hilton Joseph interview, Chicago, August 3, 2002. Also see Krebs, *Fighting for Rights*; Mettler, "'The Only Good Thing Was the G.I. Bill'"; Onkst, "First a Negro"; and Julius A. Thomas, "The Negro Veteran in the Economy," in Guzman, Foster, and Hughes, *Negro Year Book*, 151.

16. Quoted in Sitkoff, *New Deal for Blacks*, 63.
17. Brinkley, *End of Reform*, 62–63.
18. Gerstle, "Protean Character of American Liberalism."
19. See Sullivan, *Days of Hope*.
20. In addition to Biondi, see Countryman, *Up South*; Theoharis and Wood-ard, *Freedom North*; Self, *American Babylon*; and Thompson, *Whose Detroit?*
21. See Shockley, "We, Too, Are Americans"; and Kersten, *Race, Jobs, and the War.*
22. Sugrue, *Origins of the Urban Crisis*, 10.
23. Mary Watters gives a detailed explanation of Chicago's participation in war production. In one example, Watters details how the Dodge Corporation opened the largest airplane engine manufacturer in the world. See Watters, *Illinois in the Second World War*, 21–32.
24. See essays in Goings and Mohl, *New African American Urban History*; Bauman, Biles, and Szylvian, *From Tenements to the Taylor Homes*; Hirsch and Mohl, *Urban Policy*; and Sugrue, *Origins of the Urban Crisis.*
25. Hirsch, *Making the Second Ghetto.*
26. Similar examinations can be found in Biondi, *To Stand and Fight*; Korstad, *Civil Rights Unionism*; Denning, *Cultural Front*; and Sitkoff, *New Deal for Blacks.*
27. Grossman, *Land of Hope*, 8.
28. Philpott, *The Slum and the Ghetto*; Spear, *Black Chicago*; Hirsch, *Making the Second Ghetto*; Tuttle, *Race Riot*; Chicago Commission on Race Relations, *Negro in Chicago*; Seligman, *Block by Block*; Washington, *Packing Them In.*
29. For example, Chicago alderman Earl Dickerson, although not a member of the Communist Party, was frequently quoted in the *Daily World* and endorsed by the paper in his aldermanic races. Horace Cayton, also not a Communist, came from a family that was active in Communist politics in Seattle. Richard Wright was a member of the Communist Party but left, feeling that white Communists were too rigid in their understanding of black folk culture and too stifling of a native black radicalism. See Wright, *American Hunger*; Mullen, *Popular Fronts*, 8. Also see Kelley, *Hammer and Hoe*; P. Smith, "Quest for Racial Democracy," 134–35; and Naison, *Communists in Harlem.*
30. Bunche and Grantham, *Political Status of the Negro*, 575.

1. Black Belts Insult Us: Equal Housing and Contested Liberalism during the Depression

1. Notes on "Negroes Live in Chicago" by Horace Cayton, the Negro in Illinois Papers, box 37, folder 10, Vivian G. Harsh Research Collection,

Woodson Regional Library, Chicago Public Library (hereafter NIP). This article was reprinted in the Urban League's *Opportunity* in December 1937 with a second part, "No Friendly Voice," appearing in January 1938.

2. W. Dennis Keating and Janet Smith, "Past Federal Policy for Urban Neighborhoods," in Keating, Krumholz, and Star, *Revitalizing Urban Neighborhoods*, 50.

3. Duncan and Duncan, *Negro Population of Chicago*, 96.

4. See Roediger, *Wages of Whiteness*; and Jacobson, *Whiteness of a Different Color*.

5. Philpott, *Slum and the Ghetto*, 189.

6. Letter to Forty-First Ward alderman William J. Conley from the Office of the Corporation Counsel of the City of Chicago, July 28, 1938, Papers of the NAACP, Campaign against Residential Segregation, 1914–1955, reel 1, frame 1329, College of Law Library, University of Iowa. Also see *Buchanan v. Warley*, 245 U.S. 60 (1917).

7. U.S. Federal Housing Administration, *Underwriting Manual*, part 2, section 2, Rating of Location.

8. Weaver, *Negro Ghetto*, 72; Jackson, *Crabgrass Frontier*, 198–99.

9. Schietinger, "Real Estate Transfer," 14.

10. Chicago Commission on Race Relations, *Negro in Chicago*, 192.

11. Washington, *Packing Them In*, 140. Also see Myrdal, *American Dilemma*, 624.

12. Weaver, *Negro Ghetto*, 39; Drake and Cayton, *Black Metropolis*, 179.

13. Plotkin, "'Hemmed In,'" 42.

14. Plotkin, "Deeds of Mistrust," 99.

15. James L. Reid, "Restrictive Pact Cited in Race Bar," *Chicago Defender*, July 16, 1938.

16. Ibid.

17. Claude A. Barnett Papers, series A, reel 10, frame 385, Vivian G. Harsh Research Collection, Woodson Regional Library, Chicago Public Library.

18. "The Hansberrys of Chicago: They Join Business Acumen with Social Vision," *Crisis*, April 1941, 106–7. Also see Cooley, "Moving On Out."

19. "Denial of Equal Advantages by Public Officers. Chapter 38, Section 128K, Laws of 1937," Campbell C. Johnson Papers, box 51-5, folder 115, Moorland-Spingarn Research Center, Howard University, Washington, D.C. (hereafter MSRC).

20. "What People Say; Chicago Housing," *Chicago Defender*, November 6, 1937.

21. Philpott, *Slum and the Ghetto*, 165. See also work on the Great Migration: Grossman, *Land of Hope*; Hendricks, *Gender, Race, and Politics in*

the Midwest; Marks, *Farewell—We're Good and Gone;* and Trotter, *Great Migration in Historical Perspective.*

22. Grossman, *Land of Hope,* 145.
23. Best, *Passionately Human, No Less Divine,* 55.
24. Boyd, *Jim Crow Nostalgia,* 21.
25. T. Reed, *Not Alms but Opportunity,* 7.
26. Wolcott, *Remaking Respectability,* 7.
27. "A Successful Experiment in Neighborhood Improvement," Papers of the Chicago Urban League, folder 143, Chicago Urban League Records, Special Collections and University Archives, University of Illinois at Chicago (hereafter PCUL).
28. "1935 Annual Report," ibid., folder 40.
29. Philpott, *Slum and the Ghetto,* 166.
30. J. Smith, *Visions of Belonging,* 286.
31. Weaver, *Negro Ghetto,* 68.
32. "Background for Housing," PCUL, folder 702.
33. "City Harbors Worst Slums in the West; Unbelievable Squalor Located in Race Sections," *Chicago Defender,* January 30, 1937.
34. Hoyt, *One Hundred Years of Land Values in Chicago,* 476.
35. Committee on Negro Housing, "Negro Housing in Northern Cities," NIP, box 37, folder 6.
36. Abbott and Breckinridge, *Tenements of Chicago,* 124.
37. Robert Taylor, "Restrictive Covenants Challenge to Candidates Seeking Support of Race," *Chicago Defender,* January 14, 1939.
38. Ibid.; Report of the Committee on Negro Housing, "Housing Conditions and Delinquency in Chicago," NIP, box 37, folder 16.
39. Keating, Krumholz, and Star, *Revitalizing Urban Neighborhoods,* 50.
40. It was estimated that by 1937 there were six thousand Communists in the state of Illinois. Of that, two thousand were African American, and 90 percent of that population lived in Chicago. Drake, *Churches and Voluntary Associations,* 262. Conversely, Henderson wrote, "There were one thousand colored members in the city out of a total (white and colored) state roll of eight thousand by 1938." Henderson, "Study of the Basic Factors," 89.
41. Storch, *Red Chicago,* 111.
42. See Bates, "New Crowd."
43. Travis, *Autobiography of Black Chicago,* 48.
44. Abbott and Breckinridge, *Tenements of Chicago,* 443.
45. For more information regarding the creation of the association, see Manning, *William L. Dawson and the Limits of Black Electoral Leadership,* 77–78.
46. Greenberg, *Or Does It Explode?,* 96.

47. "Race Tenants are Winners in Rent Rift; Strike May Be Forerunner of Others Here," *Chicago Defender*, February 20, 1937.

48. Manning, *William L. Dawson and the Limits of Black Electoral Leadership*, 77.

49. "Fight Unfair Landlords," *Chicago Defender*, December 7, 1940.

50. "Pickets Bring Pressure after Tenant's Eviction," *Chicago Defender*, September 6, 1941.

51. "Real Estate Firm Files Suit against Tenants: League Chiefs Face Charges of Rent Group; Ishmael Flory, J. Johnson Named In Corporation's Bill of Complaint," *Chicago Defender*, August 16, 1941.

52. Philpott, *Slum and the Ghetto*, 266. Also see "Model Flats to Be Built in Mich. Ave.; Project to Cost Two Million," *Chicago Defender*, July 14, 1928; and "Grant Permit for Rosenwald Apartments," *Chicago Defender*, January 19, 1929.

53. Philpott, *Slum and the Ghetto*, 269.

54. Notes on the Michigan Boulevard Garden Apartments, from Rosenwald Annual Reports, 1935, 1937, NIP, box 37, folder 27.

55. Watters, *Illinois in the Second World War*, 297. Also see Gelfand, *Nation of Cities*.

56. Historian Arnold Hirsch, for instance, argued, "In the 1930s, and continuing thereafter, the operation of national agencies such as the Homeowners Loan Corporation . . . and the Federal Housing Authority reflected prevailing segregationist attitudes. Indirectly at least, they furthered racial segmentation of metropolitan America and inner city decay." Hirsch, *Making the Second Ghetto*, 10.

57. Gail Radford, *Modern Housing for America*, 104.

58. Williams, *Politics of Public Housing*, 10.

59. "Kelly Appoints Five to Form a Housing Authority for City," *Chicago Tribune*, January 6, 1937.

60. See Hunt, *Blueprint for Disaster*, 53.

61. See Harold Ickes, "Activities of Housing Division of the Federal Emergency Administration of Public Works," report submitted to the Senate Committee on Education and Labor, 75th Cong. (1937), Hearing on S. 1685.

62. Drake and Cayton, *Black Metropolis*, 660.

63. Bontemps and Conroy, *Anyplace but Here*, 102.

64. "Horner Paves Way for New Attack on Housing; Governor Calls Law Illegal," *Chicago Defender*, July 16, 1938.

65. "Appeals Court Halts Seizure of Slum Lands: New Deal's Practice Held Illegal," *Chicago Tribune*, July 16, 1935.

66. Strickland, *History of the Chicago Urban League*, 79.

67. Blakely and Shepard, *Earl B. Dickerson*, 79.

68. Bunche and Grantham, *Political Status of the Negro*, 98.

69. Sitkoff, *New Deal for Blacks*, 67.

70. "White in Move to Block U.S. House Projects: Government Proceeds in Face of Protests," *Chicago Defender*, August 3, 1935.

71. Ibid.

72. Ibid.

73. "South Siders in Fight for Housing Plan," *Chicago Defender*, August 17, 1935.

74. Weiss, *Farewell to the Party of Lincoln*, 52.

75. Letter from John Fitzpatrick, Chicago Federation of Labor, to Warren Clark, Commission of Church and Industry, May 26, 1937, box 25, folder Xerox copies, Negroes and Civil Rights, Papers of the Chicago Federation of Labor, Chicago History Museum.

76. Ibid.

77. Ibid.

78. Enoc P. Waters Jr., "Housing Authority Snubs Race to Give Ousted Member Planning Job," *Chicago Defender*, September 17, 1938.

79. Enoc P. Waters Jr., "Duplicity of Housing Board Disclosed through Dealings with Race Technicians Seeking Jobs: Story of Negotiations Shows How the Officials Try to Appease Race with Empty Promises for Delay," *Chicago Defender*, September 24, 1938.

80. Waters, "Housing Authority Snubs Race to Give Ousted Member Planning Job."

81. Ibid.

82. Biles, *Big City Boss in Depression and War*, 91. See also Claude A. Barnett Papers, series A, reel 11, frame 696.

83. "First Race Man on Body," *Chicago Defender*, December 3, 1938.

2. Poor but Not Poverty Stricken: Equal Employment Campaigns in 1930s Chicago

1. A. L. Foster, "Twenty Years of Interracial Goodwill through Social Services," M. H. Bickman Papers, University of Illinois at Chicago Special Collections.

2. Henderson, "Study of the Basic Factors," 56.

3. Strickland, *History of the Chicago Urban League*, 104.

4. Letter from B. J. Jennings, American Consolidated Trade Council, to President Roosevelt, July 18, 1935, Papers of the Works Progress Administration, box 119-6, folder 84, Manuscript Division, Moorland-Spingarn Research Center, Howard University, Washington, D.C (hereafter PWPA).

5. Myrdal, *American Dilemma*, 209.
6. Wolters, *Negroes and the Great Depression*, 91.
7. Piven and Cloward, *Poor People's Movements*, 74.
8. Taped interview with Sam Parks, October 3, 1985, United Packinghouse Workers of America Oral History Project, State Historical Society of Wisconsin, tape 30.
9. Strickland, *History of the Chicago Urban League*, 123.
10. C. Reed, *Chicago NAACP*, 84.
11. "Plan to Boycott Stores Refusing Employment," *Chicago Defender*, October 27, 1928.
12. Ibid.
13. Albert Barnett, "Mr. Abbott's Civil Rights Program of 1905 'Bears Fruit' in 1956," *Chicago Defender*, September 22, 1956. Richard Durham discusses the campaign of the *Chicago Whip* in his essay "Don't Spend Your Money Where You Can't Work!," NIP, box 41, folder 7.
14. *Origin of Direct-Action Protest among Negroes*, 28.
15. C. Reed, *Chicago NAACP*, 81.
16. Cox, *Origin of Direct-Action Protest among Negroes*, 40.
17. See debate over the direction of these activities in Drake and Cayton, *Black Metropolis*, 84–85.
18. Naison, *Communists in Harlem During the Depression*, 85.
19. Strickland, *History of the Chicago Urban League*, 104.
20. Glick, *Illinois Emergency Relief Commission*, 23–33.
21. Sitkoff, *New Deal for Blacks*, 69.
22. Quoted in ibid., 70.
23. Letter from Wallace Pettigrew to Harry Hopkins, June 26, 1937, PWPA, box 119-2, folder 39.
24. Letter from Robert Lewis to Mr. M. N. McIntyre, July 2, 1937, ibid.
25. Ibid.
26. Drake and Cayton, *Black Metropolis*, 512.
27. Letter from Sarah Harris to President Franklin D. Roosevelt, July 1937, PWPA, box 119-3, folder 48.
28. Letter from Vera Simmons to Franklin D. Roosevelt, June 1937, ibid., folder 47.
29. Letter from Frank Ferrill to Harry L. Hopkins, September 17, 1938, ibid., folder 40.
30. Letter from Jessie Taylor to Harry Hopkins, June 1937, ibid., folder 47.
31. Drake and Cayton, *Black Metropolis*, 220–21.
32. "Labor Department in Big Job Campaign," *Chicago Defender*, January 19, 1935.

33. Bureau of Employment Security, USES Records of Lawrence A. Oxley, Reports of Investigations on Negro Employment and Public Procurement Facilities for Negroes, 1937–1939, Alabama–Illinois, Record Group 183, box 1385, National Archives and Research Administration (hereafter NARA), College Park, Md.

34. Letter from L. S. Gregory to Franklin Delano Roosevelt, January 4, 1936, PWPA, box 119-6, folder 85.

35. Letter from George A. M. Webster, M.D., to Franklin Delano Roosevelt, April 22, 1937, ibid., box 119-3, folder 40.

36. Letter from Clarence Lymore to Franklin Roosevelt, July 18, 1935, ibid., box 119-8, folder 84.

37. Letter from Lawrence Oxley to Mr. Burr, December 14, 1937, Records of the Bureau of Employment Security, USES Records of Lawrence A. Oxley, RG 211, folder Survey—Illinois State Employment Service, NARA.

38. Memo from S. B. Danley to Administrative Office of the War Manpower Commission, Bureau of Employment Security, USES Records of Lawrence A. Oxley, Reports of Investigations on Negro Unemployment and Public Procurement Facilities for Negroes, 1937–1939, Alabama–Illinois, RG 183, box 1385, NARA.

39. Figures compiled by the South Parkway office of the Illinois State Employment Service, "Analysis of Placements for Year Ending June 30th 1936 by Type and Year," ibid.

40. Memo from S. B. Danley to Administrative Office of the War Manpower Commission.

41. Affidavit of William McMillan, March 26, 1938, PWPA, box 119-4, folder 119.

42. Letter from Clarence C. Carraway Jr., Cook County Young Democrats Executive Committee Chairman, to Harry Hopkins, n.d., ibid., box 119-6, folder 92.

43. Ibid.

44. Chicago Commission on Race Relations, *Negro in Chicago*, 393.

45. Unpublished paper by Debra L. Newman, "Urban Policy of Lawrence A. Oxley, Chief, Division of Negro Labor of the Department of Labor with a Case Study of Chicago, 1934–1939," New Deal Agencies and Black America, reel 9, frame 451, Vivian G. Harsh Research Collection, Woodson Regional Library, Chicago Public Library.

46. Interview with Timuel Black, Chicago, December 19, 2000.

47. Ibid.

48. Taped interview with Richard Saunders, September 13, 1985, United Packinghouse Workers of America Oral History Project, tape 11, State Historical Society of Wisconsin.

49. "Workers Say Coca-Cola Company Drew Color Line; Fired Race Laborers," *Chicago Defender*, February 16, 1935. Another example occurred in August 1938. White workers replaced six African American workers on a WPA job just before they qualified for a salary increase.

50. J. Levirt Kelly, "Says Sam White Is Asking Donations," *Chicago Defender*, October 5, 1935.

51. Strickland, *History of the Chicago Urban League*, 116.

52. Ibid., 117.

53. Northrup, *Organized Labor and the Negro*, 23–25.

54. "Orders Milk Drivers' Helpers Fired; Labor Union Head against 'Black Aides,'" *Chicago Defender*, August 27, 1938. In addition to the milk protests, the league was also successful in securing positions for African Americans as motion picture operators in area movie theaters and as telephone operators with the Illinois Bell Telephone Company, among other positions. "Theater Hires Race Operator after Sunday Demonstration," ibid., September 24, 1938; "Labor League and the Utilities," ibid., June 10, 1939.

55. *"Orders Milk Drivers' Helpers Fired."*

56. "Unions New Objective in Fight for Race Milkmen," *Chicago Defender*, August 6, 1938.

57. Foner, *Organized Labor and the Black Worker*, 216.

58. Ibid.

59. See Barrett, *Work and Community in the Jungle*; Halpern, *Down on the Killing Floor*; Halpern and Horowitz, *Meatpackers*; Horowitz, "Negro and White, Unite and Fight!"; M. Reed, *Seedtime for the Modern Civil Rights Movement*; and Stromquist and Bergman, *Unionizing the Jungles*.

60. Grossman, *Land of Hope*, 210.

61. "Life Membership Given Chicagoan for Loyalty to CIO Packinghouse Workers," *Chicago Defender*, June 30, 1939.

62. Quoted in Drake and Cayton, *Black Metropolis*, 315.

63. Street, "'Best Union Members,'" 212.

64. Quoted in Drake and Cayton, *Black Metropolis*, 240–41.

3. Housing the Soldiers of the Home Front

1. "Fire Traps Claim 3rd Life in Week: Baby Burns to Death, Sister May not Live," *Chicago Bee*, January 23, 1944.

2. Marion W. Baxter, "Slum Housing Again! More Lives Endangered," *Chicago Bee*, February 6, 1944.

3. Ibid.

4. Ibid.

5. "1942 Annual Report," Papers of the Metropolitan Housing Council, box, 2, folder 21, Special Collections Department, University of Illinois at Chicago (hereafter, PMHC).

6. "Race Relations in Chicago," 12, Report of the Committee on Race Relations, December 1944, Municipal Reference Collection, Harold Washington Library Center, Chicago (hereafter MRC).

7. Jacob Crane to Coleman Woodbury, Housing Policy of the War Manpower Commission, August 22, 1942, General Records of the Housing and Home Finance Agency, Record of the National Housing Agency Program, April 30, 1943, RG 207, box 3, folder War Manpower Commission, NARA.

8. Weaver, *Negro Ghetto*, 144.

9. Lusignan, "Public Housing in the United States," *Cultural Resource Management*, 37.

10. Crane to Woodbury, August 22, 1942.

11. Historian Gail Radford has argued that one of the drawbacks of federal housing policy after 1937 was that "[public housing] legislation . . . did not provide possibilities for democracy or self determination for the residents." This may have well been true. However, when one considers that the creation of public housing offered African Americans better housing and hope that the federal government was concerned with providing housing for its citizens, it becomes clear that some public housing residents could look past many of the limitations associated with public housing construction. See Radford, *Modern Housing for America*, 198.

12. Crane to Woodbury, August 22, 1942.

13. Ibid.

14. United Committee on Emergency Housing to Mr. Blandford and Mr. Divers, "The problem of Negro housing and the program of the National Housing Agency," January 14, 1944, PMHC.

15. "John B. Blandford and Nat'l Housing," *Chicago Defender*, January 12, 1943.

16. United Committee on Emergency Housing to Mr. Blandford and Mr. Divers, January 14, 1944.

17. "Federal Housing Administration Directive PR 76," General Records of the Housing and Home Finance Agency, Record of the National Housing Agency Program, August 19, 1942, RG 207, box 3, folder War Manpower Commission, NARA.

18. Ibid.

19. Eugene O. Shauds to John B. Blandford, December 16, 1944, PMHC, box 16, folder 185.

20. "CHA Promises Low Rents to Soldiers' Kin," *Chicago Bee*, December 5, 1943.
21. "Chicago Housing Center Closes after Providing Living Accommodations for 400,000 People in 6 Years," PMHC, box 16, folder 182.
22. Ibid.
23. "Race Relations in Chicago," 13.
24. Ibid.
25. "Biennial Report," PMHC, box 2, folder 27.
26. Ibid.
27. One case can be seen in Allen, *People Wasn't Made to Burn*. Also see Hirsch, *Making the Second Ghetto*, 25–26.
28. Weaver, *Negro Ghetto*, 351.
29. "1942 Annual Report."
30. Quoted from "Some Light of Truth on the Negro Housing Nightmare," by Paul T. Gilbert and J. M. Klein (1945), reprinted by the *Chicago Sun*, January 1945. George Cleveland Hall Branch Vertical File compiled by Vivian Harsh, box 29, Vivian G. Harsh Research Collection, Woodson Regional Library, Chicago Public Library.
31. "Paralytic Rat Victim Dies," *Chicago Defender*, February 7, 1942.
32. "Biennial Report."
33. Ibid.
34. "Chicago Housing Center Closes after Providing Living Accommodations for 400,000 People in 6 Years."
35. "Housing Condition in the Low Rent Negro Area on the South Side of Chicago," PMHC, box 16, folder 184.
36. "Slum Homes Hit; 3 More Children Die in Fire. Probe of Fire Traps Demanded," *Chicago Bee*, August 13, 1944.
37. Ibid.
38. "Recommends 3 Held for Jury in Fire Deaths," *Chicago Tribune*, September 7, 1944.
39. "Building Owner to Jail in Fire Quiz, Open War on South Side Fire Traps," *Chicago Bee*, September 10, 1944.
40. Ibid.
41. Ibid.
42. "1942 Annual Report."
43. "Food Costs Rise Despite Curbs, Report Reveals: Chicago Reflects Trend in National," *Chicago Tribune*, March 16, 1943.
44. "Biennial Report."
45. Housing Application, Chicago Housing Authority, Housing and Renting Office, n.d., MRC.
46. Drake and Cayton, *Black Metropolis*, 207.

47. See Chicago Plan Commission, *Report of the Chicago Land Use Survey*. Also see Weaver, *Negro Ghetto*, 110.

48. See chart, "Median Income of Those Earning $1,000 or More and Median Rent by Race in Communities," in *Chicago Defender*, January 3, 1942. *Chicago Defender*, March 14, 1942, "The Inner Zone of Chicago Where Median Income Was under $1,500 in 1939," found in Weaver, *Negro Ghetto*, 109. Original material found in Louis Wirth and Associates, *Recent Population Trends in Metropolitan Chicago*, table 39.

49. Weaver, *Negro Ghetto*, 109.

50. "Landlord Gets in Trouble for Evicting Pair," *Chicago Bee*, May 15, 1943.

51. "U.S. May Put Ceiling on South Side Rents; Real Estate Lobby Fights Pending Move," *Chicago Defender*, April 4, 1942.

52. "Tenants to Get More Time for Moving Decision," *Chicago Tribune*, February 28, 1942.

53. "Cleveland Fair-Rent Meet Launches Active Drive," *Chicago Defender*, January 3, 1942.

54. "U.S. May Put Ceiling on South Side Rents."

55. Weaver, *Negro Ghetto*, 118.

56. Hirsch, *Making the Second Ghetto*, 271.

57. Records of the FEPC, Headquarter Files, Division of Review and Analysis Tension Files, July 1943–October 1945, Idaho–Indiana, RG 228, box 446, folder Adequacy and Housing, NARA.

58. "South Side Aroused by Mecca Fate; Crisis Looms as 1500 Face Homes Ouster," *Chicago Bee*, May 23, 1943.

59. George Tagge, "Bill to Curtail Razing of Negro Homes Passed," *Chicago Tribune*, April 28, 1943.

60. "South Side Aroused by Mecca Fate."

61. "Ask Congress to Stop Homes," *Chicago Bee*, October 10, 1943.

62. "Judge Stops Mecca Evictions; Decision May Set Precedent," *Chicago Bee*, June 6, 1943.

63. "Race Relations in Chicago," 27–28.

64. Bowly, *Poorhouse*, 41–42.

65. "5 War Homes a Day: A Story of War Housing," MRC.

66. Bowly, *Poorhouse*, 43.

67. Weaver, *Negro Ghetto*, 96.

68. "Whites Fight South Side War Homes; Ask Federal Aid to Keep Out Negro," *Chicago Bee*, September 19, 1943.

69. "New Move On to Halt War Homes; South Siders Ask Mayor's Aid; White Protest," *Chicago Bee*, October 17, 1943.

70. Ibid.

71. "Chi Teachers Endorse War Homes Fight," *Chicago Bee*, November 7, 1943.
72. See P. Smith, "Quest for Racial Democracy."
73. "Home Owners Fight Invasion by U.S. Plan," *Chicago Tribune*, August 19, 1944.
74. Ibid.
75. Richard Durham, "Ku Kluxers Join Fight on Chicago's West Chesterfield Housing Project," *Chicago Defender*, September 9, 1944. Also see Lands, *Culture of Property*; Rubinowitz, Rosenbaum, and Dvorin, *Crossing the Class and Color Lines*; and Michael Galvin, "Ghetto in the Sky."
76. Durham, "Ku Kluxers Join Fight."
77. Lillian E. Bates, "Project Dweller Proud of Home," *Chicago Defender*, March 31, 1945.
78. Leo H. Ellis Jr., "Reply to Letter on West Chesterfield," *Chicago Defender*, April 28, 1945.
79. "Protest Rally Shows Mass Support of Controversial War Homes," *Chicago Bee*, September 17, 1944.
80. Durham, "Ku Kluxers Join Fight."
81. Karen Ferguson argues that efforts by black homeowners to improve and protect the integrity of their communities were "all part of an effort to demonstrate black citizenship through respectability in face of white-imposed conditions that denied that possibility." See Ferguson, *Black Politics in New Deal Atlanta*, 193.

4. The Greatest Negro Victory since the Civil War: Fair Employment Policy during World War II

Portions of this chapter appeared in the article "I Too Serve America: African American Women War Workers in Chicago, 1940–1945," *Journal of the Illinois State Historical Society* 93, no. 4 (2000–2001): 415–34.

1. See Barbeau and Henri, *Unknown Soldiers*; Berlin, Reidy, and Rowland, *Freedom's Soldiers*; Nalty, *Strength for the Fight*; and Wynn, *Afro-American and the Second World War*.
2. News from Earl B. Dickerson newsletter, January 9, 1941, Papers of the Brotherhood of Sleeping Car Porters, box 6, folder 1, Chicago History Museum.
3. See also Scott and Womack, *Double V*; Jefferson, *Fighting for Hope*.
4. "News from Earl B. Dickerson," November 14, 1941, Earl B. Dickerson Papers, box 1, folder Book II, Chicago Historical Society.

5. Dalfiume, "'Forgotten Years,'" 106.

6. Ibid.

7. Dalfiume, *Desegregation*, 2.

8. Ibid.

9. Kersten, *Race, Jobs, and the War*, 12.

10. Ibid. Also see Moreno, *From Direct Action to Affirmative Action*, 7; M. Reed, *Seedtime for the Modern Civil Rights Movement*; and Ruchames, *Race, Jobs and Politics*.

11. John J. Gorson to All Regional Representatives and State Directors of the United States Employment Service, USES Information Bulletin No. B-4, Records of the War Manpower Commission, USES Information Bulletin, RG 211, box 11, National Archives and Records Administration, College Park, Md. (hereafter USES).

12. Ibid.

13. Ransom, "Combating Discrimination," 414.

14. See Garfinkel, *When Negroes March*; and Lewis, "Role of Pressure Groups."

15. George F. McCray, "12,000 at Coliseum Voice Demands for Democracy," *Chicago Defender*, July 4, 1943.

16. Bates, *Pullman Porters*, 199.

17. Moreno, *From Direct Action to Affirmative Action*, 68; and Ransom, "Combating Discrimination," 412.

18. Philip Franchine, "Earl B. Dickerson, 95, Named Civil Rights Leading Lawyer," *Chicago Sun-Times*, September 4, 1986.

19. George F. McCray, "The Labor Front: This Is Our War," *Chicago Defender*, February 6, 1943.

20. "End Quiz of 14 Defense Job 'Traitors,'" *Chicago Defender*, January 24, 1942.

21. "Defense Fight Carried to Washington Front," *Chicago Defender*, April 5, 1941.

22. Biles, *Big City Boss in Depression and War*, 113.

23. Ibid., 126.

24. "Mayor Kelly's Race Commission," *Chicago Defender*, August 7, 1943.

25. Report of the Committee on Race Relations, December 1944, MRC. Others members of the committee were Edwin C. Embree, president of the Rosenwald Foundation; Ruth Moore Smith, executive secretary of the South Parkway YWCA; Robert Taylor, chairman of the Chicago Housing Authority; and Willard S. Townsend, international president of the United Transport Service Employees Union (CIO).

26. Ruchames, *Race, Jobs and Politics*, 179.

27. Letter from Frank W. McColloch to Milton Webster, July 28, 1941, Frank McColloch Papers, box 9, Chicago History Museum.

28. Kersten, *Race, Jobs, and the War*, 47.

29. Drake and Cayton, *Black Metropolis*, 215.

30. Ibid.

31. For information regarding wartime strikes, see Glaberman, *Wartime Strikes*; Winslow, *Waterfront Workers*; Fraser, *Labor Will Rule*; Harris, *Harder We Run*; Lichtenstein, *Labor's War at Home*; Milkman, *Gender at Work*; Pope, "Worker Lawmaking"; Boyle, "Kiss"; and Korstad, "Opportunities Found and Lost."

32. Richard Durham, "Race Hate Strike Sweeps Big Pullman Shipyard," *Chicago Defender*, December 16, 1944.

33. Ibid.; "Pullman Hate Strikers Lose," *Chicago Defender*, December 23, 1944.

34. "Pullman Hate Strikers Lose."

35. Records of the FEPC, U.S. Committee on Fair Employment Practices (1941–1945), reel 74FRA, College of Law Library, University of Iowa.

36. "100 Whites Stage Walkout; Strike over Washroom," *Chicago Bee*, June 20, 1943.

37. Records of the FEPC, reel 76FR.

38. Ibid.

39. "Bee Hails Surface Line Victory; Bus Jobs Now Open," *Chicago Bee*, October 31, 1943.

40. "Mass Meeting Opens Fight for Street Car Jobs for Negroes," *Chicago Bee*, August 29, 1943.

41. Weaver, *Negro Labor*, 182.

42. "Bee Hails Surface Line Victory."

43. Abe Noel, "'No Jobs Yet' in Street Car Fight; Confab Fails When Chief Evades Issue," *Chicago Bee*, September 5, 1943; "Lines End 'L' Jim Crow; 7 Are Upgraded," *Chicago Bee*, December 5, 1943.

44. Weaver, *Negro Labor*, 155.

45. "Expect Order Freezing City's War Contracts: Fear Labor Scarcity in Six Months," *Chicago Tribune*, March 14, 1943.

46. This information was derived from a newsletter published by the Office of War Services, Records of the FEPC, Headquarters Files, Division of Review and Analysis Tension Files, July 1943–October 1945, Idaho–Indiana, RG 228, box 446, NARA.

47. Watters, *Illinois in the Second World War*, 272.

48. Affidavit found in the Records of the Committee of Fair Employment Practices, Region VI, Government Agencies, RG 228, entry 68, Chicago Vocational School, National Archives Research Administration, Great Lakes Branch, Chicago (hereafter CFEP).

49. Ibid.

50. Letter from Henry Tapley to George M. Johnson, assistant executive secretary, War Manpower Commission, November 9, 1942, ibid.
51. Affidavit found in the Records of the Committee of Fair Employment Practices, ibid.
52. Ibid.
53. "A Brief of Unfair Practices at the Chicago Post Office," entry 68, Post Office Chicago No. 1, ibid.
54. Ibid.
55. The summary of remedies to discriminatory practices in the post office were outlined in a letter from the president of the Chicago branch of the National Alliance of Postal Employees, Ashby B. Carter, to Lawrence Cramer, executive secretary of the FEPC, July 23, 1944, ibid.
56. For more details, see Meyer, *Creating GI Jane*, 11–13.
57. Ernestine D. Tyler to Alderman Benjamin Grant, June 2, 1942, entry 68, U.S. Civil Services Commission, Tyler, Ernestine D., CFEP.
58. Ibid.
59. Ibid.
60. "FEPC Begins Probe of Armour Charges," *Chicago Defender*, July 18, 1942.
61. Records of the FEPC, reel 75FRA.
62. Ibid.
63. "Urges Civil Disobedience Week in May; Randolph Advises Use of Passive Resistance to Jim Crow Acts," *Chicago Defender*, January 24, 1943.
64. Garfinkel, *When Negroes March*, 73.

5. From Foxholes to Ratholes: Stuggles for Postwar Housing

1. "Officials Rap Slum Conditions; Families Herded into 'Black Belt,'" *Chicago Defender*, August 31, 1946.
2. Mayor's Commission on Human Relations, "Human Relations in Chicago: Report for 1946," 62 (hereafter MCHR 1946).
3. Hirsch, *Making the Second Ghetto*, 44.
4. Ibid.
5. Factual Report on Housing, PCUL, folder 722.
6. MCHR 1946, 80.
7. Ibid.
8. "Homes in War Plants Urged to Ease Crisis," *Chicago Tribune*, November 6, 1945.
9. "Temporary Housing Need Confirmed," Papers of the Metropolitan Planning Commission of Chicago, box 16, folder 182, Special Collections Department, University of Illinois at Chicago.

10. "Plain Talk about Negroes and the Taft-Ellender-Wagner General Bill S.866," PCUL, folder 714.

11. Ibid.

12. "The Federal Housing Bill," *Chicago Defender*, January 5, 1946. Also see McEnaney, "Nightmares on Elm Street."

13. "Plain Talk about Negroes and the Taft-Ellender-Wagner General Bill S.866."

14. Weaver, *Negro Ghetto*, 131.

15. Papers of Congressman William L. Dawson, box 188-2, folder 26, MSRC.

16. "Vet Group Hits Housing Plight of Negro Ex-GI's," *Chicago Bee*, October 13, 1946.

17. Elizabeth Wood interview, Chicago State College Oral History Research Program, Chicago State University Archives and Special Collections.

18. Chicago Housing Authority, "Temporary Housing for Chicago Veterans," MRC.

19. Ibid.

20. Elizabeth Wood interview.

21. MCHR 1946, 83.

22. "10,000 Riot in Scramble for 422 Southside Homes," *Chicago Defender*, February 16, 1946.

23. MCHR 1946, 89.

24. Ibid., 90.

25. "Gains in Human Relations in the Field of Housing, 1945–1948," Chicago Conference on Civic Unity, Raymond M. Hilliard Papers, box 73, folder IPAC 1949, Chicago Historical Society.

26. Meyerson and Banfield, *Politics, Planning, and the Public Interest*, 122.

27. MCHR 1946, 119.

28. Ibid.

29. Ibid., 120.

30. "Racist Gang Threatens UPWA Vet as Housing Project," Meatpacking Commission Record Relating to Geographical Differential, RG 202, entry 371, NARA, Great Lakes Region.

31. MCHR 1946, 121.

32. Ibid.

33. "Racist Gang Threatens UPWA Vet as Housing Project."

34. Vernon Jarrett, a reporter for the *Chicago Defender*, recounted this event in a panel videotaped discussion during the seventy-fifth anniversary celebration for the Chicago Public Library's George Cleveland Hall Library and the establishment of the Vivian G. Harsh Research Collection on January 20, 2001.

35. "Mayor Acts to End Vet Homes Strife; Hits Violence: Police Ordered to Enforce Law," *Chicago Bee*, November 24, 1946.
36. MCHR 1946, 125.
37. Ibid., 121.
38. "Cops Fight Mob as Vets Occupy Homes; Preachers Aid in Unloading Furniture Vans," *Chicago Defender*, December 7, 1946.
39. Ibid.
40. Marion M. Campfield, "Race Issue Open in Vet Homes Fight; Squatters Storm City Hall," *Chicago Bee*, December 6, 1946.
41. Statement by Mayor Edward J. Kelly about Airport Housing Projects, November 20, 1946, in Mayor's Commission on Human Relations, "Airport Homes Housing Project."
42. MCHR 1946, 127.
43. Ibid., 129.
44. Ibid., 131.
45. *Chicago Defender*, December 7, 1946.
46. MCHR 1946, 133; Elizabeth Wood interview.
47. MCHR 1946, 140.
48. Halpern, *Down on the Killing Floor*, 216.
49. MCHR 1946, 149.
50. "City, FBI Probe Vet Homes Gunfire," *Chicago Bee*, February 23, 1947.
51. Halpern, *Down on the Killing Floor*, 216–27.
52. "Gains in Human Relations in the Field of Housing, 1945–1948."
53. "Memorandum on Fernwood Park Homes, 105th and Union," 1, in Mayor's Commission on Human Relations, Fernwood Park Homes Incident file.
54. "Record of Events Prior to Move-In Day at the Fernwood Park Homes," 2, in ibid., 2.
55. Ibid., 3.
56. Ibid., 4.
57. "Memorandum on Fernwood Park Homes, 105th and Union," ibid., 20.
58. Ibid., 10.
59. John Bartlow Martin, "Incident at Fernwood," *Harper's Magazine*, October 1949, 94.
60. "Memorandum on Fernwood Park Homes, 105th and Union," 10.
61. "Text of Kennelly's Address," *Chicago Bee*, March 22, 1947.
62. Meyerson and Banfield, *Politics, Planning, and the Public Interest*, 129.
63. "Demand Chicago Mayor's Ouster," *Chicago Defender*, December 3, 1949.
64. *Shelley v. Kraemer*, 334 U.S. 21.
65. Ibid., 21–22.

66. "Discrimination Ban in Housing Faces Defeat: Poll Shows Aldermen Won't Enact Law," *Chicago Tribune*, February 13, 1949.

67. For the Carey Ordinance, also see Hirsch, *Making the Second Ghetto*, 128–29; and Dickerson, *African American Preachers and Politics*.

68. "Council Heeds Mayor's Plea, Beats Carey Bill, 31–13," *Chicago Tribune*, March 3, 1949.

69. "Kennelly 'On Spot' as Council Votes 31 to 13 against Ordinance," *Chicago Defender*, March 12, 1949.

70. Cohen and Taylor, *American Pharaoh*, 83.

71. Meyerson and Banfield, *Politics, Planning, and the Public Interest*, 137.

72. Ibid., 131.

73. Ibid., 85.

74. Ibid., 85–86.

75. For the full text of the interview, see Mayor's Commission on Human Relations, "Documentary Report of the Anti-racial Demonstrations and Violence against the Home and Persons of Mr. and Mrs. Roscoe Johnson, 7153 St. Lawrence Ave., July 25, 1949," appendix A, p. 3 (hereafter MCHR 1949).

76. Ibid., appendix A, p. 2.

77. "Memorandum on Fernwood Park Homes, 105th and Union," 5.

78. P. Johnson, *Call Me Neighbor*, 16.

79. MCHR 1949, 33.

80. Ibid., 32.

81. Mayor's Commission on Human Relations, "Documentary Report on Reoccurrence of Anti-racial Disturbances in the 7100 and 7200 Blocks on St. Lawrence Avenue," 16.

82. Ibid., 17.

83. Interview with Charles A. Davis, December 12, 2002, Chicago.

84. De Rose, *Camille De Rose Story*, 1953.

85. "The Cicero Riot of 1951," Papers of the NAACP, part 5, reel 19, frame 749.

86. Ibid., frames 744–45.

87. Ibid.

88. "Contempt Action Begins against Cicero Officials," ibid., part 5, reel 19, frame 646.

89. "Cicero Riot of 1951," ibid., part 5, reel 19, frame 746.

90. Ibid.

91. Ibid., frame 89.

92. Ibid., frame 746.

93. Mayor's Commission on Human Relations, "Trumbull Park Homes Disturbances," 10.

94. See P. Smith, "Quest for Racial Democracy."
95. Mayor's Commission on Human Relations, "Trumbull Park Homes Disturbances," 11.
96. See "Chicago Public Housing Today," October 15, 1953, Papers of the Chicago Urban League, reel 28, Vivian G. Harsh Research Collection, Woodson Regional Library, Chicago Public Library; and Mayor's Commission on Human Relations, "Trumbull Park Homes Disturbances," 16.
97. Mayor's Commission on Human Relations, "Trumbull Park Homes Disturbances," 23.
98. Ibid., 23.
99. Albert Rosenberg to Elizabeth Wood, November 18, 1953, Papers of the Chicago Urban League, reel 28.
100. Mayor's Commission on Human Relations "Trumbull Park Homes Disturbances," 37.
101. Ibid., 37.
102. Kennelly's position on public housing in this instance seemingly contradicts the stance he took during his election campaign. However, Thomas O'Malley wrote in his dissertation on Kennelly that slum clearance and housing issues were "only a temporary investment of city funds" and "that the task of redeveloping the city and providing housing for its citizens was primarily the responsibility of private enterprise." O'Malley, "Mayor Martin H. Kennelly of Chicago," 104.
103. Mayor's Commission on Human Relations, "Trumbull Park Homes Disturbances," 38.
104. Ibid.
105. Cohen and Taylor, *American Pharaoh*, 101.
106. "Council OK's Group to Probe Racial Strife: Ald. Pacini Demands Miss Wood's Ouster," *Chicago Tribune*, October 15, 1953.
107. "Army Man Named to Head CHA," *Chicago Defender*, August 28, 1954.
108. "Action Labeled Victory for Mob," *Chicago Defender*, September 4, 1954.
109. "Army Man Named to Head CHA."
110. Hirsch, "Massive Resistance in the Urban North, " 540.
111. Cohen and Taylor, *American Pharaoh*, 201.
112. For more information regarding Martin Luther King and open housing drives in Chicago, see Anderson and Pickering, *Confronting the Color Line*; Hirsch, "Massive Resistance in the Urban North"; and Ralph, *Northern Protest*.

6. Picket Lines Were the Front Lines for Democracy: Black Veterans' Labor Activism in Post–World War II Chicago

1. Jacqueline Lopez, "Stockyard Pickets Strike for More Meat on Table," *Chicago Defender*, January 26, 1946.
2. Ibid.
3. Halpern, *Down on the Killing Floor*, 218.
4. Fones-Wolf, *Selling Free Enterprise*, 32.
5. Ibid., 33.
6. Sugrue, *Origins of the Urban Crisis*Princeton Studies in American Politics (Princeton, N.J.: Princeton University Press, 1996, 128.
7. Drake and Cayton, Black *Metropolis*, 750.
8. Hilton Joseph interview, Chicago, August 3, 2002.
9. Timuel Black interview, Chicago, December 20, 2000.
10. Weaver, *Negro Labor*, 173.
11. Philip Harrington, "Presentation in Behalf of the City of Chicago Relating to Plans for Post War Employment," February 8, 1944, MRC.
12. Clement, "Problems of Demobilization and Rehabilitation," 537.
13. Ibid.
14. C. Reed, *Chicago NAACP*, 119.
15. Ruchames, *Race, Jobs and Politics*, 122.
16. Bolté and Harris, *Our Negro Veterans*, 20. Also see Katznelson, *When Affirmative Action Was White*, 114–18.
17. Ruchames offers a very detailed narrative dealing with the demise of the FEPC and the activities of Theodore Bilbo. *Race, Jobs and Politics*, 121–36.
18. Ibid., 179.
19. Kersten, *Race, Jobs, and the War*, 136.
20. "Illinois Faces Increase in Job Discrimination since FEPC Termination," Claude A. Barnett Papers, part 1: Associated Negro Press and News Releases, 1928–1964, series B, 1945–1955, reel 33, frame 11.
21. The Fair Employment Practices Ordinance of the City of Chicago, with excerpts from the report of the Mayor's Commission on Human Relations in the City of Chicago and the Annual Report of the Law Department of the City of Chicago, MRC. Also see "Negro Hired, Pepsodent Workers Stay on Job," *Chicago Defender*, May 11, 1946.
22. City of Chicago, "Annual Report of the Law Department of the City of Chicago, 1946," 125–26, MRC.
23. Mayor's Commission on Human Relations, "Race Relations in Chicago," 1–2.

24. MCHR 1946, 10.
25. Colonel Campbell C. Johnson, "Employment Problems of the Negro Veteran," October 23, 1945, Campbell C. Johnson Papers, box 57-4, folder 11, MSRC.
26. "USES Appeals to Employers for Aid in Job Campaign," *Chicago Bee,* March 24, 1946.
27. Mayor's Commission on Human Relations, "Race Relations in Chicago," 15.
28. Harrington, "Presentation."
29. "Young Demos Fight to Keep Bus Jobs; Mayor Backs Moves," *Chicago Bee,* March 3, 1946.
30. "Bus Company Drops Race Hiring Ban," *Chicago Bee,* March 10, 1946.
31. Ibid.
32. "5 to Get Jobs with Bread Co.," *Chicago Bee,* March 16, 1947.
33. MCHR 1946, 12.
34. Trezzvant W. Anderson, "Negro Combat Vets Will Have More Difficulty in Post War World," Claude A. Barnett Papers, part 1: Associated Negro Press and News Releases, 1928–1964, series B, 1945–1955, reel 33, frame 84.
35. Interview with Mary McBride, Chicago, August 22, 2002.
36. C. Johnson, "Employment Problems of the Negro Veteran."
37. Ibid.
38. Colonel Campbell C. Johnson, "The Unforgotten Man," *Opportunity,* Winter 1945, 20.
39. Campbell C. Johnson, "The Employment of Negro Veterans," November 1944, Campbell C. Johnson Papers, box 57-3, folder 58, MSRC.
40. General Omar N. Bradley to Robert K. Carr, April 22, 1947, President Truman's Commission on Civil Rights, reel 2, frames 871–72, Vivian G. Harsh Research Collection, Woodson Regional Library, Chicago Public Library.
41. Ibid., frames 884–85.
42. H. Johnson, "Negro Veteran Fights for Freedom!," 434.
43. In addition to Biondi, *To Stand and Fight,* see Countryman, *Up South;* Theoharis and Woodard, *Freedom North;* Self, *American Babylon;* and Thompson, *Whose Detroit?* For the purposes of this project, the veterans' assistance activities of the Chicago Branch of the NAACP, while important, are not a central theme. Instead, substantial attention must be paid to the influence of Communists and Communist-influenced organizations that pushed for both racial equality and veterans' rights during and after the war.

44. Jacqueline Lopez, "War Vets Lash Jim Crowism at DuSable Meet," *Chicago Defender*, April 13, 1946. Also see Robert Jefferson's entry on the UNAVA in Mjagkij, *Organizing Black America*, 668–69. Also see the Papers of the National Negro Congress, series II, reel 34, frames 710–13, Vivian G. Harsh Research Collection, Woodson Regional Library, Chicago Public Library. According to UNAVA leadership, the primary mission of the group was to "organize Negro and white veterans around a program of securing for them the unqualified right to the enjoyment of the privileges and rewards which America promised her fighting men." See Kimble, "'Only Way to Get What's Coming to Us,'" 60.

45. "Not Communist, UNAVA Asserts," *Chicago Defender*, February 22, 1947.

46. Record, *Race and Radicalism*, 137; Bunche and Grantham, *Political Status of the Negro*, 578. Also see Cohen, *Making a New Deal*, 261–62. Cohen reports that five hundred black people, or half of all black individuals in the Communist Party, lived in Chicago.

47. Record, *Race and Radicalism*, 136–37, 137 n. 7.

48. "Memorandum for the President's Committee on Civil Rights," President Truman's Commission on Civil Rights, reel 3, frames 1040–46.

49. MCHR 1946, 35.

50. Ibid.

51. "Cab Companies Strike Back at Police; Ask Courts to Issue Order against Cops," *Chicago Defender*, August 3, 1935.

52. "Striking Chicago Cabbies Win Court Tilt; Judge Scolds Attorney for Owners Group," *Chicago Defender*, July 6, 1940.

53. "Cab Strike Ends; 18 Owners Sign," *Chicago Defender*, December 21, 1940.

54. "Veterans Preference Is Outlined by ODT," *New York Times*, May 15, 1945.

55. Kitch, Isaacson, and Kasper, "Regulation of Taxicabs in Chicago."

56. "GI Cab Drivers Fight Monopoly and Jim Crow," *Chicago Defender*, March 2, 1946.

57. "Vets' Cab Organization in Suit for Licenses," *Chicago Defender*, February 2, 1946.

58. Ibid.

59. Ibid.

60. "Vets to Fight Ban on Cabs; Plan March," *Chicago Bee*, February 10, 1946.

61. "Keenan in Fight Today to Get Action on Cab Law," *Chicago Sun*, February 28, 1946.

62. "Vets' Cab Organization in Suit for Licenses."
63. For additional details regarding this case, see Kitch, "Yellow Cab Antitrust Case." While Kitch outlines the case, he focuses solely on the American Cab Drivers' Association for Discharged Veterans. No mention of the Illinois Cab Drivers' Association for Discharged Veterans.
64. Chicago cabdrivers were not alone in these efforts. Similar protests occurred in other cities, such as Baltimore, Philadelphia, Pittsburgh, and Indianapolis. See "Taxi Driver Veterans Protest License Ban," *New York Times*, February 13, 1946; and "G.I. Cab Ride," *Business Week*, August 3, 1946, 31–33.
65. In Philadelphia the Veterans Taxicab Association was aided by two church congregations, St. Paul Baptist Church and McDowell Community Church. In Baltimore the efforts of the Deluxe Cab Company were greatly aided by the work of the *Baltimore Afro-American* and the FEPC. See "Yellow Cab Race Bias Played at Philly Hearing," *Chicago Defender*, December 29, 1945; "Union Will Oppose Cab Petition," *Pittsburgh Courier*, June 15, 1956; and Farrer, "Baltimore Afro-American," 97–98.
66. "$2,500 Bail of 63 Veterans in Taxi Cases Returned," *Chicago Sun*, February 20, 1946.
67. "GI Cab Drivers Fight Monopoly," *Chicago Defender*, March 2, 1946.
68. J. M. Klein, "Cab Rate Cut of $1000 a Day Sought," *Chicago Sun*, March 2, 1946.
69. Ibid. Although the Chicago City Council approved the release of 275 licenses, Mayor Kelly's office calculated that only 197 of these permits would be used. The mayor's office determined that only those drivers who could start operating immediately would receive operating licenses.
70. Biles, *Big City Boss in Depression and War*, 147.
71. Sugrue, *Origins of the Urban Crisis*, 156.
72. C. Reed, *Chicago NAACP*, 134.
73. Quoted in Schrecker, *Many Are the Crimes*, 275.
74. Ibid., 282.
75. See Fuerst, *When Public Housing Was Paradise*, 213 n. 21; and "Vote to Compel CHA Workers to Swear Loyalty: Board Members Reverse Stand under Pressure," *Chicago Tribune*, January 22, 1953.
76. "CIO Leads Loyalty Oath Foes at Hearing before CHA Board," *Chicago Tribune*, January 15, 1953.
77. "Mayor Favors Loyalty Oaths for CHA Staff," *Chicago Tribune*, January 20, 1953.
78. "Vote to Compel CHA Workers to Swear Loyalty."

79. "CHA'S Loyalty Oath Is 'Joke,' Says Clamage: Legion Official Terms It 'Meaningless,'" *Chicago Tribune*, January 23, 1953.
80. "Sykes Elected CHA Chairman; McMillen Out: Retiring Leader Assailed on Loyalty Oath," *Chicago Tribune*, March 24, 1953.
81. "CHA's Loyalty Oath Is Upheld; Ten ants Lose," *Chicago Tribune*, October 2, 1953; "CHA Anti-res Oath Voided by Supreme Court: Rules Balky Tenants Can't Be Evicted," ibid., March 13, 1954; and "Loyalty Oaths for Tenants Is Ended by CHA: Statements Voluntary since 1954," ibid., August 9, 1956.
82. Papers of the NAACP, part 13, series 3, Part C, reel 5, frame 882.
83. Ibid., frame 881.
84. Ibid.
85. See Jefferson's entry on the UNAVA entry in Mjagkij, *Organizing Black America*.
86. Tyler, "American Veterans Committee," 428.
87. Halpern and Horowitz, *Meatpackers1999*, 244.
88. Schrecker, *Many Are the Crimes*, 282. For the effects of the Cold War on the civil rights movement, see Plummer, *Window on Freedom*; Dudziak, *Cold War Civil Rights*; and Plummer, *Rising Wind*.
89. See Beth Bates, "'Double V for Victory' Mobilizes Black Detroit, 1941–1945," in Theoharis and Woodard, *Freedom North*, 32–33; and Anderson, "Last Hired, First Hired," 95.
90. Rast, *Remaking Chicago*, 101.

Conclusion

1. Weaver, *Negro Labor*, 307.
2. *Chicago Defender*, August 1, 1964.
3. See Cohen and Taylor, *American Pharaoh*, 183–215.
4. Ibid., 53.
5. *Chicago Defender*, May 14, 1960.
6. Drake and Cayton, *Black Metropolis*, 816.
7. Honey, *Southern Labor and Black Civil Rights*.

BIBLIOGRAPHY

Abbott, Edith, and Sophonisba Preston Breckinridge. *The Tenements of Chicago, 1908–1935.* Chicago: University of Chicago Press, 1936.

Allen, Joe. *People Wasn't Made to Burn: A True Story of Race, Murder, and Justice in Chicago.* Chicago: Haymarket Books, 2011.

Anderson, Karen Tucker. "Last Hired, First Hired: Black Women Workers during World War II." *Journal of American History* 69, no. 1 (July 1983): 82–97.

Anderson, Alan B., and George W. Pickering. *Confronting the Color Line: The Broken Promise of the Civil Rights Movement in Chicago.* Athens: University of Georgia Press, 1986.

Axelrod, Steven Gould, Camille Roman, and Thomas J. Travisano. *The New Anthology of American Poetry.* New Brunswick, N.J.: Rutgers University Press, 2003.

Barbeau, Arthur E., and Florette Henri. *The Unknown Soldiers: African-American Troops in World War I.* New York: Da Capo Press, 1996.

Barrett, James R. *Work and Community in the Jungle: Chicago's Packinghouse Workers, 1894–1922.* The Working Class in American History. Urbana: University of Illinois Press, 1987.

Bates, Beth Tompkins. "A New Crowd Challenges the Agenda of the Old Guard in the NAACP, 1933–1941." *American Historical Review* 102, no. 2 (April 1997): 340–77.

————. *Pullman Porters and the Rise of Protest Politics in Black America, 1925–1945.* Chapel Hill: University of North Carolina Press, 2001.

Bauman, John F., Roger Biles, and Kristin Szylvian, eds. *From Tenements to the Taylor Homes: In Search of an Urban Housing Policy in Twentieth-Century America.* University Park: Pennsylvania State University Press, 2000.

Berlin, Ira, Joseph P. Reidy, and Leslie S. Rowland. *Freedom's Soldiers: The Black Military Experience in the Civil War.* New York: Cambridge University Press, 1998.

Best, Wallace D. *Passionately Human, No Less Divine: Religion and Culture in Black Chicago, 1915–1952.* Princeton, N.J.: Princeton University Press, 2005.

Bibliography

Biles, Roger. *Big City Boss in Depression and War: Mayor Edward J. Kelly of Chicago.* DeKalb: Northern Illinois University Press, 1984.

Biondi, Martha. *To Stand and Fight: The Struggle for Civil Rights in Postwar New York City.* Cambridge, Mass.: Harvard University Press, 2003.

Blakely, Robert J., and Marcus Shepard. *Earl B. Dickerson: A Voice for Freedom and Equality.* Chicago Lives. Evanston, Ill.: Northwestern University Press, 2006.

Bolté, Charles G., and Louis Harris. *Our Negro Veterans.* Public Affairs Pamphlet. New York: Public Affairs Committee, 1947.

Bontemps, Arna Wendell, and Jack Conroy. *Anyplace but Here.* New York: Hill and Wang, 1966.

Bowly, Devereux. *The Poorhouse: Subsidized Housing in Chicago, 1895–1976.* Carbondale: Southern Illinois University Press, 1978.

Boyd, Michelle R. *Jim Crow Nostalgia: Reconstructing Race in Bronzeville.* Minneapolis: University of Minnesota Press, 2008.

Boyle, Kevin. "The Kiss: Racial and Gender Conflict in a 1950s Automobile Factory." *Journal of American History* 84, no. 2 (1997): 496–523.

Brinkley, Alan. *The End of Reform: New Deal Liberalism in Recession and War.* New York: Alfred A. Knopf, 1995.

Brown, Earl Louis, and George Ross Leighton. *The Negro and the War.* Public Affairs Pamphlet. New York: Public Affairs Committee, 1942.

Brown, Frank London. *Trumbull Park; A Novel.* Chicago: Regnery, 1959.

Bunche, Ralph J., and Dewey W. Grantham. *The Political Status of the Negro in the Age of FDR.* Chicago: University of Chicago Press, 1973.

Chicago (Ill.). Committee on Sub-Standard Housing. *The Chicago Program for Demolition and Rehabilitation of Sub-Standard Housing: Operating through the Fire Department, the Board of Health, the Department of Law, the Department of Buildings, the Department of Public Works, in Conjunction with the Illinois Emergency Relief Commission and Co-Operating Agencies.* Chicago, 1935.

———. Department of Law. *Annual Report of the Law Department of the City of Chicago, 1946.* Chicago, 1946.

———. Department of Welfare. *Final Report on a Demonstration Conducted by the Chicago Relief Administration in Cooperation with the Illinois Council on Public Assistance and Employment and the Illinois Emergency Relief Commission, February through April, 1938.* Chicago, 1938.

Chicago Commission on Race Relations. *The Negro in Chicago: A Study of Race Relations and a Race Riot.* Chicago: University of Chicago Press, 1922.

Chicago Plan Commission. *Report of the Chicago Land Use Survey.* Ann Arbor: University of Michigan Library, 1942.

Clement, Rufus E. "Problems of Demobilization and Rehabilitation of the Negro Soldier after World Wars I and II." *Journal of Negro Education* 12, no. 3 (Summer 1943): 533–42.

Cohen, Adam, and Elizabeth Taylor. *American Pharaoh: Mayor Richard J. Daley; His Battle for Chicago and the Nation.* Boston: Little, Brown, 2000.

Cohen, Lizabeth. *Making a New Deal: Industrial Workers in Chicago, 1919–1939.* Cambridge: Cambridge University Press, 1990.

Cooley, William. "Moving On Out: Black Pioneering in Chicago, 1915–1950." *Journal of Urban History* 36, no. 4 (July 2010): 485–506.

Countryman, Matthew. *Up South: Civil Rights and Black Power in Philadelphia.* Philadelphia: University of Pennsylvania Press, 2006.

Cox, Oliver Cromwell. *Origin of Direct-Action Protest among Negroes.* New York: Bell and Howell, 1973.

Dalfiume, Richard M. *Desegregation of the U.S. Armed Forces: Fighting on Two Fronts, 1939–1953.* Columbia: University of Missouri Press, 1969.

———. "The 'Forgotten Years' of the Negro Revolution." *Journal of American History* 55, no. 4 (1968): 90–106.

Denning, Michael. *The Cultural Front: The Laboring of American Culture in the Twentieth Century.* The Haymarket Series. New York: Verso, 1996.

De Rose, Camille. *The Camille De Rose Story.* Chicago: De Rose, 1953.

Dickerson, Dennis C. *African American Preachers and Politics: The Careys of Chicago.* Jackson: University Press of Mississippi, 2010.

Dombrowski, Theodore. "Methods of Direct Relief Used by the Illinois Emergency Relief Commission in Cook County." MA thesis, University of Chicago, School of Social Service Administration, August 1940.

Drake, St. Clair. *Churches and Voluntary Associations in the Chicago Negro Community: By St. Clair Drake.* Chicago: Works Progress Administration, 1940.

Drake, St. Clair, and Horace Roscoe Cayton. *Black Metropolis: A Study of Negro Life in a Northern City.* New York: Harper and Row, 1962.

Dudziak, Mary L. *Cold War Civil Rights: Race and the Image of American Democracy.* Princeton: Princeton University Press, 2000.

Duncan, Otis Dudley, and Beverly Duncan. *The Negro Population of Chicago: A Study of Residential Succession.* Monograph Series of the Chicago Community Inventory of the University of Chicago. Chicago: University of Chicago Press, 1957.

Fairbanks, Robert B. *For the City as a Whole: Planning, Politics, and the Public Interest in Dallas, Texas, 1900–1965.* Urban Life and Urban Landscape Series. Columbus: Ohio State University Press, 1998.

Farrer, Hayward. *The "Baltimore Afro-American": 1892–1950.* New York: Praeger, 1998.

Ferguson, Karen. *Black Politics in New Deal Atlanta.* Chapel Hill: University of North Carolina Press, 2002.

Foner, Philip S. *Organized Labor and the Black Worker, 1619–1981.* New York: International Publishers, 1982.

Fones-Wolf, Elizabeth A. *Selling Free Enterprise: The Business Assault on Labor and Liberalism, 1945–60*. Urbana: University of Illinois Press, 1994.

Fraser, Steve. *Labor Will Rule: Sidney Hillman and the Rise of American Labor*. New York: Free Press, 1991.

Fuerst, J. S. *When Public Housing Was Paradise: Building Community in Chicago*. With the assistance of D. Bradford Hunt. Urbana: University of Illinois Press, 2005.

Galvin, Michael. "Ghetto in the Sky": Race, Class, and Housing in the Twin Cities. Saarbrücken, Germany: VDM Verlag, 2009.

Garfinkel, Herbert. *When Negroes March: The March on Washington Movement in the Organizational Politics for FEPC*. New York: Atheneum, 1968.

Gelfand, Mark I. *A Nation of Cities: The Federal Government and Urban America, 1933–1965*. New York: Oxford University Press, 1975.

Gerstle, Gary. "The Protean Character of American Liberalism." *American Historical Review* 99, no. 4 (October 1994): 1043–73.

Gilbert, Mary Louise. "District Variations in Relief Standards: An Analysis of Statistical Data of the Illinois Emergency Relief Commission for the City of Chicago, for the Period of July 1, 1934, through June 30, 1935." MA thesis, University of Chicago, School of Social Service Administration, 1937.

Glaberman, Martin. *Wartime Strikes: The Struggle against the No-Strike Pledge in the UAW during World War II*. Detroit: Bewick, 1980.

Glick, Frank Ziegler. *The Illinois Emergency Relief Commission: A Study of Administrative and Financial Aspects of Emergency Relief*. Chicago: University of Chicago Press, 1940.

Glover, Lydia M. "A Study of Work Relief in La Salle County, Illinois, under the Illinois Emergency Relief Commission." MA thesis, University of Chicago, School of Social Service Administration, 1936.

Goings, Kenneth W., and Raymond A. Mohl, eds. *The New African American Urban History*. Thousand Oaks, Calif.: Sage, 1996.

Green, Adam. *Selling the Race: Culture, Community, and Black Chicago, 1940–1955*. Chicago: University of Chicago Press, 2007.

Greenberg, Cheryl Lynn. *Or Does It Explode? Black Harlem in the Great Depression*. New York: Oxford University Press, 1997.

Grossman, James R. *Land of Hope: Chicago, Black Southerners, and the Great Migration*. Chicago: University of Chicago Press, 1989.

Guzman, Jessie Parkhurst, Vera Chandler Foster, and William Hardin Hughes, eds. *Negro Year Book: A Review of Events Affecting Negro Life, 1941–1946*. Tuskegee, Ala.: Department of Records and Research, Tuskegee Institute, 1947 (microform).

Halpern, Rick. *Down on the Killing Floor: Black and White Workers in Chicago's Packinghouses, 1904–54*. Urbana: University of Illinois Press, 1997.

Halpern, Rick, and Roger Horowitz. *Meatpackers: An Oral History of Black Packinghouse Workers and Their Struggle for Racial and Economic Equality*. New York: Monthly Review Press, 1999.

Harris, William Hamilton. *The Harder We Run: Black Workers since the Civil War*. New York: Oxford University Press, 1982.

Henderson, Elmer William. "A Study of the Basic Factors Involved in the Change in the Party Alignment of Negroes in Chicago, 1932–1938." MA thesis, University of Chicago, 1939.

Hendricks, Wanda A. *Gender, Race, and Politics in the Midwest: Black Club Women in Illinois*. Blacks in the Diaspora. Bloomington: Indiana University Press, 1998.

Hirsch, Arnold R. *Making the Second Ghetto: Race and Housing in Chicago, 1940–1960*. Interdisciplinary Perspectives on Modern History. New York: Cambridge University Press, 1983.

———. "Massive Resistance in the Urban North: Trumbull Park, Chicago, 1953–1966." *Journal of American History* 82, no. 2 (1995): 522–50.

Hirsch, Arnold R., and Raymond A. Mohl, eds. *Urban Policy in Twentieth-Century America*. New Brunswick, N.J.: Rutgers University Press, 1993.

Honey, Michael K. *Southern Labor and Black Civil Rights: Organizing Memphis Workers*. Urbana: University of Illinois Press, 1993.

Horowitz, Roger. *"Negro and White, Unite and Fight!": A Social History of Industrial Unionism in Meatpacking, 1930–90*. Urbana: University of Illinois Press, 1997.

Hoyt, Homer. *One Hundred Years of Land Values in Chicago*. New York: Arno Press, 1970.

Hunt, D. Bradford. *Blueprint for Disaster: The Unraveling of Chicago Public Housing*. Chicago: University of Chicago Press, 2009.

Jackson, Kenneth T. *Crabgrass Frontier: The Suburbanization of the United States*. New York: Oxford University Press, 1985.

Jacobson, Matthew Frye. *Whiteness of a Different Color: European Immigrants and the Alchemy of Race*. Cambridge, Mass.: Harvard University Press, 1999.

Jefferson, Robert F. *Fighting for Hope: African American Troops of the 93rd Infantry Division in World War II and Postwar America*. Baltimore: Johns Hopkins University Press, 2008.

Johnson, Howard. "The Negro Veteran Fights for Freedom!" *Political Affairs*, May 1947, 429–40.

Johnson, Philip A. *Call Me Neighbor, Call Me Friend: The Case History of the Integration of a Neighborhood on Chicago's South Side*. Garden City, N.Y.: Doubleday, 1965.

Katznelson, Ira. *When Affirmative Action Was White: An Untold History of Racial Inequality in Twentieth-Century America*. New York: W. W. Norton, 2005.

Keating, W. Dennis, Norman Krumholz, and Philip Star, eds. *Revitalizing Urban Neighborhoods*. Lawrence: University Press of Kansas, 1996.

Kelley, Robin D. G. *Hammer and Hoe: Alabama Communists during the Great Depression*. Chapel Hill: University of North Carolina Press, 1990.

Kersten, Andrew Edmund. *Race, Jobs, and the War: The FEPC in the Midwest, 1941–46*. Urbana: University of Illinois Press, 2000.

Kimble, Lionel, Jr. "I Too Serve America: African American Women War Workers in Chicago, 1940–1945." *Journal of the Illinois State Historical Society* 93, no. 4 (2000–2001): 415–34.

———. "'The Only Way to Get What's Coming to Us': African American Coalition Building and Veterans' Rights in Post–World War II Chicago." *Journal of Illinois History* 12, no. 1 (Spring 2009): 53–70.

Kitch, Edmund W. "The Yellow Cab Antitrust Case." *Journal of Law and Economics* 15 no. 2 (October 1972): 327–36.

Kitch, Edmund W., Marc Isaacson, and Daniel Kasper. "The Regulation of Taxicabs in Chicago." *Journal of Law and Economics* 14, no. (October 1971): 285–350.

Knupfer, Anne Meis. *The Chicago Black Renaissance and Women's Activism*. Urbana: University of Illinois Press, 2006.

Korstad, Robert Rodgers. *Civil Rights Unionism: Tobacco Workers and the Struggle for Democracy in the Mid-Twentieth-Century South*. Chapel Hill: University of North Carolina Press, 2003.

———. "Opportunities Found and Lost: Labor, Radicals, and the Early Civil Rights Movement." *Journal of American History*, 75, no. 3 (December 1988): 786–811.

Krebs, Ronald R. *Fighting for Rights: Military Service and the Politics of Citizenship*. Ithaca: Cornell University Press, 2006.

Lands, LeeAnn. *The Culture of Property: Race, Class, and Housing Landscapes in Atlanta, 1880–1950*. Athens: University of Georgia Press, 2009.

Lewis, Roscoe E. "The Role of Pressure Groups in Maintaining Morale among Negroes." *Journal of Negro Education* 12, no. 3 (Summer 1943): 464–73.

Lichtenstein, Nelson. *Labor's War at Home: The CIO in World War II*. Philadelphia: Temple University Press, 2003.

Logan, Rayford Whittingham, ed. *What the Negro Wants*. Chapel Hill: University of North Carolina Press, 1944.

Lusignan, Paul R. "Public Housing in the United States, 1933–1949." *Cultural Resource Management*, no. 1 (2002): 36–37.

Manning, Christopher. *William L. Dawson and the Limits of Black Electoral Leadership*. DeKalb: Northern Illinois University Press, 2009.

Marks, Carole. *Farewell—We're Good and Gone: The Great Black Migration*. Bloomington: Indiana University Press, 1989.

Martin, John Barlow. "Incident at Fernwood." *Harper's Monthly,* October 1949, 86–98.

Mayor's Commission on Human Relations. "Airport Homes Housing Project, November 20, 1946." Chicago, 1946.

———. "Documentary Report of the Anti-racial Demonstrations and Violence against the Home and Persons of Mr. and Mrs. Roscoe Johnson, 7153 St. Lawrence Ave., July 25, 1949." Chicago, 1949.

———. "Documentary Report on the Reoccurrence of Anti-racial Disturbances in the 7100 and 7200 Blocks on St. Lawrence Avenue." Chicago, 1950.

———. Fernwood Park Homes Incident file, 1947.

———. "Human Relations in Chicago: Report for 1946." Chicago, 1946.

———. "Memorandum on Fernwood Park Homes, 105th and Union." Fernwood Park Incident file, Chicago, 1947.

———. "Race Relations in Chicago." Chicago, 1945.

———. "The Trumbull Park Homes Disturbances: A Chronological Report, August 4, 1953 to June 30, 1955." Chicago, 1955.

McEnaney, Laura. "Nightmares on Elm Street: Demobilizing in Chicago, 1945–1953." *Journal of American History* 92, no. 4 (2006): 1265–91.

Mettler, Suzanne. "'The Only Good Thing Was the G.I. Bill': Effects of the Education and Training Provisions on African-American Veterans' Political Participation." *Studies in American Political Development* 19, no. 1 (2005): 31–52.

———. *Soldiers to Citizens: The G.I. Bill and the Making of the Greatest Generation.* New York: Oxford University Press, 2005.

Meyer, Leisa D. *Creating GI Jane: Sexuality and Power in the Women's Army Corps during World War II.* New York: Columbia University Press, 1996.

Meyerson, Martin, and Edward C. Banfield. *Politics, Planning, and the Public Interest: The Case of Public Housing in Chicago.* Glencoe, Ill.: Free Press, 1955.

Milkman, Ruth. *Gender at Work: The Dynamics of Job Segregation by Sex during World War II.* Urbana: University of Illinois Press, 1987.

Mjagkij, Nina. *Organizing Black America: An Encyclopedia of African American Associations.* New York: Routledge, 2001.

Moreno, Paul D. *From Direct Action to Affirmative Action: Fair Employment Law and Policy in America, 1933–1972.* Baton Rouge: Louisiana State University Press, 1997.

Mullen, Bill V. *Popular Fronts: Chicago and African-American Cultural Politics, 1935–46.* Urbana: University of Illinois Press, 1999.

Myrdal, Gunnar. *An American Dilemma: The Negro Problem and Modern Democracy.* New York: Harper, 1944.

Naison, Mark. *Communists in Harlem during the Depression.* Urbana: University of Illinois Press, 1983.

Nalty, Bernard C. *Strength for the Fight: A History of Black Americans in the Military.* New York: Free Press, 1986.

Northrup, Herbert R. *Organized Labor and the Negro.* New York: Harper and Bros., 1944.

O'Malley, Peter Joseph. "Mayor Martin H. Kennelly of Chicago: A Political Biography." Ph.D. diss., University of Illinois at Chicago Circle, 1980.

Onkst, David H. "'First a Negro . . . Incidentally a Veteran': Black World War Two Veterans and the G.I. Bill of Rights in the Deep South, 1944–1948." *Journal of Social History* 31, no. 3 (1998): 517–44.

Phillips, Kimberley L. *AlabamaNorth: African-American Migrants, Community, and Working-Class Activism in Cleveland, 1915–45.* The Working Class in American History. Urbana: University of Illinois Press, 1999.

Philpott, Thomas Lee. *The Slum and the Ghetto: Blacks, Immigrants, and Reformers in Chicago, 1880-1930.* Belmont, Calif.: Wadsworth Publishing Company, 1991.

Piven, Frances Fox, and Richard A. Cloward. *Poor People's Movements: Why They Succeed, How They Fail.* New York: Vintage, 1979.

Plotkin, Wendy. "Deeds of Mistrust: Race, Housing, and Restrictive Covenants in Chicago, 1900–1953." Ph.D. diss., University of Illinois at Chicago, 1999.

———. "'Hemmed In': The Struggle against Racial Restrictive Covenants and Deed Restrictions in Post–World War II Chicago." *Journal of the Illinois State Historical Society* 94, no. 1 (Spring 2001): 39–69.

Plummer, Brenda Gayle. *Rising Wind: Black Americans and U.S. Foreign Affairs, 1935–1960.* Chapel Hill: University of North Carolina Press, 1996.

———, ed. *Window on Freedom: Race, Civil Rights, and Foreign Affairs, 1945–1988* Chapel Hill: University of North Carolina Press, 2007.

Pope, Jim. "Worker Lawmaking, Sit-Down Strikes, and the Shaping of American Industrial Relations, 1935–1958." *Law and History Review* 24, no. 1 (Spring 2006): 45–113.

Purdy, G. Flint. *A Preliminary Report on the Investigation of School Library Resources, Administration and Use in the Metropolitan Area of Chicago. Conducted by the Graduate Library School of the University of Chicago, with the Cooperation of the Federal C.W.E.S. Administration and the Illinois Emergency Relief Commission. Preliminary Report of Sept. 20, 1934.* Chicago, 1934.

Radford, Gail. *Modern Housing for America: Policy Struggles in the New Deal Era.* Chicago: University of Chicago Press, 1996.

Ralph, James R., Jr. *Northern Protest: Martin Luther King, Jr., Chicago, and the Civil Rights Movement.* Cambridge, Mass.: Harvard University Press, 1993.

Ransom, Leon A. "Combating Discrimination in the Employment of Negroes in War Industries and Government Agencies." *Journal of Negro Education* 12, no. 3 (1943): 405–16.

Rast, Joel. *Remaking Chicago: The Political Origins of Urban Industrial Change.* DeKalb: Northern Illinois University Press, 1999.

Record, Wilson. *Race and Radicalism: The NAACP and the Communist Party in Conflict.* Communism in American Life. Ithaca: Cornell University Press, 1964.

Reed, Christopher Robert. *The Chicago NAACP and the Rise of Black Professional Leadership, 1910–1966.* Bloomington: Indiana University Press, 1997.

Reed, Merl Elwyn. *Seedtime for the Modern Civil Rights Movement: The President's Committee on Fair Employment Practice, 1941–1946.* Baton Rouge: Louisiana State University Press, 1991.

Reed, Touré F. *Not Alms but Opportunity: The Urban League and the Politics of Racial Uplift, 1910–1950.* Chapel Hill: University of North Carolina Press, 2008.

Rodgers, Lawrence R. *Canaan Bound: The African-American Great Migration Novel.* Chicago: University of Illinois Press, 1997.

Roediger, David R. *The Wages of Whiteness: Race and the Making of the American Working Class.* New York: Verso, 1999.

Rubinowitz, Leonard S., James E. Rosenbaum, and Shirley Dvorin. *Crossing the Class and Color Lines: From Public Housing to White Suburbia.* Chicago: University of Chicago Press, 2000.

Ruchames, Louis. *Race, Jobs and Politics: The Story of FEPC.* New York: Columbia University Press, 1953.

Schietinger, Egbert Frederic. "Real Estate Transfer during Negro Invasion." Unpublished master's thesis, University of Chicago, 1948.

Schrecker, Ellen. *Many Are the Crimes: McCarthyism in America.* Boston: Little, Brown, 1998.

Scott, Lawrence P., and William M. Womack. *Double V: The Civil Rights Struggle of the Tuskegee Airmen.* East Lansing: Michigan State University Press, 1994.

Self, Robert O. *American Babylon: Race and the Struggle for Postwar Oakland.* Princeton: Princeton University Press, 2003.

Seligman, Amanda I. *Block by Block: Neighborhoods and Public Policy on Chicago's West Side.* Chicago: University of Chicago Press, 2005.

Seltzer, Sydney. "The Problem of Client Fraud: A Study of Ninety-Nine Cook County Families Who Have Made No Restitution for Aid Fraudulently Obtained from the Illinois Emergency Relief Commission and Retained upon the Relief Rolls between July 1929 and August 1937." MA thesis, University of Chicago, School of Social Service Administration, 1938.

Shockley, Megan Taylor. *"We, Too, Are Americans": African American Women in Detroit and Richmond, 1940–54.* Urbana: University of Illinois, 2004.

Sitkoff, Harvard. *A New Deal for Blacks: The Emergence of Civil Rights as a National Issue.* New York: Oxford University Press, 1978.

Smith, Judith E. *Visions of Belonging: Family Stories, Popular Culture, and Postwar Democracy, 1940–1960*. New York: Columbia University Press, 2004.

Smith, Preston H., II. "The Quest for Racial Democracy: Black Civic Ideology and Housing Interests in Postwar Chicago." *Journal of Urban History* 26, no. 2 (2000): 131–57.

———. *Racial Democracy and the Black Metropolis Housing Policy in Postwar Chicago*. Minneapolis: University of Minnesota Press, 2012.

Spear, Allan H. *Black Chicago: The Making of a Negro Ghetto, 1890–1920*. Chicago: University of Chicago Press, 1967.

Storch, Randi. *Red Chicago: American Communism at Its Grassroots, 1928–35*. Urbana: University of Illinois Press, 2007.

Street, Paul. "'The Best Union Members': Class, Race, Culture, and Black Worker Militancy in Chicago's Stockyards during the 1930s." *Journal of American Ethnic History* 20, no. 1 (Fall 2000): 18–49.

Strickland, Arvarh E. *History of the Chicago Urban League*. Urbana: University of Illinois Press, 1966.

Stromquist, Shelton, and Marvin Bergman. *Unionizing the Jungles: Labor and Community in the Twentieth-Century Meatpacking Industry*. Iowa City: University of Iowa Press, 1997.

Sugrue, Thomas J. *The Origins of the Urban Crisis: Race and Inequality in Postwar Detroit*. Princeton: Princeton University Press, 1996.

Sullivan, Patricia. *Days of Hope: Race and Democracy in the New Deal Era*. Chapel Hill: University of North Carolina Press, 1996.

Theoharis, Jeanne, and Komozi Woodard, eds. *Freedom North: Black Freedom Struggles outside the South, 1940–1980*. New York: Palgrave Macmillan, 2003.

Thompson, Heather Ann. *Whose Detroit? Politics, Labor, and Race in a Modern American City*. Ithaca: Cornell University Press, 2001.

Travis, Dempsey. *An Autobiography of Black Chicago*. Chicago: Urban Research Institute, 1981.

Trotter, Joe William. *The Great Migration in Historical Perspective: New Dimensions of Race, Class, and Gender*. Bloomington: Indiana University Press, 1991.

Tuttle, William M. *Race Riot: Chicago in the Red Summer of 1919*. New York: Atheneum, 1970.

Tyler, Robert L. "The American Veterans Committee: Out of a Hot War and into the Cold." *American Quarterly* 18, no. 3 (Autumn 1966): 419–36.

U.S. Federal Housing Administration. *Underwriting Manual: Underwriting and Valuation Procedure under Title II of the National Housing Act*. Washington, D.C.: Government Printing Office, 1936.

Von Eschen, Penny M. *Race against Empire: Black Americans and Anticolonialism, 1937–1957*. Ithaca: Cornell University Press, 1997.

Washington, Sylvia Hood. *Packing Them In: An Archaeology of Environmental Racism in Chicago, 1865–1954.* Lanham, Md.: Lexington Books, 2005.

Watters, Mary. *Illinois in the Second World War.* Vol. 2, *The Production Front.* Springfield: Illinois State Historical Library, 1951.

Weaver, Robert C. *The Negro Ghetto.* New York: Harcourt, Brace, 1948.

———. *Negro Labor: A National Problem.* New York: Harcourt, Brace, 1946.

Weiss, Nancy J. *Farewell to the Party of Lincoln: Black Politics in the Age of FDR.* Princeton: Princeton University Press, 1983.

Williams, Rhonda Y. *The Politics of Public Housing: Black Women's Struggles against Urban Inequality.* New York: Oxford University Press, 2004.

Winslow, Calvin. *Waterfront Workers: New Perspectives on Race and Class.* The Working Class in American History. Urbana: University of Illinois Press, 1998.

Wolcott, Victoria W. *Remaking Respectability: African American Women in Interwar Detroit.* Gender and American Culture. Chapel Hill: University of North Carolina Press, 2001.

Wolters, Raymond. *Negroes and the Great Depression: The Problem of Economic Recovery.* Contributions in American History 6. Westport, Conn.: Greenwood, 1970.

Wright, Richard. *American Hunger.* New York: Harper and Row, 1977.

———. *Native Son.* New York: Harper and Brothers, 1940.

Wynn, Neil A. *The Afro-American and the Second World War.* New York: Holmes and Meier, 1976.

———. "War and Racial Progress: The African American Experience during World War II." *Peace and Change* 20 (July 1995): 348–63.

Young, Paul Clinton. "Race, Class, and Radicalism in Chicago, 1914–1936." Ph.D. diss., University of Iowa, 2001.

INDEX

Page numbers in italics indicate illustrations.

Index

Index

Index

LIONEL KIMBLE JR. is an associate professor of history at Chicago State University, where he teaches twentieth-century American history with an emphasis on African Americans in Chicago. His essays have appeared in the *Journal of the Illinois State Historical Society* and the *Journal of Illinois History.*